CHOOSE FLORIDA

FOR RETIREMENT

Help Us Keep This Guide Up to Date

Every effort has been made by the author and editors to make this guide as accurate and useful as possible. However, many things can change after a guide is published—establishments close, phone numbers change, facilities come under new management, housing costs fluctuate, and so on.

We would love to hear from you concerning your experiences with this guide and how you feel it could be made better and be kept up to date. While we may not be able to respond to all comments and suggestions, we'll take them to heart and we'll make certain to share them with the author. Please send your comments and suggestions to the following address:

The Globe Pequot Press
Reader Response/Editorial Department
P.O. Box 833
Old Saybrook, CT 06475

Or you may e-mail us at:

editorial@globe-pequot.com

Thanks for your input, and happy travels!

Choose Retirement™ Series

CHOOSE FLORIDA
FOR RETIREMENT

Retirement Discoveries for Every Budget

JAMES F. GOLLATTSCHECK

The Globe Pequot Press

Old Saybrook, Connecticut

Cover Photos: Images © PhotoDisc, Inc.
Cover and text design: Laura Augustine
Maps: Daniel Murray and Lisa Reneson

Library of Congress Cataloging-in-Publication Data

Gollattscheck, James F.
   Choose Florida for retirement / by James F. Gollattscheck. — 1st ed.
      p. cm. — (Choose retirement series)
   Includes bibliographical references and index.
   ISBN 0-7627-0311-3
   1. Florida—Guidebooks,   2. Retirement, Places of—Florida—Guidebooks.
   3. Cost and standard of living—Florida. I. Title. II. Series.
   F309.3.G65   1998
   646.7'9'09759—dc21   98-38321
                                                                CIP

Manufactured in the United States of America
First Edition/First Printing

DEDICATION

This book is dedicated to those in my family who have been part of Florida for more than 150 years: those who came to north Florida from Georgia and South Carolina in the early 1800s seeking land to farm and finding themselves in the midst of the Seminole Indian Wars; those who left their homes in Illinois to look for a new life in south Florida in 1880; my grandfather, who left Germany in 1888 alone at age fifteen to "seek his luck" in the jungle of what is now Miami; and my mother and father, born in north and south Florida at the turn of the century. These adventurous, pioneering men and women and all who came with them lived through wonderful times and terrible times, through prosperity and financial ruin and back again, through delightful sunny winters and deadly summer hurricanes. Their bravery and determination helped create the Florida of today. I invite you to make it your new home.

ACKNOWLEDGMENTS

I am indebted to countless public officials, community leaders, and retirees who gave me information, suggestions, and advice. I wish to thank the many employees of chambers of commerce throughout Florida for their willingness to send materials, answer my questions, and give so graciously of their time. I am grateful to volunteers at many senior centers for their help. I appreciate the assistance of those representatives of state, county, and municipal agencies who gave so willingly of their time and expertise. Most of all, I wish to thank my good friend and colleague, Daniel Murray, for his assistance with research, illustrations, proofreading, questioning, criticizing, and—most of all—for his patience with a computer neophyte. This book would not have been possible without his help. I am most deeply indebted to Gail Gavert at The Globe Pequot Press not only for her many helpful suggestions and careful editing of this book, but also for her understanding and patient hand-holding throughout the editing process.

Contents

INTRODUCTION

In *Choose Florida for Retirement*, the most popular retirement destinations in America's most popular retirement state have been visited, studied, and profiled. The greatest difficulty in organizing this book was deciding which cities and towns to include, since there is hardly a spot in Florida that doesn't have its share of devoted retirees who are quite certain they have found the perfect place. Another challenge was drawing boundaries around the communities to be included. I very often found clusters of adjacent communities that were equally attractive and equally popular with retiring Americans. In such cases I usually profiled one and listed others as neighboring communities. You should consider the city or town profiled as representative of several nearby retirement possibilities.

Choose Florida for Retirement is a guide to Florida's most popular retirement locations that focuses on those areas research has shown to be of greatest concern to retirees. It is not based on a rating system in which one community scores higher than another. Such schemes are by their nature highly subjective. They are based on criteria someone has selected, criteria that may be very different from yours. One thing I have learned in talking with retirees across the state is that there is a wide variety of preferences. No one rating system can hope to reflect such diversity. In this book I will give you as much information as possible about Florida's most popular retirement communities and let you select those that appeal to you.

As thorough as the authors of the "Choose" books have tried to be, there is no substitute for your own research into the communities you find most attractive. For this reason, I have included lists of resources and other contacts from whom you may request more detailed information. Since firsthand knowledge about the community you are seriously considering for retirement is so very important, I urge you to make your own visit to the "Sunshine State," because no guide can ever cover completely all the personal considerations you will have regarding a new community.

As a fourth-generation Floridian and now a retiree myself, I am proud to have been asked to write this guide to the many retirement possibilities in my state. I am convinced—and I hope to convince you—that Florida has a community to suit the tastes and financial status of every retiree. Your leisure interests and the lifestyle you prefer will determine the very best Florida retirement communities for you, but even after applying your own selective criteria, you will probably find that there are a number of "near perfect" choices. Your very pleasant challenge will be to narrow those cities and towns down to one that is exactly right for you. Best wishes in making that very important choice, and welcome to Florida!

> The prices and rates listed in this book were confirmed at press time. We recommend, however, that you call establishments before traveling to obtain current information.

WHERE AMERICA RETIRES

In 1513 the peninsula of land we know as the state of Florida enchanted its first recorded visitor. At Easter time in that year the Spanish explorer Ponce de León, seeking gold and a fabled fountain of youth, found instead a shore so verdant he called it *La Florida*—the land of flowers. Lured by Ponce de León's reports and a continuing search for gold, more explorers followed, then came residents. In 1565 St. Augustine, the first permanent European settlement in what would become the United States, was founded. For almost 500 years Florida has continued to enchant its visitors and in the process has attracted millions of new residents. In this century it has become increasingly popular as a vacation spot, and each year many of its visitors choose to return as residents. So many of these new residents are retirees that, according to a study recently published as *Retirement Migration in America*, Florida is clearly America's first choice as a retirement destination.

Florida's Unknown History

Unlike the predominantly English colonization of the thirteen original states, Florida was established and governed for many years by Spain. Since schoolchildren are led to believe that European (read English-speaking) civilization took root in North America in Virginia in 1607 and in Massachusetts in 1620, the early history of Florida has been largely ignored. However, when the Pilgrims landed on Plymouth Rock, St. Augustine, North America's oldest city, had been established for fifty-five years. While northern settlers were barely surviving their first harsh New England winter, third-generation Spanish colonists in Florida were enjoying mild weather and all the amenities of a small town in what would eventually become the "Sunshine State." La Florida continued mainly under Spanish rule until 1819 when it was purchased by the United States. As the noted Florida historian Michael Gannon has pointed out, "Not until the year 2055 will the American flag have flown over Florida as long as did the flag of Spain." Even after Florida became

FLORIDA

a state in 1845, it was another fifty years before its lower half became accessible by rail and automobile and thus known to the rest of the nation. With the coming of Henry Flagler's railway in the late nineteenth century, Palm Beach was created and the legend of Florida as a paradise with no winter began.

Because the southern half of Florida has been developed since the 1920s by northerners seeking a warmer climate and because the northern half was settled in the early 1800s by southern homesteaders looking for land to farm (my ancestors among them), a curious phenomenon exists: North Florida is southern and south Florida is northern! Much of north Florida was settled before the Civil War and you find antebellum mansions and an "old South" feeling throughout the area. In south Florida, native Floridians are a small minority and northern accents drown out southern drawls.

Why Consider Florida?

If you are reading this book you may not have decided exactly where you plan to retire. If that's the case and unless there are personal reasons why you must choose another part of the United States, you should not ignore Florida as a retirement destination. Just the fact that more Americans have chosen to retire in Florida than in any other state is an indication of the advantages Florida offers. If you are curious about where your fellow retirees have been retiring in the past thirty or so years, you should read *Retirement Migration in America*, a very scholarly but also very readable study of how America's sixty-plus population moves around. The figures for the years 1985–1990 (the most recent tabulations available for this book) are astounding. During that period 1,901,105 persons over age sixty moved from one state to another. Of that number, 451,709 or 23.8 percent moved to Florida. More than three times as many retirees moved to Florida as to California, the second most popular state. While the attractiveness of various counties in Florida to incoming retirees will be covered in subsequent chapters, it is indicative of the entire state's appeal to retirees that of the top twenty-five most popular counties for retirement in the United States, eighteen were in Florida. America's retirees have voted with their moving vans, and it is safe to say that Florida has more of what people look for in a retirement destination than any other state.

Florida's geography and climate work together to provide pleasant surroundings for the leisure that retirement brings. A fairly narrow peninsula thrust far into the sea, Florida is blessed with the moderate climate that comes from being nearly surrounded by the warm waters of the Gulf of Mexico and the powerful Gulf Stream of the Atlantic Ocean. These waters also provide the beaches and the many outdoor activities for which Florida is justly famous. With taxes and a cost of living lower than most states, Florida is an economical state in which to retire, and the large number of voting retirees in Florida guarantees that taxes will remain relatively low for those living on fixed incomes. Finally, Florida is so diverse there is a city or town to satisfy every taste and financial situation.

Florida's Mild Climate

It is not surprising that Florida has become such a popular place to vacation and eventually to retire. Three mild climatic zones allow flowers and greenery to thrive even in midwinter and encourage year-round outdoor activities. Winter in the northern third of the state, a little warmer than southern Georgia and Alabama, may bring frost and an occasional mild freeze, giving residents a pleasant taste of four seasons. However, if you are accustomed to northern winters, you will be pleased to find that even the coldest days in Florida usually come with bright sunshine, and often in January and February you will have weeks of mild weather in the 70s and 80s. A subtropical climate prevails in the middle third of the state with little or no frost, and the very rare drop below freezing is considered an agricultural disaster. There citrus trees thrive in backyards, and residents go much of the winter in shorts and shirtsleeves. The southernmost third of the state is tropical, and it is there that coconut palms grow wild, hibiscus and orchids flourish outdoors, and winter offers only a slight variation in temperature. Throughout the state temperatures are always milder—warmer in the winter and cooler in the summer—nearer the coasts than inland.

You may have heard that Florida summers are unpleasant with excessive heat and humidity. People who have moved here are divided on the subject. Some will tell you it is not a problem; others complain that summers were more pleasant "back home." Perhaps it depends on what summer weather was truly like in one's former home. I have lived most of my life in one or another part of Florida, and I can honestly say that I have never experienced summer heat and humidity as unpleasant here as I have in New York City, Chicago, or Washington, D.C. Humidity may be high in some parts of Florida, but there is almost always a breeze, air pollution is virtually nonexistent, and temperatures rarely go above the mid-90s on the hottest days anywhere in the state. Will you need air-conditioning? Certainly. And you will probably use it for more of the year than you might in a northern climate, but you will use far less heat during the brief winters. "Snowbirds"—those fortunate enough to be able to spend their winters in Florida and their summers in some cooler spot—probably have the best of both worlds. The rest of us must choose, and for many retirees Florida summers are happy trade-offs for long, dark winters with ice and snow. The following chapters will describe as accurately as possible the year-round weather patterns in each area of Florida. Weather data will be taken from the National Oceanic and Atmospheric Administration's (NOAA) report *Comparative Climatic Data for the United States through 1995.* This report gives data from thirteen stations around the state. Data from the nearest NOAA station is provided for each county profiled.

Florida's Gentle Geography

One feature of Florida that attracts both visitors and retirees is that no part of it is far from water. Wherever you may be in the state, you are rarely more than an hour away from a coast and Florida's famed beaches. While state promotional literature proclaims 1,200 miles of coastline on the Atlantic Ocean and the Gulf of Mexico, it has been estimated that if one considers all its bays, islands, and inlets, Florida's actual waterfront exceeds 8,000 miles in length! The nature of Florida's beaches varies from region to region. The extremely fine sand along the northern Atlantic coast of Florida (from south of Daytona Beach north to Jacksonville Beach) is so hard-packed by the tides that you may drive and park your car on the wide beaches. Coconut trees sway over the soft, sink-to-your-ankles, gold-colored sand of the beaches on the southern Atlantic coast. The water is warmer, the sand is sugary white, and one finds as many pines as palms on Florida's Gulf beaches. While some beaches—those at Miami Beach, for example—are almost completely hidden from view by high-rise condominiums and hotels, there are still miles of open public beaches in Florida and many areas where the beaches have been preserved in their natural state.

Most of Florida's beaches are on long, narrow barrier islands separated from the mainland by rivers, lagoons, and lakes. Along much of the east and west coasts of Florida these natural bodies of water have been connected by canals or by dredging marshy areas to become the Intracoastal Waterway, a riverlike channel that allows smaller boats to travel safely along the coasts without venturing into the Atlantic Ocean or the Gulf of Mexico. These protected waters are the site of many marinas for an ever-growing number of small pleasure boats, as well as major ports such as Port Everglades in Fort Lauderdale where freighters, tankers, cruise ships, and even ships the size of the *Queen Elizabeth II* dock. Frequent inlets allow access to the Gulf and the Atlantic.

The state's 54,135 square miles of land include 4,425 square miles of lakes and rivers. To one flying over the state, much of the landscape below resembles Swiss cheese. More than 30,000 lakes range in size from the gigantic 700-square-mile Lake Okeechobee to thousands of little round lakes, many smaller than a city block, that dot woodlands and residential neighborhoods. Larger lakes in Florida's central highlands, many connected by canals to form chains of lakes, are touted by both residents and local chambers of commerce as having the best bass fishing in the nation. Neighborhood lakes allow you to live near the center of many bustling cities yet see herons, egrets, fish, turtles, and even an occasional alligator.

Florida's limestone substructure makes it a land of freshwater springs. Thousands of small springs line and feed great rivers such as the Suwannee and the St. Johns, while others are huge subterranean rivers in their own right. Flowing from under northern mountains, they surface in Florida, forming above-ground rivers with millions of gallons of clear, cold water daily. Several of these—Silver Springs, for example—have been developed as commercial attractions while others have become state parks and recreational areas providing swimming, scuba diving, canoeing, tubing, fishing, and camping for residents and visitors.

Just as with its climate, changes in Florida's geography are subtle. There are no towering mountains and no deep canyons. The highest point in the state is only 345 feet in elevation and the lowest points— most of the coastal regions—are at sea level. A ridge that runs down the center of the state from its northern border to near Lake

Okeechobee gives that part of the state low rolling hills. Much of that area is heavily wooded with oak and pine trees. More than a million acres of these woodlands are protected in three national forests containing public recreational sites and campgrounds. South of Lake Okeechobee the ridge gives way to a great, flat expanse of water and sawgrass. This swampland spreads southwestward from near the Atlantic to the far side of the state where it becomes the Ten Thousand Islands, a marshy area of small islands and mangrove-covered mud flats in the Gulf of Mexico. Known generally as the Everglades, this vast swampland really is, as author Marjorie Stoneman Douglas named it, a great "river of grass" 50 miles wide, less than a foot deep, and flowing almost imperceptibly toward the Gulf of Mexico. Only a small part of this swampland of more than 2,000 square miles is protected in the 1.5 million-acre Everglades National Park.

The Economics of Retiring in Florida

If you are like most retirees looking for a new home, in addition to pleasant weather and attractive surroundings you are concerned about living costs in your new area. Overall you will find Florida an economical state in which to live. As in any state, your cost of living will vary from area to area, but it will depend more than anything else on your choice of lifestyle. Very wealthy retirees are happy with the luxurious homes and amenities they find in Florida, while those of more modest means are equally happy with the lifestyles they can afford. Often both are in the same community. Information on the general cost of living will be given for each region in subsequent chapters. For this book I have used the comparative costs of living determined annually for each county in Florida by the Office of Education Budget and Management of the Florida Department of Education. The 1996 Florida Price Level Index compares each of the state's sixty-seven counties to the statewide average, shown as 100. For example, rural Washington County, in the middle of the Panhandle but away from the coast, ranks sixty-seventh in cost with an index of 89.03, or 10.97 percent below the statewide average. Monroe County, which includes the Florida Keys and Key West, ranks highest with an index of 108.40 or 8.4 percent above the statewide average. In the statewide average cost of living, housing accounts for 38.24 percent of each dollar, food for 21.86 percent, transportation for

17.9 percent, health, recreation, and personal services for 15.54 percent, and apparel for 6.46 percent.

Housing. The most difficult cost to report meaningfully in a book such as this is the cost of housing. An average cost tells you very little when a large home or luxury condominium may sell for several million dollars and a bungalow in the same community for well under $50,000. So many variables come into play that even the median cost is somewhat meaningless unless it can be broken down by type and location of housing. In coastal areas, for example, a general rule is that prices will go up as you get closer to the water; however, some beach communities have many small, inexpensive cottages, while open land a few miles from the water has been turned into gated communities of large, expensive homes. In most of the areas covered in subsequent chapters you will have a choice of every type of housing in almost every price range. Its ranking in the above-mentioned Price Level Index will give you an idea as to how a particular county compares to all other counties in the state with regard to the general cost of housing. Information will be given regarding housing that is unique to an area such as the many well-established communities of manufactured homes in north central Florida and condominiums in many coastal towns and cities.

I took information from real estate web sites, and when I visited each of the cities and towns covered in the following chapters, I culled information from local realtors, the real estate sections of local newspapers, and from the many real estate brochures found in chambers of commerce and in front of every supermarket. Samples of listings of various types of housing are included for every community profiled. When a very specific listing is described, the price I quote is the price that was asked in the listing. You may assume that in almost every case there was room for negotiation. In the area of housing, you are urged to work closely with a qualified realtor serving as a buyer's agent to get information concerning the range of prices for the type and location of housing you prefer.

What about Land Fraud? Florida gained a bad reputation during the land development boom of the 1920s (and again to a lesser extent in the 1940s and early 1950s) when unscrupulous developers promoted through magazine and newspaper ads "pie in the sky" communities and even cities that never materialized. Many trusting souls from out of state bought lots sight unseen only to find out, after their checks had cleared and the developer had vanished or gone bankrupt, that the lots were underwater or nonexistent. Could this happen now? There will always be con men preying on the naive, but much has been done in Florida and throughout the nation to eliminate such fraudulent activities. Even today, however, anyone gullible enough to buy land in any state on the basis of an advertisement and without a thorough on-site inspection is asking to be taken for a ride. Condominiums and planned communities are always marketed before construction begins. In some areas an entire building or the very best lots are sold long before groundbreaking, and it isn't necessarily foolish to get in early on such developments. But before putting your money down on a speculative venture, you should know as much as possible about the developer's background, finances, and track record, and you should have made a personal visit to the site.

Home Insurance. Since Hurricane Andrew struck south Florida in 1992, causing several billion dollars worth of damages, insurance companies have often been reluctant to insure houses and condos near the Atlantic Ocean or the Gulf of Mexico, and rates have soared in some of those areas. Hurricanes are very unpredictable and you may never encounter one, but finding yourself in the path of one is a possibility everywhere in Florida. Hurricanes may do wind damage inland, but they lose strength over land. It is on the coast that winds are usually strongest and where tidal surges do so much damage. I was told recently that rates in Fort Lauderdale are 60 percent higher if your residence is between the Atlantic Ocean and Interstate 95, more than 2 miles inland. I found when I moved to Sarasota recently that the company with whom I had all my insurance for years would not provide me with renters insurance because my apartment building was less than 2,500 feet from water, in this case a quiet little bayou about a half mile inland from Sarasota Bay. Just as you should, I shopped around and found another company that would write the policy I needed.

Before signing a contract on a house or condo near the coast, you should find out what your options are for insurance, including the Florida Residential Property and Casualty Joint Underwriting Association, an insurance program created by the Florida Legislature to assist property owners in high-risk areas. A booklet titled *Insuring Your Home, Consumers' Guide 1997–98,* available from the Florida Department of Insurance, will answer many of your questions (see Additional Resources for details). For new homes in many coastal areas, living areas are now required to be a specified number of feet above sea level. Along the Gulf Coast beaches you see a great many houses, condominiums, and apartment buildings built on posts with only garages and storage at the ground level.

Taxes. Keeping in mind its image as a desirable location for new businesses as well as new residents, Florida has found ways to keep taxes low for its residents by spreading them out to include its millions of tourist visitors from other states and countries. One very important consideration for you as a retiree is that there is no state or local income tax. Instead, many state services are funded by a 6 percent state sales tax paid by both residents and visitors. Unlike some states with a sales tax, Florida exempts groceries, prescription drugs, and medical services. To the 6 percent state sales tax, residents of individual counties may vote to add a local sales tax. This will be reported where applicable. Additional local "tourist taxes," such as those applied to hotel and motel rooms, help communities provide services and facilities such as public buildings, entertainment and sports venues, and the upkeep of beaches enjoyed by residents and visitors alike.

A tax that may be new to many prospective residents is Florida's intangible tax. The state collects an annual tax on stocks, bonds, and other nonexempt securities at a rate of $1.00 per thousand dollars of value. Only individuals with intangible assets greater than $20,000 and couples with greater than $40,000 are affected by this tax. Intangible assets greater than $100,000 for individuals and $200,000 for couples are taxed at $2.00 per thousand dollars of value. Your intangible tax is assessed on the value of your taxable assets as of January 1 of each year and must be paid by June 30 to avoid penalties. For further information on Florida taxes, you should contact the Florida Department of Revenue (see Additional Resources for details).

Many public services such as road construction and maintenance, police and fire protection, and funding for public schools beyond a state minimum are supported by local property taxes. All real estate is theoretically assessed at 100 percent of its value, but many local exemptions come into play. You will want to check very carefully into local property taxes before you commit to buy. Other than a statewide homestead exemption of $25,000 off the assessed value of a home for permanent residents, these taxes vary from county to county and from area to area within a county. Information concerning local property taxes will be given in each of the following chapters.

To qualify for the homestead exemption, you must prove you own the home, declare it your permanent residence, and file an application at the office of the county property appraiser by March 1 of the year for which you are seeking an exemption. If you do not meet this deadline, you may not receive an exemption for that year. Approval of your application for homestead exemption is up to the county property appraiser who will simply require you to prove your residency status. In addition to your proof of home ownership, the most important documents for proof of residency are a Florida driver's license and Florida automobile registration. Other considerations are a Florida voter registration card, filing of Florida intangible tax if applicable, and filing your annual federal income tax as a Florida resident. You must file for homestead exemption in person the first time. After that it may be done by mail each year. Since actual procedures may vary from county to county, you should contact the office of the county property tax appraiser as soon as you have purchased your Florida residence to begin the application process and make sure you have proof of all requirements.

Another statewide limitation on property taxes, fueled mainly by fears of retirees on fixed incomes that they might lose their homes due to rising tax assessments, took effect in 1995 via a constitutional amendment. Known as "Save Our Homes," the amendment caps increases in property tax assessments at 3 percent or at the rate of inflation, whichever is lower. The cap applies as long as a person owns and lives in the house, and here the same rules apply as those for homestead exemption. When a house is sold, it is reassessed at full value and if the new owner qualifies, the cap starts over again.

Housing Choices in Florida

Because they no longer have children at home, wish to live more economically, or simply desire less housework and responsibility for upkeep, many retirees choose to downsize their living accommodations when they move to a retirement location. Others, perhaps more affluent, want space for entertaining and room for out-of-town guests and so look for a spacious retirement residence. Some look for open spaces; others want to be in the middle of a city. All will find what they are looking for in almost every region of Florida. A continuous influx of new residents has caused builders and developers to maintain a large inventory of houses, condominiums, and apartments in almost every style, size, and price range.

New or Old? As a new resident looking for a home you will have a choice of a new or an older residence. Each has advantages and disadvantages. An older house or apartment is likely to be in a neighborhood or building whose character is already established, where landscaping has had time to mature, and where flaws in construction may have become apparent. You will find excellent bargains in "fixer-uppers," sometimes listed as "handyman's specials," throughout Florida. Unless you truly are a handyman who can do the renovation work yourself, you will want to get a thorough inspection and professional estimates of the cost to make such a house meet your standards before you agree to purchase. New houses and buildings will, of course, reflect contemporary styles and contain more modern conveniences. Older residences are more likely than newer developments to be closer to a town center and on a public transportation route.

House or Condo? Another important consideration is whether you prefer a house or a condominium. Because so many retirees do not want the responsibility of maintaining a house yet want to own their retirement residence, and because they feel safer in a building with other residents, condominiums have developed rapidly throughout Florida. Again, there are advantages and disadvantages. When you buy into a condominium building, you also assume obligations and responsibilities, many beyond your control. You will not be responsible for maintaining or improving other than the inside of your particular unit, but neither will you have the right to make decisions concerning the building in which you own your home. In a condominium all matters concerning the building as a whole and even rules by which you as a resident must abide are made by a board of directors elected by and from residents of the condominium. As a condominium resident you pay a monthly fee for the upkeep of the building, but such fees are decided by the board and may be increased at any time. Additional maintenance and improvement expenses are borne by all the residents in the form of assessments. A new condominium, like a new house, is not likely to need major repairs in the immediate future, and therefore you might not expect increases or assessments. On the downside, however, the type of residents the building will attract will be unknown and there will be no record of the actions of a newly elected board of directors.

There are many things to consider when buying into an older condominium. You may be pleased at the low monthly fees but find the reason they are low is because needed maintenance has been deferred, sometimes for years. In that case you may find yourself responsible for high assessments to pay for a new roof, painting of the building, or other major repairs and upkeep. Some condominiums are run like a happy family, but others seem filled with residents determined to fight each other and the board governing the building. You should know all you can about a building in which you are thinking of renting an apartment or a neighborhood in which you are considering buying a house, but it is even more important for you to know as much as you can about the condominium in which you are considering buying a unit. A tenant in a rented apartment can move out at the end of a lease if for some reason the building becomes unsatisfactory, but the owner of a condominium unit can only sell. If a condominium building has problems or if assessments have become too high, you may have to sell at a loss. As a prospective resident, you should be allowed to read the minutes of recent meetings of the condominium board. Issues being discussed at board meetings will reveal matters of concern to the unit owners, and the tone of such meetings will tell you much about the atmosphere of the building. You will also want to look at the annual budget and monthly treasurer's reports to determine the financial stability of the condominium, as well as the condominium documents including the rules established by the board of directors. For example, may you have pets in the building, are there limits to the number of guests you may have, and may you rent out your unit if you choose? You will do well to talk with residents of the building if that is possible. You cannot know too much about a condominium building before you buy! It is far easier to ignore neighbors you don't like and unpleasant neighborhood issues when you live in a house than it is when you live in a condominium where you share lobbies, hallways, elevators, garages, and many other common facilities with your neighbors and where those neighbors have the right to make decisions directly affecting you, your property, and your pocketbook.

Mixed or Retiree Only? Increasingly you will find condominiums, apartment buildings, and entire communities restricted to residents above a certain age, frequently age fifty-five. Whether you will be happier in such an arrangement than in a diverse neighborhood of young and old is entirely a matter of personal preference. I have spoken with many retirees and found very strong opinions on both sides of the issue.

Some relish the idea of being in a community or a building limited to other adults and fellow retirees. Others cannot imagine being around only people their own age. If you are considering an age-restricted community for the first time, you should find out as much about such an arrangement as you can. Look carefully at the rules. For how long may a younger guest stay with you? What happens if you marry or choose to live with a younger person? How much time would you have to sell if you no longer meet the requirements? You should also consider very realistically the chances that a younger member of the family may need to move in with you. There have been extremely bitter court battles between older residents and the board of directors of a development or building when the residents suddenly find they must take in a grandchild. The nature of these developments ranges from age-restricted through various levels of assisted living to complete nursing care.

Planned Communities. Particularly in those areas where land is readily available, entire communities developed specifically for retirees are springing up. In a drive down I–75, I recently counted billboards advertising nine different retirement communities in the area immediately south of Ocala. Most of these stated in their advertising that they are restricted to those over age fifty-five. Some are communities of developer-built individual homes; others are duplexes or triplexes. Many contain only manufactured homes or double-wide mobile homes. Most have swimming pools, clubhouses, and other amenities.

Golf Course Communities. In Florida you do not have to belong to an expensive country club to live on or near the beautiful greens and open spaces of a golf course. Because so many retirees are avid golfers, many communities—even some with very modest prices—have been developed around golf courses.

What about Manufactured and Mobile Homes? If you have only negative opinions of manufactured homes and mobile-home parks, you may want to reconsider those options when you consider retiring in Florida. There are many pleasant communities of manufactured (also called modular or prefabricated) homes and others of mobile homes—mobile only in the sense they were towed to the site—throughout Florida. Many are beautifully landscaped with swimming pools, clubhouses, golf courses, bike trails, and other amenities. Some are on lakes or rivers and a few of the most desirable front on the Atlantic Ocean or the Gulf of

Mexico. Many fall into the category of age-restricted discussed above. Costs of such residences are generally, but not always, lower than other types of homes. Just as with a condominium, you will want to look carefully at all of the covenants, restrictions, and financial obligations before settling on property in such a community. For an idea of the options available in one community you might request a copy of *Mobile Home Lifestyles of Pinellas*, a booklet distributed by the Pinellas County members of the Florida Manufactured Housing Association, Inc. (see Additional Resources for details.)

Rent or Own Your Retirement Residence? You will also have to decide whether owning a house or condominium unit makes more sense for you than renting. One consideration is how it will affect your tax situation, and you will want to check with your accountant or with the Internal Revenue Service to get up-to-date information on tax laws pertaining to your specific case. Unless you have visited your favorite area of Florida enough to be certain it is where you want to live, you may want to rent for a few months or even a year while you get to know your new community. Otherwise you could have to sell at a loss if you discover you have made a mistake in the first few years of owning your home or apartment. While this book can help you narrow your choices, only personal experience over a period of time will determine how happy you will be in any new city or town.

Is Florida Too Crowded? A concern of some who are considering retiring to Florida is that the state may be overcrowded. An honest answer must be that some coastal areas are indeed crowded, especially during that area's busy season, but there are trade-offs. If you choose to live in an oceanfront condominium with a spectacular view, your building will likely be a high-rise, side by side with many others. Oceanfront property in popular beach communities is so expensive that developers will almost always build for maximum usage. However, even if you wish to live in a beach area—Fort Lauderdale, for example—you have a choice of a high-rise condominium on the beach or, only a short distance inland, a house or an apartment with more open spaces but still only a few minutes from the beach. Other than beach areas, which are always the most heavily populated, much of Florida is uncrowded and many areas are yet to be developed.

Your Personal Safety

As a retiree you will be wise to make your personal safety a high priority in your choice of a retirement destination, for it is no secret that older persons are often the target of crime wherever they live. Throughout this book the rate of crime in each community profiled will be given as the number of criminal offenses per 1,000 residents. These numbers have been provided by the Statistical Analysis Center of the Florida Department of Law Enforcement and are for the year 1996. They will give you a good sense of the relative safety of the areas you are considering. It should be noted, however, that crime rates are calculated using the number of year-round residents in a community and do not include visitors. Areas with large numbers of tourists or winter-only residents will suffer in such comparisons. In these communities the number of reported offenses actually took place amid a far larger seasonal population than is shown in the data. This is also true of towns with a large college or university population, such as Tallahassee or Gainesville, where students from out of town are not included in the population base. It should be noted, too, that the publicity given to crime in a particular area is often misleading. One crime against an international tourist or a well-known figure, while certainly serious and regrettable, may generate banner headlines across the nation, creating an image of rampant crime. When crime statistics are lumped together, the picture presented may be misleading. Crimes such as petty theft are of far less concern than crimes of violence such as assault or murder. Before considering a move to a new location anywhere, you will do well to talk with local law enforcement officials to find out as much as possible about the number and types of crimes reported in their jurisdiction. It is safe to say that law enforcement and crime prevention are high priorities throughout the state, and Florida has many police and sheriffs departments with national reputations for excellence and state-of-the-art systems. Most recently I heard about the installation in some communities of a new proactive telephone system by which residents are automatically called to alert them to possible severe weather, neighborhood criminal activity, or other dangerous situations.

Retirement Lifestyles

Unlike Florida's climate and geography, there is no sameness to the lifestyles of Florida's retirees. The seven regions of the state covered in the following chapters vary greatly in their offerings and the type of retirees they attract. Indeed, even individual communities within a region may vary greatly. Predominant retiree lifestyles in Florida communities will be discussed in each of the following chapters, but you are urged to visit and make your own judgment as to whether a particular community will be compatible with your preferences.

Entertainment and Cultural Activities. As you would expect in a state with such a large number of retirees, most communities have a wide range of cultural activities and entertainment designed to suit the preferences of an older population, whether those preferences include opera, bingo, or both. Dinner theaters abound and are popular with older residents and visitors. Practically every town big enough to have an adequate auditorium is on the itinerary of traveling companies from hit Broadway shows. Popular entertainers and groups tour the state, and because of Florida's older population you are as likely to be offered Robert Goulet singing show tunes from the 1950s as you are the latest rock band. Art and history museums, public libraries, choral groups, local symphonies and opera companies, dance ensembles, lectures, botanical gardens, and commercial art galleries round out the cultural and entertainment opportunities of many Florida communities.

While most larger communities will offer all the above, many communities have developed a cultural and entertainment image that causes them to attract residents with similar interests. Some retirees choose a community where residents take pride in their city's image as the cultural capital of the state, while others seek a town with bragging rights to the nation's best bass fishing and golf courses. Those wishing a livelier nightlife will probably find Fort Lauderdale preferable to Naples, and those whose main desire is to be involved in the community activities of a small town will be happier in Live Oak or Mount Dora than in Orlando. Fortunately for many couples who do not share the same tastes, in most of Florida it is possible to live in one and be within an easy drive of the other. Choosing the right community will guarantee not only that you will find the kind of entertainment and cultural activities you enjoy but that you will find other like-minded retirees you will enjoy getting to know.

Sports and Outdoor Recreation. Many retirees choose Florida because the state's climate makes year-round outdoor sports and recreation possible. However, if your mental image of retiree sports is a leisurely game of shuffleboard, you are in for a surprise. Florida's retirees play golf and tennis, scuba dive, skate, swim, water-ski, run, fish, hunt, and work out in gyms. In fact, you will find retirees in Florida involved in every sport that doesn't require ice, snow, or a mountain, and even ice is increasingly a possibility given the growing number of indoor skating rinks. To meet the wishes of these very active retirees, most communities provide a variety of sports and recreational facilities.

Avid sports spectators will be delighted to find that most of Florida's larger cities have one or more sports franchises, and the number of professional baseball, basketball, football, and hockey teams seems to grow every year. As of now the following cities have professional teams: Jacksonville (football), Miami (football, baseball, basketball, and hockey), Orlando (basketball), Tampa (football and hockey), and St. Petersburg (baseball). The new sport of arena football has already found a home in Orlando and Tampa. In addition, many major-league baseball teams from all over the nation have spring training headquarters in a Florida community. Known as the Grapefruit League, the games between these teams give baseball fans an economical opportunity to watch their favorite teams and players every year. As of this writing the following teams practice in Florida: Atlanta Braves, Lake Buena Vista; Baltimore Orioles, Fort Lauderdale; Boston Red Sox, Fort Myers; Cincinnati Reds, Sarasota; Cleveland Indians, Winter Haven; Detroit Tigers, Lakeland; Florida Marlins, Melbourne; Houston Astros, Kissimmee; Kansas City Royals, Davenport; Los Angeles Dodgers, Vero Beach; Minnesota Twins, Fort Myers; Montreal Expos, West Palm Beach; New York Mets, Port St. Lucie; New York Yankees, Tampa; Philadelphia Phillies, Clearwater; Pittsburgh Pirates, Bradenton; St. Louis Cardinals, West Palm Beach; Tampa Bay Devil Rays, St. Petersburg; Texas Rangers, Port Charlotte; and Toronto Blue Jays, Dunedin.

Many of Florida's colleges and universities have nationally ranked baseball, basketball, and football teams with exciting state rivalries, and several Florida cities play host to end-of-the-year college football bowl games. Begun in 1935, the oldest is Miami's Orange Bowl. Jacksonville's Gator Bowl and Orlando's Citrus Bowl celebrated fifty-year anniversaries in 1996. The two newest are Tampa's Outback Bowl, begun in 1986 as the Hall of Fame Bowl, and Miami's seven-year-old Carquest Auto Parts Bowl.

Because they are so popular with tourists and retirees, a number of Florida communities now offer pari-mutuel betting at greyhound and horse racetracks and at jai alai frontons. Bingo, another well-attended "sport," is widely available throughout Florida.

The following guides, available free from the state of Florida, provide a great deal of up-to-date information about spectator and participant sports in the Sunshine State: *Florida Camping Directory; Florida Fishing; Florida Sports Vacation Guide; Grapefruit League Spring Training Guide; Destination: Florida Golf, 1998; and Florida Vacation Guide.* (see Additional Resources for details.)

Educational Opportunities

Florida's public school, community college, and university systems have responded to the needs and wishes of the state's burgeoning retiree population with continuing-education programs for adult members of their communities. Florida's university system comprises ten state universities with a total of twenty-five campuses spread rather evenly over the state. Twenty-five private colleges and universities range in size from the 12,000-student University of Miami to the 500-student Edward Waters College in Jacksonville and provide many kinds of specialized degrees such as art and design, business, theology, and aeronautics. While not many retirees expect to enroll in a four-year degree program at a university, the presence of a college or university campus has many advantages for the residents of a community. In addition to a diversity of noncredit community-education courses and seminars (many designed expressly for retirees), a university almost always brings with it concerts, lectures, art shows, athletic programs, and a general level of culture.

The Florida community college system is made up of twenty-eight community colleges with a total of eighty-seven campuses and a great many off-campus centers. Wherever you live in Florida you will not be far from a superb community college facility. As the name implies, Florida's community colleges are not junior colleges but true community institutions offering programs that prepare students to transfer to a university for a four-year degree, any number of two-year degrees leading to highly technical fields of work, and a range of noncredit educational programs and services based on the lifelong learning needs and wishes of the community. It is not unusual for retirees to return to a community college to pursue a two-year degree, sometimes to prepare for a second (or third) career but often simply for their own satisfaction. Many community colleges allow senior citizens to enroll in any class free of charge if the class has not been filled with tuition-paying students by the time classes begin. Some community colleges operate centers or programs developed for the senior population of the college's district. Older students outnumber recent high school graduates in community colleges, making these institutions very comfortable places for retirees.

All of Florida's sixty-seven county public school systems provide adult education, offering—at very low cost—courses in foreign languages, the arts, computers, health and nutrition, and citizenship education, to name but a few. Since adult education classes are held throughout most counties, either in adult centers or in regular school classrooms, you can usually find a convenient location. Classes offered in public schools are most often held at night or in the late afternoon. In every Florida community you will find the retiree population heavily involved in public school adult-education programs.

Military Retirement

Florida has long been a popular choice for military retirees who look for proximity to active military bases and Veterans Administration medical facilities for the services they provide. It should be noted, however, that not only are military bases closing across the nation but services to retirees are being curtailed at many installations. As a military retiree you should check carefully to find out what services are possible in a particular location. As of this writing the following Florida cities and towns are host to military bases or Veterans Administration facilities:

Cocoa Beach	Cape Canaveral Air Force Station
Destin, Fort Walton Beach	Eglin Air Force Base
Gainesville	Veterans Administration Medical Center
Jacksonville	Mayport U.S. Navy Station
	Jacksonville Naval Air Station

Key West	Key West Naval Air Station
Melbourne	Patrick Air Force Base
Miami	Veterans Administration Medical Center
Panama City	Tyndall Air Force Base
Pensacola	Pensacola Naval Air Station
St. Petersburg	Bay Pines Veterans Administration Medical Center
Tampa	MacDill Air Force Base
West Palm Beach	Veterans Administration Medical Center

Can You Work?

Retirees who wish to work full- or part-time will find that it is not difficult to get a job in Florida. Employers here have discovered that retirees are reliable, are hard workers, and get along well with the older population the business serves. Whether it is at the checkout counter in the grocery store, at SeaWorld, or in a restaurant, you are as likely to see a sixty-year-old as a teenager holding down a job. In all facets of the tourist and hospitality industries a great many jobs are part-time and seasonal, providing excellent work opportunities for seniors who wish to supplement their incomes but are not seeking full-time or year-round employment.

Senior Activities

Because of the great number of retirees, practically every community of any size in Florida has one or more "senior centers." Funded through private philanthropy and/or a combination of local, state, and federal grants, these centers provide a variety of services such as entertainment and social activities, health services, educational programs, financial and legal counseling, and sometimes meals. They often serve to coordinate volunteer efforts for the community, linking seniors who wish to volunteer with organizations and agencies in need of help. Access to a senior center will be discussed in many of the communities profiled in the following chapters.

Getting around the State

Partly because of its interest in promoting tourism and partly because of its efforts over the years to bring in business and industry, Florida has an excellent system of well-maintained and attractive highways. I–10 runs east and west across the Panhandle from Pensacola to Jacksonville; I–95 is the north-south connector for the cities and towns on the east coast of the state; I–4 crosses the middle of the state from Tampa to Daytona Beach; and I–75 connects the north central part of the state with Tampa and the lower west coast. As I-75 swings east from Naples and crosses the Everglades to connect with Fort Lauderdale and Miami, it is known as "Alligator Alley," a name carried over from before it became a fenced-in superhighway. In those earlier days alligators sleeping on the road were a very real nighttime hazard. The Florida Turnpike, a toll road running from its connection with I–75 just south of Ocala to Miami, speeds traffic through that part of the state. Well-maintained federal and state highways connect other cities and towns throughout Florida. This network of highways makes it possible for you to reside anywhere in the state—perhaps enjoying the amenities of small-town living—yet take advantage of all that a nearby city has to offer.

What about All Those Tourists?

Some of you who have visited one or more of Florida's tourist attractions along with crowds of other visitors may wonder if tourists are a big problem to those who live here. The answer really depends on where you live. Plus, there is a difference between tourists and part-time residents, who are often winter-only residents. Cities such as Sarasota and Naples on the Gulf Coast, Dade City and Zephyrhills in central Florida, and Boca Raton on the Atlantic have some tourist visitors but the greatest increase in their population comes from winter residents. Places like Orlando with its theme parks, Panama City with its popular beach, and Key West with its funky atmosphere are literally swamped with tourists at certain times of the year. During the season snowbirds become residents, frequenting the same restaurants, grocery stores, and movie theaters as year-round residents. Those who live year-round in cities with large numbers of winter residents do experience more crowded conditions in the busiest season, but in most cases the host city has provided for these fluctuations in its long-range planning.

Tourists are usually easier to avoid, because they tend to flock to tourist attractions. Friends who have visited Orlando as tourists have asked me how I could bear to live there with such crowds. I usually find that those asking the question came to Orlando as tourists and stayed in a motel on International Drive, a several-block-long street of motels, fast food restaurants, and tourist attractions. They spent all of their time at SeaWorld and Walt Disney World, along with a few hundred thousand other tourists at the busy time of the year. From my experience I know that if you live in Orlando, you are almost unaware of tourists "out there." No resident would think of going to International Drive other than somewhat reluctantly to pick up guests, and residents seldom go to the theme parks at the busiest time of the year if they can avoid it.

On the positive side of the ledger, tourists and seasonal residents benefit year-round residents. The taxes they pay help keep taxes low for residents. A town committed to tourism will want to ensure the community is clean and visually attractive. Roads, beaches, and parks will be better maintained. Tourists and winter visitors help support community amenities such as theaters, galleries, restaurants, golf courses, and museums that might not be able to exist on the support of year-round residents alone.

If you prefer a community with a stable, year-round population and no tourists, there are a great many in Florida, and they are easy to find. Before you pass up an attractive community because it draws tourists and seasonal residents, however, you might want to talk to some year-round residents to find out how much of a problem it really is.

Will You Be Welcome in Florida?

The answer to this question is a resounding yes. You will be welcomed by both state and local officials and by other residents. State and local officials recognize that retirees are a valuable asset to the community. A recent study by an Orlando-based economic research firm found that Florida's growing retiree population (the 2.65 million residents over age sixty-five) spent $37 billion in 1997. This was exceeded only by the $42 billion spent by Florida's tourists. It was also pointed out that retirees contributed $1.04 billion in school taxes, a great benefit since they rarely impact the state's school systems. Elected officials realize the power of retiree votes and are always ready to welcome a new addition. Since practically everyone you will meet in popular retirement communities came from somewhere else, there is almost never a native-versus-newcomer attitude. In many communities you will find retiree clubs and organizations ready to extend a very warm welcome.

What to Do When the Grandkids Visit

At the beginning of each chapter you will find a section devoted to some interesting, very often inexpensive, and local things to do when the grandkids visit you in your new retirement home. Because Florida has been a popular family vacation destination for so many years, there is no shortage of entertaining attractions, and the lists given barely scratch the surface of things to do. It almost goes without saying that Florida's beaches will provide the most inexpensive fun for the grandkids wherever you may choose to live. Even the more landlocked parts of the state are not more than an hour or so from a coast, and many of those areas have lakes, rivers, and springs. Florida's many state and national parks provide ample opportunities for camping, hiking, swimming, diving, canoeing, and tubing. Florida's sunshine and warm weather make outdoor activities popular. Water parks abound, and there is hardly a spot in the state without one or more miniature golf courses for you and your young duffers. A few of Florida's major attractions—such as Walt Disney World, SeaWorld, Universal Studios, Busch Gardens, and the Kennedy Space Center—are so popular it will be worth a little longer drive to visit them. They may be listed in several regions with distances indicated. Where possible, admission fees have been included, but they are subject to change and often vary with the time of year. It will always be worth a phone call to get up-to-date information about admission fees as well as hours of operation. Check your local newspapers and your chamber of commerce for flyers with discount coupons for many attractions.

A Word about Sources of Information

A variety of sources has been used to compile the information in this book. In many instances you will want to use these same sources as you conduct your own research into Florida's many retirement destinations. Since so many of you are now using computers and are familiar with the Internet, E-mail and web site addresses have been included wherever available.

Chambers of Commerce. It is one of the missions of chambers of commerce to attract new residents and businesses, and most Florida chambers of commerce have very complete and informative relocation packets, frequently including community directories, maps, real estate brochures, and newcomer information pamphlets. In every city and town profiled in the following chapters information concerning the local chamber of commerce has been given. You should be aware, however, that since Florida's chambers of commerce are often inundated with requests for information, many have begun to charge a modest fee to recover the costs of expensive relocation materials. To avoid delays, you might want to call or E-mail a chamber to find out what kinds of materials are available and whether payment is required. In many cases where there is a charge you may pay by credit card.

Can you rely on information provided by a chamber of commerce? The answer is yes—with one important caveat. You may be quite certain that the information a chamber of commerce provides will be truthful, but it may be somewhat one-sided. You will not find negative aspects of the community presented, and your attention will not be called to potential community problems. Read chamber of commerce literature to get an idea of all the good things about a community, but talk to local citizens and read the local newspaper to find out the problems and issues the community is facing.

State Agency Reports and Other Materials. Because of Florida's great interest in attracting new residents as well as tourists, many of its state agencies provide a wealth of valuable and up-to-date information about the state. These reports, guides, and pamphlets will help you decide if Florida is the state for you and, if it is, where in Florida you will be happiest. Some of these have been mentioned in this chapter and others will be referred to as we go into more detail about various regions, cities, and towns in the following chapters. Most of these materials are free for the asking.

Books, Magazines, and Newspapers. Your local bookstore will probably have a selection of books about Florida, both fiction and nonfiction. A few of these have been referred to in this and other chapters. I urge you to find these and other books in your bookstore or in your library and read as much as you can about the state you are considering for your retirement. Several magazines cover the state as a whole and many cities and regions have their own magazines. These periodicals are usually glossy and colorful, most often focusing on designer homes, glittering social occasions, and leading citizens. Even if those things are not your cup of tea, you might wish to read an issue or two to acquaint yourself with what a particular community thinks of itself. Nothing, however, will acquaint you with a city or town as quickly or as thoroughly as reading the local newspaper. I urge you to subscribe for several months to the newspaper of the community you are seriously considering, at least to the weekend papers, which contain the most complete real estate and entertainment information. Increasingly you will find local newspapers available on the Internet.

Internet Sources. Many Internet sources provide free access to information and services you may find helpful in your further research on retirement locations in Florida. Two that I find particularly helpful and easy to use are:

The Florida Living Network (http://fl.living.net/community/), a marketing and information service owned and operated by the Florida Association of Realtors. It provides current profiles of forty-three Florida cities, towns, and counties with information on the real estate market, demographics, weather, major employers, public school education, transportation, things to do in the outdoors, amateur and professional sports, culture and entertainment, shopping, higher education, and information for senior citizens. The information is cleverly written and, from my experience, right on the money.

Realtor.com (http://realtor.com/) is the official Internet site of the National Association of Realtors. It provides detailed information on millions of homes for sale nationwide along with helpful links to real estate–related sites, including mortgage information and moving and relocation service suppliers.

1996 Florida Statistical Abstract. The *1996 Florida Statistical Abstract* must be singled out in terms of the information it has provided for this book. It is published annually by the Bureau of Economic and Business Research of the University of Florida. Data concerning the population of cities and towns, average purchase price of homes, average rents, and many other bits of information are based on the current edition of this helpful book.

Local Residents. I have spoken with local residents, particularly retirees, in every community profiled in this book and so should you. There is no substitute for talking with others who have already made such a move, particularly those with interests, tastes, and levels of income similar to yours. Visiting churches, senior centers, public libraries, or clubs will put you in touch with many retirees in any Florida community.

Our Route around Florida

Following this overview chapter, we will begin at the western border of the Panhandle, take a counterclockwise route around the entire coast, and then proceed from north to south down the middle of the state. For this book Florida has been divided into seven regions with corresponding chapters as follows: the Panhandle, the Central Gulf Coast, the Southwest Gulf Coast, the Southeast Atlantic Coast, the Mid-Atlantic Coast, Northeast Florida, and Central Florida.

THE PANHANDLE

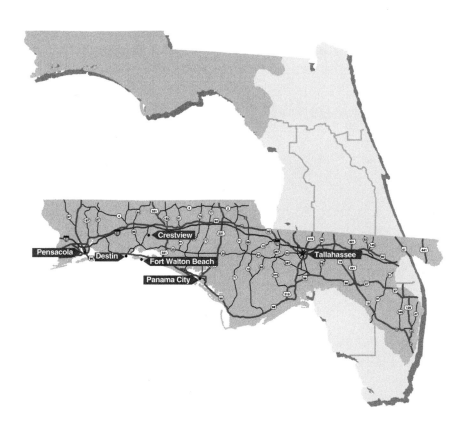

THE PANHANDLE

The Panhandle of Florida is a narrow strip of land—300 miles wide but only 30 to 60 miles deep—between the Gulf of Mexico and the Alabama and Georgia state lines. It begins at Florida's western boundary, the Perdido River, and ends unofficially where the Suwannee River twists and turns its way southwesterly from the Okefenokee Swamp in Georgia to the Gulf of Mexico. East and south of the Panhandle, Florida becomes a peninsula. The Panhandle may be narrow, but its twenty-two counties are geographically and economically diverse. In fact it almost seems there are three panhandles. There are beaches, then coastal cities and towns on the mainland, and finally rural areas to the north. From west to east, the cities and counties most popular with retirees are: Escambia County (Pensacola), Okaloosa County (Fort Walton Beach, Destin, and Crestview), Bay County (Panama City), and Leon County (Tallahassee).

The beaches here have been declared the most beautiful in the world. The sand, which really is finely crushed quartz, is so unbelievably white and the usually calm Gulf water is such a bright blue-green that the coast's nickname, "the Emerald coast," seems entirely appropriate. The beaches are on barrier islands, separated from the mainland by bays, bayous, and lagoons. All of the Panhandle's beaches are popular summer resorts. Winter, mild and sunny as it is, finds only residents and a few hardy tourists (very often Canadians) enjoying the Gulf air. Some tourist-oriented businesses close in the winter. On these Gulf beaches you find many condominiums, apartments, and tourist accommodations, but few houses. The beach homes you do find are likely to be very expensive, and many are summer retreats. The community of Seaside, on the beach between Panama City and Destin, is certainly the most publicized residential development in recent years. Its beautiful and colorful adaptations of old southern summer houses with front porches and picket fences have been featured in many architectural and home magazines. One-bedroom apartments in Seaside begin at $200,000, and most houses are in the $500,000 to $800,000 range. While most of the Panhandle's beach communities are not likely to attract other than the wealthiest retirees, they contribute to the beauty of the area and provide recreation to all who live nearby.

The Panhandle's coastal cities and towns developed on those parts of the coast where barrier islands created protected harbors for shipping and naval installations and where well-formed beaches attracted both tourists and residents. With land more readily available than on the beaches, these communities have clusters of residential developments at all price levels. Generally speaking, however, you will find that housing costs are lower in this part of Florida than in many other coastal areas. The Panhandle is home to several large military installations, and its towns attract a great many military retirees.

The "third" Panhandle begins just a short distance inland from the coast. Here the land is hilly, sparsely populated, and agriculture rather than tourism is the economic base. The towns in this area will remind you of rural communities throughout the South. Retirees looking for small-town living in friendly communities away from urban problems (and lacking some urban amenities) will do well to look at Chipley, Marianna, De Funiak Springs, Milton, or any one of several others in the northern part of the Panhandle. All are within a short drive of larger coastal cities and towns. The large area inland from the "Big Bend," where the coast turns southward, contains low-lying wetlands and pine forests with only a few communities. Here there are no barrier islands, and the coast more often consists of marshes with a few man-made beaches. Retirees looking for affordable acreage and a rural lifestyle have found the towns of Perry, Chiefland, and Cross City appealing.

One major inland city in the Panhandle is Tallahassee, Florida's capital city. It may seem strange that a city less than 20 miles south of the Georgia state line and more than 500 miles from heavily populated southeast Florida is the state capital, but in 1823 when the capital was selected there were very few settlements south of the narrow strip of land on the northern edge of the state. Tallahassee was centrally located, almost equidistant from Pensacola and St. Augustine, Florida's only two cities at the time.

Although winter is mild and very brief, those who like four comfortable seasons enjoy the weather in this part of Florida. While the Gulf of Mexico moderates temperatures near the coast, northern areas of the Panhandle may expect occasional frost. Infrequently during the winter season the thermometer may drop below freezing, but it is only a few hours before the bright Florida sun warms things up again.

When Grandkids Visit. Throughout this region of Florida you may have trouble getting the grandkids away from the beautiful white-sand beaches. Running the length of the Panhandle, they are free and accessible. When you can get the kids into something other than their bathing suits, there is much to see and do. In Pensacola the *National Museum of Naval Aviation* has dozens of exhibits tracing the history of flight from the earliest airplanes to the Skylab Module. An adjoining IMAX theater shows "The Magic of Flight" featuring the Navy's Blue Angels. The museum is free but the theater costs $4.50 with discounts for children and seniors.

A half-hour from Pensacola is the little town of Milton, famous for its springs, rivers, and creeks. More than 100,000 visitors come here each year to paddle canoes and kayaks or simply drift in tubes down clear rivers with white sand bottoms. You will have a choice of quiet streams ideal for family canoeing and tubing or some with rapids for the more adventuresome. Canoes, kayaks, and tubes are available from several rental companies.

Between Pensacola and Fort Walton Beach is *The Zoo*, a 50-acre nature park with more than 700 animals and the Safari Line train. Admission is $9.75 for adults and $5.75 for children ages 3 to 11. Children under 3 are free.

Near Fort Walton Beach and Eglin Air Force Base is the *Air Force Armament Museum* with aircraft and armament dating back to World War I. The museum is free. Famous as a family vacation spot, Panama City Beach has just about everything you could want to amuse and interest the grandkids, including several miniature golf courses, an amusement park with more than thirty rides, and one of the largest water parks in the South.

In Tallahassee you can give the grandkids a lesson in civics by touring the Capitol building and watching the Florida Legislature in operation or let them experience one of the largest and deepest springs in the world at nearby *Wakulla Springs State Park* with glass-bottom boats and swimming. Entrance to the park is $3.25 per vehicle with up to eight people and $1.00 for each additional person. Boat tours are $4.50 for adults and $2.25 for kids. About an hour west of Tallahassee is *Florida*

Caverns State Park. Entrance to the park is $3.25 per vehicle with up to eight people and $1.00 for each additional person. A guided one-hour tour of the caverns is $4.00 for adults and $2.00 for kids over age 3.

ESCAMBIA COUNTY: Pensacola

Escambia County (population 286,301) is the gateway to Florida for anyone coming from the west on I–10 or old U.S. 98. Like much of the Panhandle, it has a popular Gulf coast with wonderful beaches and—not very far inland—hills, forests, and farming communities. Here, creeks, bayous, and small rivers take the place of the coast's bays and open Gulf. All of Escambia County is popular with retirees. Those looking for a more urban environment choose Pensacola, while those who prefer a small-town ambience choose one of the many rural communities only a few miles away. In recent years Escambia County (lumped with neighboring Santa Rosa County in the statistics) ranked fifty-eighth among all U.S. counties in the number of retirees moving in from out of state.

Cost of Living. Adding to its appeal to retirees is Escambia County's low cost of living. Escambia County ranks thirty-eighth in the state with a cost of living 93.83 percent of the state average. Escambia County citizens have voted to add a 1 percent sales tax to the state's 6 percent. The cost of housing is 10.84 percent below the state average. The average purchase price of a house is $79,000. Escambia County ranks thirtieth in the state with an average monthly rent for an apartment of $531.

Climate. Escambia County's proximity to so much water moderates winter temperatures even though it is about as far north as you can go in Florida. Throughout Florida, temperatures are more moderate nearer the coast than inland. The chamber of commerce in Pensacola reports 343 days of sunshine a year.

Pensacola–Escambia County Weather

| | In degrees Fahrenheit | | | | |
	Jan.	Apr.	July	Oct.	Annual Rainfall
DAILY HIGHS	59.8	76.6	89.9	79.1	62.25"
DAILY LOWS	41.4	58.5	74.2	59.4	

Medical Care. Escambia County is served by three major hospitals with a total of 1,463 beds. The Pensacola Naval Hospital, a 138-bed acute-care medical and surgical hospital, provides care for retired military personnel.

Transportation. The Pensacola Regional Airport has direct flights to only a few cities in the Southeast. A larger airport in Mobile, Alabama, an hour away, provides more direct flights to other parts of the country. Local transportation is provided by Escambia County Area Transit with thirty buses and eighteen routes plus a trolley service in downtown Pensacola.

Opportunities for Continuing Education. Two state institutions of higher education, the University of West Florida and Pensacola Junior College, offer many courses and programs aimed at the needs and interests of retirees in the community. The Escambia County public school system offers a complete program of adult education.

Pensacola

It isn't widely known, even in Florida, that Pensacola is one of the state's most beautiful and historic cities. Built on several hills overlooking broad bays and lagoons, Pensacola may remind you of San Francisco. Further, its many colorfully renovated Queen Anne, Tudor Revival, Victorian, and Craftsman bungalow homes in the historic North Hill Preservation District need not take a back seat to San Francisco's "painted ladies." With its hills, bays, and sparkling white beaches that run for miles along the Gulf of Mexico, it is hard to beat Pensacola's natural assets. Historically, however, Pensacola has always had to yield to St. Augustine. Although settled six years earlier (1559), Pensacola's earliest settlement did not survive a disastrous hurricane, and St. Augustine claims the title of the oldest *continuous* European settlement in the United States. Pensacola was permanently settled in 1698 and now considers itself America's "First Place City." Like much of Florida, the flags of Spain, France, England, the Confederate States of America, and the United States have flown over it, and Pensacola has done a fine job of preserving its illustrious past in the Seville and Palofox historic districts.

About 1,000 new residents are added each year to the city's population of approximately 60,000. In July 1997, *Money* magazine rated

Pensacola as the thirty-third best place to live in the United States. Of Escambia County's total resident population of 286,301, more than 35,000 are retirees. It is no secret that servicemen and -women often retire to the area they found most pleasant while on active duty, and many of Pensacola's new citizens are ex-military who remember the city fondly. Now, in retirement, they wish to be near the facilities of Pensacola Naval Air Station and Eglin Air Force Base. The chamber of commerce reports 30,000 military retirees in the general area.

Housing. In Pensacola and all of Escambia County your real estate dollars go a long, long way. Newcomers are pleased to learn that the gorgeous older homes in the North Hill Preservation District are priced affordably when compared to similar properties in other parts of the country. Other areas a home buyer may want to consider are the historic districts, architecturally interesting East Hill, and the neighborhoods near the Scenic Highway with wonderful views from a bluff high above Escambia Bay. Pensacola is a city with many tree-shaded older neighborhoods, beautiful modern developments, and luxurious condominiums and houses on its Gulf beaches.

In its offerings, Pensacola's low end ranges from large, modern, one-bedroom downtown condos in the low $30,000s to neighborhoods of bungalows and small homes below $40,000 in the most affordable areas. Restored historic homes with extraordinary views and prime locations (homes that would be listed for more than a million dollars in other cities) often sell for well under $300,000. Recently a large, award-winning, restored 1895 Queen Anne home with several bedrooms, original pine floors, and six fireplaces listed for $239,000. In the middle range, a handsome three-bedroom home with a pool will probably sell for about $90,000 in many locations. You can find a three-bedroom three-bath luxury townhouse with 12-foot ceilings near the Pensacola Country Club for just $89,900 or a unique three-bedroom courtyard home with a complete artist's studio for $139,900. Whether you prefer a simpler, scaled-down lifestyle or seek something approaching absolute luxury, Pensacola will delight you with the quality and abundance of housing it provides. In recent years the average sale price for a home sold by owners and through agents has been $92,790. Property taxes in Pensacola are about $21 per $1,000 nonexempt valuation.

Culture and Entertainment.   Pensacola has more cultural and entertainment opportunities than you might expect in a city of 60,000 people.

A section of the downtown area has been redeveloped as a cultural center with several old buildings turned into galleries, museums, studios, and performance facilities. The University of West Florida and Pensacola Junior College provide gallery space, performance venues, and a full calendar of events open to the community. The new Pensacola Cultural Center, brilliantly built in a renovated old jail, contains a 500-seat theater that houses the Pensacola Little Theater. The city also boasts the Pensacola Symphony Orchestra, a choral society, and the Pensacola Opera all of which offer several performances each season. Broadway shows, the New York City Opera, and Florida Ballet come to the beautifully restored Saenger Theatre. The Pensacola Museum of Art, several commercial galleries, and three artist cooperatives—including Quayside, the south's largest cooperative gallery—bring the visual arts to the community.

Sports and Recreation. As would be expected in a city that seems surrounded by water, much of Pensacola's recreation focuses on fishing, swimming, diving, waterskiing, boating, and other water sports. The bays offer protected water for the small-boat fisherman, and numerous charter boats provide opportunities for sport fishing farther from shore. Miles of public beaches, many preserved in their natural state, bring residents to the shore for picnics, swimming, and lounging in the sun. Sixteen public golf courses, many tennis courts, and bike and jogging trails keep the landlubber active.

Law Enforcement and Safety. In 1996 there were sixty-eight criminal offenses reported per 1,000 year-round residents in Pensacola. Since Pensacola is a tourist resort with a much larger summer population, this figure is somewhat misleading.

Senior Centers. Bayview Senior Center, operated by the Department of Leisure Services of the City of Pensacola, is a public facility open to all seniors over the age of fifty. The center offers a variety of programs, activities, and classes, including health screening, dances, fitness classes, luncheons, and courses offered by Pensacola Junior College.

Nearby Communities. Just across Escambia Bay from Pensacola is the rapidly growing town of **Pace**, population 17,000. Located near three military installations, Pace is popular with military retirees. The little rural town of **Milton**, population 7,500, is only thirty minutes away in nearby Santa Rosa County, but many miles away in spirit and atmosphere. Milton is typical of many north Florida towns with its town square, historic courthouse, and big old Victorian houses in the middle of the town. With several rivers nearby, Milton has been called the "Canoe Capital" of the state as more than 100,000 visitors come to paddle the area's heavily wooded waterways each year.

Addresses and Connections

Chamber of Commerce: Pensacola Area Chamber of Commerce, P.O. Box 550, Pensacola, FL 32953-0550; (800) 608–3479; http://www.chamber.pensacola.fl.us; E-mail: information@chamber.pensacola.fl.us

Newspaper: Pensacola News Journal (daily), P.O. Box 12710, Pensacola, FL 32574; (904) 435–8500

OKALOOSA COUNTY: Fort Walton Beach, Destin, and Crestview

Okaloosa County (population 165,319) stretches from the Alabama state line to the Gulf of Mexico. On the Gulf coast you find a very narrow strip of land with beaches and two of Florida's most popular beach communities. Inland and just above the coast is gigantic Eglin Air Force Base. North of the base you are once again in rural north Florida. Since almost half of the county's 936 square miles is taken up by Eglin, it is not surprising that this part of Florida has an obvious military orientation.

Cost of Living. In spite of the expensive elements of its beach communities, Okaloosa County ranks twenty-fourth in the state with an overall cost of living 96.26 percent of the state average. The cost of housing is 8.26 percent below the state average. The average home purchase price in Okaloosa County is about $85,500. There will certainly be a wide variation in apartment rents between beach areas and inland neighborhoods in an area so impacted by tourism as Fort Walton Beach and Destin. Okaloosa County ranks fifteenth in the state with an average apartment rent of $598.

Climate. The weather in Okaloosa County is typical Panhandle weather: cooler in summer and warmer in winter on the coast than inland. Northern areas can expect frost and now and then a brief nip of freezing temperatures in the winter.

Pensacola–Okaloosa County Weather

| | In degrees Fahrenheit | | | | |
	Jan.	Apr.	July	Oct.	Annual Rainfall
DAILY HIGHS	59.8	76.6	89.9	79.1	62.25"
DAILY LOWS	41.4	58.5	74.2	59.4	

Medical Care. Okaloosa County is served by three hospitals with a total of 432 beds, plus a geriatric hospital with 120 beds. Several medical centers have physicians on call in practically every specialty. Military retirees are served by the excellent medical facilities at Eglin Air Force Base.

Transportation. Okaloosa County Air Terminal offers direct flights to a few southeastern cities. There is no public transportation in either Fort Walton Beach or Destin.

Opportunities for Continuing Education. Okaloosa-Walton Community College provides many courses and activities for senior citizens in the community.

Fort Walton Beach and Destin

East along the coast of the Panhandle, 40 miles from Pensacola, are the "twin" cities of Fort Walton Beach (population 22,037) and Destin (population 9,802). These towns share a beautiful Gulf setting and great numbers of summer tourists. Few cities adjacent to large military installations (and 724-square-mile Eglin Air Force Base is the largest U.S. installation in the world) are able to maintain their unique personal character as successfully as Fort Walton Beach. Further, in spite of its name and its 26 miles of spectacular beaches, it is not just a beach community. From the Gulf up into the "highlands" north and east of Eglin, Fort Walton Beach establishes itself as the backbone community of one of the most appealing and scenic areas in Florida. If you imagine combining the freshness and natural vitality of a city like Portland, Oregon, with the watery beauty of the Louisiana bayous, and season the combination with a dash of dazzling white beaches, you might have Fort Walton Beach. Add to this wonderful environment an advanced infrastructure that supports the military establishment here and the educational legacy of a highly skilled military population and you have a perfect setting for a comfortable retirement. In May 1997, *Money* magazine rated Fort Walton Beach the tenth best place to live in the United States.

Destin is a much smaller community, and the impact of summer tourism and summer residents is much more obvious than on nearby Fort Walton Beach. Destin is visibly more upscale than its neighbors along the Panhandle. Its posh condominiums, elegant shops, and landscaped parkways prompted one visitor to label it "Boca on the Gulf." Neighboring communities to the north, however, bring you back to the real Panhandle with their hills, bays, and wooded residential neighborhoods. With affordable housing, all the amenities of nearby towns, and access to the gorgeous beaches and water activities of Destin, this area has become very appealing to retirees. In the November 1996 issue of *Southern Living* magazine, Destin was voted as having the best beaches in the South.

Housing. The fact that the cost of housing in Okaloosa County is 8.26 percent below the state average is even more heartening when you consider that it is inflated by terribly expensive houses and condominiums in the more elegant beach communities. Most retirees to this area will be interested in the affordable homes in neighborhoods away from the coast, and there are a great many attractive and very inexpensive possibilities.

Fort Walton Beach's bays and bayous reach out in many directions, creating a great deal of natural waterfront and water-view property. As a result, the abundance of affordable and gorgeous homes is amazing. A "waterfront" getaway with three bedrooms, two baths, a community pool, and community docks was listed for $58,900. An immaculate four-bedroom three-bath cottage-style home with raised ceilings and hardwood floors in a very nice neighborhood was for sale for $102,900. If you need elbow room, a four-bedroom contemporary on six acres with in-ground pool, workshop, and office was recently listed for $114,900. In a family neighborhood snuggled near a state park just north of the Mid-Bay Bridge you can find modern three-bedroom homes for less than $100,000. For around $170,000 you might find a four-bedroom Georgian home with a pool in an established older community like Niceville, a hilly peninsula of land jutting into Choctawhatchee Bay. In Mary Esther near downtown Fort Walton Beach, three-bedroom three-bath homes list for less than $110,000. In all of these neighborhoods you are never far from water. The Mid-Bay Bridge allows residents of newer neighborhoods north of the bay to hop over to Destin and Henderson

Beach State Park in just a few minutes. Property taxes in Fort Walton Beach are about $17.80 per $1,000 nonexempt valuation.

Of course, if it's rather exclusive beach living you're after, Destin will be very hard to beat. Although it is more expensive than Fort Walton Beach or other nearby areas, there is a return on your real estate investment. Destin is a beautifully developed modern beach community with a year-round population of around 10,000. It absolutely bustles during the busy season when summer residents and tourists abound, yet it is very subdued during the mild winter months. Most residents live in mid-rise and high-rise condominiums fronting on the Gulf. While $200,000 to $400,000 condominium apartments are the rule in Destin, there are interesting alternatives such as the new "Beach Street Cottages," a development of condominium apartments in a beach-cottage style priced at just over $100,000. Stunning new Mediterranean homes near the beach with limestone floors and 9-foot ceilings are being built for around $150,000. Large new homes full of beach character are still being built. A 3,300-square-foot five-bedroom four-bath home with a view of the Gulf of Mexico recently listed for $179,900. For those with more modest needs, an energetic real estate shopper can still locate bargains in this beach area. When I was there last a modest home with an in-ground pool listed for $99,500. Destin also offers an abundant supply of million-dollar penthouses on the Gulf. For those of you who choose to spend your retirement dollars in other ways, Destin will be a place to visit from your comfortable, affordable home a few minutes away from the beach. For those who can't live without sand in their shoes, those wonderful views, and a chance to rub elbows with well-to-do folks from around the world, Destin is just the place! Property taxes in Destin are about $14.90 per $1,000 of nonexempt valuation.

Culture and Entertainment. Residents of Fort Walton Beach, Destin, and neighboring communities can take advantage of all the cultural and entertainment opportunities of Pensacola, less than an hour away. In addition, the spectacular new $20-million Arts Center of Okaloosa-Walton Community College provides art galleries; art, music, and theater instruction; and a 1,650-seat main theater for concerts, dance performances, and touring shows open to the community. The Fort Walton Beach Art Museum and several commercial galleries promote the visual arts.

Sports and Recreation. The Gulf of Mexico, Choctawhatchee Bay, and numerous bayous and rivers make the Destin–Fort Walton Beach area a water sports capital, and its residents take advantage of all the possibilities. Destin calls itself the "World's Luckiest Fishing Village." More than one hundred charter and party boats, ranging in size from six passengers to more than one hundred, are on call. Bottom fishing in the Gulf is the specialty, but fishing from smaller boats in the area's many rivers, bays, and bayous is also very popular. Just being lazy on one of the world's most beautiful beaches is an attraction for residents and visitors. Seven golf courses with 189 holes keep golfers busy and challenged.

Law Enforcement and Safety. In the 1996 statewide annual crime report there were fifty-four criminal offenses per 1,000 year-round residents in the city of Fort Walton Beach. For Niceville, a residential community less impacted by summer tourism, the rate was twenty-six, and for unincorporated Okaloosa County the rate was twenty-six.

Senior Centers. The Fort Walton Beach Senior Citizens Center provides a range of services to the area's over-age-fifty-five population, including classes in art, crafts, dance, and bridge; activities such as bowling, card parties and tournaments, pool tournaments, square dancing, and bingo; health services such as blood pressure checks and flu shots; and regular events such as covered-dish luncheons and parties. A number of facilities in the community offer several levels of assisted living.

Nearby Communities. **Niceville** (population 11,705) is a lovely residential community across the bay from Destin. Niceville has some of the most attractive building sites in the Panhandle. **Crestview** (population 12,429) is a small town north of Eglin Air Force Base and the county seat of Okaloosa County. If it were not for the base, Crestview would probably be a sleepy hamlet more concerned with crops and livestock than with new neighborhoods and affordable housing. As it is, however, Crestview is a magnet for off-base military housing and for retirees, especially military retirees. Housing here is plentiful and very affordable. For example, a four-bedroom home on five acres was recently listed for $134,900. If you don't need that much land to tend, a remodeled three-bedroom two-bath house with a barn and one acre of land was listed for $51,500. Attractive homes on treed lots abound in the $60,000 to $70,000 range. The terrain around Crestview is hilly and heavily forested, with many creeks and small rivers. For those of you who would like to keep a little touch of four seasons in your future and would like to live in beautiful natural surroundings, Crestview may be just the place for you.

Addresses and Connections

Chambers of Commerce: Destin Area Chamber of Commerce, P.O. Box 8, Destin, FL 32540-0008; (850) 837–6241; http://www.destinfl. com/chamber.htm

Greater Fort Walton Beach Chamber of Commerce, P.O. Box 640, Fort Walton Beach, FL 32549-0640; (904) 244–8191; Fax, (904) 244–1935; http://interlead.com/fwb.chamber/index.html

Crestview Area Chamber of Commerce, 502 South Main Street, Crestview, FL 32536; (904) 682-3212

Newspapers: The Northwest Florida Daily News (daily), P.O. Box 2949, Fort Walton Beach, FL 32549; (850) 863–1111

The Walton Sun (weekly, free), P.O. Box 2363, Santa Rosa Beach, FL 32459; (850) 267–4555; Fax, (850) 267–0929

BAY COUNTY: Panama City

Bay County (population 142,159) is another Panhandle county heavily impacted by the military and by summer tourism. Both have a generally beneficial effect on the county and those who live here year-round. Tyndall Air Force Base and the Coastal Systems Station are the county's largest employers. The military presence creates a demand for and a turnover in housing as well as providing the amenities military retirees seek. Panama City Beach actively courts tourism and is inundated with crowds in the summer, but tourism provides funds for community beautification and renewal throughout the county. Panama City and other communities in the area enjoy the benefits of the tourism economy, but are not always in the thick of it.

Cost of Living. Bay County ranks thirtieth in the state with a cost of living 95.28 percent of the state average. Bay County has a 7 percent sales tax. The cost of housing is 10.43 percent below the state average. The average house purchase price is about $81,300. Bay County ranks twenty-first in the state with an average apartment rent of $565 a month.

Climate. Bay County's climate is moderated by its proximity to the Gulf of Mexico and St. Andrew Bay with all its tributaries.

Pensacola–Bay County Weather

| | In degrees Fahrenheit | | | | |
	Jan.	Apr.	July	Oct.	Annual Rainfall
DAILY HIGHS	59.8	76.6	89.9	79.1	62.25"
DAILY LOWS	41.4	58.5	74.2	59.4	

Medical Care. Two hospitals with a total of 529 beds serve the
Panama City area. The twenty-bed hospital on Tyndall Air Force Base
serves military retirees and dependents.

Transportation. The Panama City/Bay County International Airport
provides service to several larger cities in the Southeast. The Bay Town
Trolley System provides limited public transportation within the city for
a nominal fare.

Opportunities for Continuing Education. Gulf Coast Community
College's Office of Lifelong Learning offers a variety of courses for residents over age fifty. The fee for most courses is $20. The Panama City
campus of Florida State University offers undergraduate and graduate
degree programs.

Panama City

Panama City is 50 miles east of Destin on U.S. 98. The easternmost
of the Panhandle's popular beach communities, Panama City is another
coastal town developed around a large protected bay. St. Andrew Bay
branches into Grand Lagoon, West Bay, and North Bay, and these bays
spread out into nearly twenty fingerlike bayous reaching far inland, so
that wherever you go in Panama City and its adjacent towns you seem
to find a body of water. This, of course, creates miles of beautiful waterfront and water-view property for residential development. In fact, the
second most striking aspect of Panama City, after the wonderful views of
St. Andrew Bay and the open Gulf beyond, is the large number of beautiful and affordable waterfront homes. Most neighborhoods away from
the bay and bayous are heavily wooded.

With a population of 37,236 (and another 4,554 in Panama City
Beach), Panama City is large enough to have the amenities most retirees
seek. Like the other Panhandle towns we have discussed, Panama City
draws its share of military retirees. Tyndall Air Force Base is the city's

major employer and provides services to 8,500 retirees. Panama City is well laid out and even during the busier spring and summer tourist season, traffic circulates well. Wherever you live there is quick access to the downtown area and the Gulf beaches.

Housing. Chats with retirees who have moved to the Panhandle have convinced me that inexpensive housing is its most important drawing card. The cost of housing in Bay County is only 89.57 percent of Florida's already low average, making it immediately clear that Panama City is among the most affordable retirement towns in Florida. This is a sleepier town than many in Florida, and quiet middle-class neighborhoods abound. As a result, homes—even those on the waterfront—are priced tens of thousands (sometimes hundreds of thousands) of dollars below similar areas in other Gulf communities. Waterfront homes with three and four bedrooms, a pool, and a boathouse may be listed for around $200,000. And a modest three-bedroom beach cottage may come on the market for around $80,000! A two- or three-bedroom house in a wooded community north of downtown Panama City may sell for as little as $65,000. On the outskirts of Panama City a four-bedroom home on five acres nestled among flowering bushes, including a detached guest cottage and a greenhouse, listed for $117,500. For those who long for an older home, I recently saw a 2,600-square-foot five-bedroom home built in 1912 (but in great condition) on an oversize lot in Lynn Haven that was listed for $109,000.

Retirees from California, New York, or Boston will suffer reverse "sticker shock" when they see that for less than the price of their two-bedroom co-op or three-bedroom house back home they can purchase a beach duplex—a pair of two-bedroom two-bath town homes with a beautiful in-ground pool and Jacuzzi, and a private garden overlooking the Gulf—for $180,000. Or you might consider a colonial home on a manicured estate with circular drive, paneled wainscoting, crown molding, Italian chandeliers, silk wallpaper, an in-ground pool, four bedrooms and four baths for $249,950. Here you can enjoy water views, the amenities of an attractive small city, low real estate taxes, clean air, a wonderfully mild climate, and the world's most magnificent sunrises and sunsets. In between you can try to imagine how all these rewards are possible while not paying a single dollar in state income tax. Property taxes in Panama City are about $20 per $1,000 of nonexempt valuation.

Culture and Entertainment. The impressive Marina Civic Center, on the bay in downtown Panama City, provides a venue for all the performance arts including touring Broadway shows, operas, dance, and concerts. Ticket prices are modest and many events are free. The Visual Arts Center of Northwest Florida provides several gallery spaces for shows of local and out-of-town artists' work as well as touring art shows. There are many active civic groups dedicated to enriching the quality of life in Panama City. Among them are the Art Association, the Bay Arts Alliance, the Panhandle Writers Guild, the Panama City Music Association, the Audubon Society, and the Historical Society.

Sports and Recreation. Like all the coastal Panhandle cities and towns, recreation in Panama City tends to focus on its abundance of water. Fishing is very big here, in the bays and bayous and far out in the Gulf of Mexico. Freshwater fishing enthusiasts will delight in the many lakes and rivers that are said to be the home of trophy-size largemouth bass. St. Andrew State Park offers 1,260 acres of natural beach dunes and pine woods for picnicking and camping. For those who think Florida's beaches are too crowded and overdeveloped there is Shell Island. Accessible only by boat, Shell Island is an unspoiled barrier island with miles of natural beaches. Six golf courses are open to the public in Panama City.

Law Enforcement and Safety. In 1996 there were eighty-nine reported criminal offenses per 1,000 year-round residents in Panama City. An example of how distorted such figures can be in an area where there is a high nonresident population, the rate for Panama City Beach was 324 offenses per 1,000.

Senior Centers. An active chapter of the National Association of Senior Friends provides many activities for its members in Panama City including get-acquainted meetings for newcomers, health screenings, a weight-loss support group, breakfasts and luncheons, trips and tours, fashion shows, and classes in arts and crafts, exercise, dance, computers, safe driving, and financial affairs.

Nearby Communities. **Panama City** is surrounded by separately incorporated small towns such as **Callaway** (pop. 14,044), which has attracted a great many military retirees, **Cedar Grove** (pop. 2,102) east of Panama City and close to Tyndall Air Force Base, and **Lynn Haven** (pop. 11,353) with its many lovely residential areas. All are worthy of your interest. **Panama City Beach** (pop. 4,554) has a great many motels, condominiums, and other resort accommodations but few residential neighborhoods.

Addresses and Connections

Chamber of Commerce: Bay County Chamber of Commerce, P.O. Box 1850, Panama City, FL 32402-1850; (888) 229–7483; Fax, (850) 763–6229; http://www.interoz.com/edchome.htm; E-mail: baycnty @interoz.com

Newspaper: Panama City News Herald (daily), P.O. Box 1940, Panama City, FL 32401; (850) 747–5000

LEON COUNTY: Tallahassee

Leon County (pop. 221,621) reaches from the Georgia state line to within 10 miles of the Gulf of Mexico. Tallahassee, Florida's capital city, is almost in the middle. If you are coming from other parts of Florida, the most striking thing about Leon County is its many hills. Actually they are the first of the foothills of the Appalachian Mountains. While there are large rural areas in Leon County (some would really be considered "backwoods"), Tallahassee with its dual focus on government and higher education is the dominant factor in this area.

Cost of Living. In spite of Tallahassee's reputation as a city where a great many people have seemingly unlimited expense accounts, Leon County ranks twentieth in the state with a cost of living only 96.79 percent of the state average. The cost of housing in Leon County is 8.5 percent below the state average. The average purchase price of a home in Leon County is $83,695. Leon County ranks twentieth in the state with an average monthly apartment rent of $567.

Climate. Tallahassee is 20 miles inland from the Gulf of Mexico and therefore does not enjoy the maximum benefit of its moderating effect. Temperatures will be slightly colder in the winter and warmer in the summer than in nearby Panama City, for example. Northern areas of Leon County will be considerably colder in winter.

Tallahassee Weather

| | In degrees Fahrenheit | | | |
	Jan.	Apr.	July	Oct.	Annual Rainfall
DAILY HIGHS	62.9	80.4	91.3	81.5	65.71"
DAILY LOWS	38.1	52.2	71.1	55.9	

Medical Care. Two full-service hospitals with a total of 950 beds and one 70-bed specialty hospital provide medical care for the residents of Leon County.

Transportation. Tallahassee Regional Airport provides service to other cities in Florida and to other airline hubs in the Southeast. The Taltran public bus system provides transportation within the city. The free Old Town Trolley provides service in the downtown area.

Opportunities for Continuing Education. Both state universities, Tallahassee Community College, and Leon County schools provide courses and activities for Tallahassee's senior citizen population.

Tallahassee

Tallahassee is undoubtedly one of the most interesting, historic, and beautiful cities in Florida. Built on several hills that create spectacular views in all directions, the city is also blessed with ancient moss-draped oak trees, antebellum mansions, broad avenues, and all the amenities that come with being the state capital and the home of two state universities. Its year-round population of 132,000 does not include well over 50,000 students at Florida State and Florida Agricultural and Mechanical Universities nor the thousands of legislators, lobbyists, and others associated with the state government who come to the city when the Florida Legislature is in session each year.

Designated the state capital in 1823, Tallahassee is a city much concerned with its history. In 1539 the Spanish conquistador Hernando de Soto celebrated the first Christmas in North America here. There are significant archaeological digs and a Civil War battlefield in the area. Throughout the city you will find historic houses, churches, and public buildings. The Old Capitol built in 1845 has been beautifully restored. Since the opening of the new capitol building in 1977, the old building has served primarily as a visitor center. Even the local chamber of commerce is housed in a home built in 1830.

Housing. One factor that distinguishes housing in Tallahassee is the demand on the real estate market made by legislators, lobbyists, state employees, and the faculty, staff, and students of the two universities. These major elements of Tallahassee's economy and population have created an inventory of houses at all levels of affordability. Further, the population's transient nature causes a frequent turnover of housing. In spite of the demand for upscale homes, the huge need for student housing and the large number of midlevel state and university employees seeking more modest homes keep the overall cost of housing down in the area.

For the upper echelons of state government and the faculty and administrators of the university there are a great many distinctive, beautifully appointed homes reflecting the tastes of these residents. This demand for quality housing combined with Tallahassee's outstanding natural beauty make this city an extraordinarily appealing place to live. Nestled among its many hills and lakes are tree-canopied streets with neighborhoods built to take advantage of the area's natural beauty. Many homes in these neighborhoods are listed in the low $200,000 range.

On the other hand, the demand for lower-cost housing has created a huge inventory of apartments in both high-rise buildings and in small, duplex and triplex houses. Some of these are rental units and others are condominiums. Also for this market there are neighborhoods of modest homes, many in attractive wooded settings, where houses list for $60,000 to $90,000 or even less. A quaint Victorian-style two-bedroom cottage on a huge lot recently listed for $52,900. A stunning four-bedroom Williamsburg colonial with an English garden, heart of pine floors, and two fireplaces went on the market for $129,000.

Tallahassee also offers many unique country-living opportunities. Just a few miles outside the city limits you will find charming homes, both old and new, on two or three acres of wooded land for less than $200,000. Many of these homes, just minutes from town, have rural amenities such as horse barns, kennels, and ponds stocked with trout. A 3,500-square-foot home on a one-acre lot with terra-cotta tile floors, high ceilings, two fireplaces, an office, a den, a gym, and a pool with a massive deck recently went on the market for $229,900. Property taxes in Tallahassee are about $22.50 per $1,000 nonexempt valuation.

Culture and Entertainment. Tallahassee has no shortage of cultural and entertainment venues and events. When I was in Tallahassee last, I had a choice of a touring Broadway show at the Tallahassee–Leon County Civic Center, a concert of classical guitar at Florida A&M University's Lee Hall Auditorium, the University Symphony in Florida State University's Ruby Diamond Auditorium, a faculty art show at FSU's Museum of Fine Arts, a performance of *The Threepenny Opera* in The Lab at the FSU School of Theater, and a play at the Tallahassee Little Theater. The Museum of Fine Art, touring art shows in the Old Capitol, and several commercial galleries bring the visual arts to the community.

Sports and Recreation. The two local universities bring intercollegiate sports to town throughout the year. Freshwater fishing is popular in several large lakes in Leon County, and for saltwater fishing the Gulf of Mexico is only 20 miles south. Three eighteen-hole and two nine-hole golf courses are open to the public. More than thirty tennis courts are available in public parks throughout the city. For football fans, Tallahassee boasts two outstanding university teams. FSU's Seminoles and FAMU's Rattlers provide exciting home games throughout the fall.

Tallahassee residents have access to one of the state's most unique recreational sites. Wakulla Springs, twenty minutes from Tallahassee, is reportedly the world's largest and deepest spring. It is 185 feet deep and flows at the rate of 600,000 gallons per minute. The spring is open for swimming and scuba diving. Wakulla Springs Lodge, built in 1937, has been refurbished and is once again open to guests. The entire 2,888-acre site is now owned and protected by the Florida Park Service.

Law Enforcement and Safety. The 1996 annual crime report shows 101 criminal offenses per 1,000 year-round residents. You should keep in mind that this figure is misleading for a city such as Tallahassee, where the population is greatly increased by nonresident visitors, business and government travelers, and students.

Senior Centers. The Tallahassee Senior Center is one of the most active centers in the state. The March 1998 issue of its newspaper, the *Golden Review*, listed more than forty classes ranging from beginning line dancing to calligraphy; twenty activities such as bridge, yoga, and square dancing; meals; and health screenings. The Retired Senior Volunteer Program (RSVP) coordinates volunteer activities of retirees.

Nearby Communities. While there are many suburbs around Tallahassee, there are few nearby towns of great interest to retirees. Two interesting exceptions are small towns in nearby counties. **Monticello** (pop. 2,884) in Jefferson County and **Madison** (pop. 3,463) in Madison County are of interest to retirees who look for charming small towns in rural America. Both communities are in areas of hills, farms, and old southern mansions, but neither is more than an hour from Tallahassee via I–10.

Addresses and Connections

Chamber of Commerce: Tallahassee Area Chamber of Commerce, P.O. Box 1639, Tallahassee, FL 32302; (904) 224–8116; Fax, (904) 561–3860

Newspaper: *Tallahassee Democrat* (daily), 227 N. Magnolia Drive, Tallahassee, FL 32302; (850) 599–2100; Fax, (850) 599–2231

Other Resources: Tallahassee Area Convention and Visitors Bureau, P.O. Box 1369, Tallahassee, FL 32302; (800) 628–2866; Fax, (850) 487–4621; http://www.co.leon.fl.us/cvb/homepage.htm.

THE CENTRAL GULF COAST

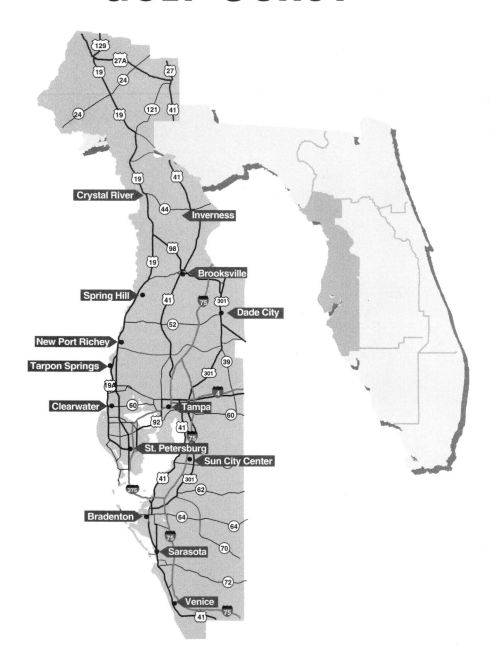

THE CENTRAL GULF COAST

No part of Florida is more popular with retirees than the Central Gulf Coast, an area stretching for more than 200 miles along the Gulf of Mexico and including, from north to south, the following counties and their cities and towns most popular with retirees: Citrus County (Crystal River and Inverness), Hernando County (Brooksville), Pasco County (Dade City and New Port Richey), Pinellas County (Tarpon Springs, Clearwater, and St. Petersburg), Hillsborough County (Tampa and Sun City Center), Manatee County (Bradenton), and Sarasota County (Sarasota and Venice). Recently these seven counties all ranked in the top twenty-five among U.S. counties attracting new retirees from other states. Prospective residents have a choice of many small and midsize towns and the larger cities of Clearwater, St. Petersburg, Tampa, and Sarasota. The nearby Gulf and broad Tampa Bay moderate the region's climate. The cities and towns profiled here are a sample of the dozens of communities which share in the region's superb climate, interesting topography, and quality of life.

Two kinds of typical Florida coastline are found here. From the mouth of the Suwannee River southward for more than 100 miles along the coasts of Citrus, Hernando, and Pasco Counties, there are no barrier islands, and beaches for sunning and swimming are rare. Rather, the coast is a patchwork of marshes, wetlands, small islands, and forests through which numerous spring-fed rivers and streams meander into the Gulf of Mexico. This area is one of the richest and most important estuarine refuges in the United States, providing a protected environment for many endangered species of animal life.

The barrier islands that run the length of the coast of Pinellas, Manatee, and Sarasota Counties—in some places several city blocks wide and in others so narrow you can see both the Gulf on one side and the Intracoastal Waterway on the other—provide the excellent white sand beaches for which this area is so well known. These islands contain side-by-side small beach communities where residents have a choice of high-rise condominiums, small apartment complexes, luxurious beach homes, or simple cottages, frequently next door to each other and all within view of or walking distance from the Gulf of Mexico. Bridges and causeways link these communities with nearby cities and towns on the mainland.

Just a few miles inland from the coastal cities and towns, large tracts of land that until very recently were orange groves, ranches, or farms are being turned into communities of interest to retirees. Some are developments of less expensive manufactured or mobile homes. Most of these are being developed primarily for the retiree market and many have age restrictions. Some are new communities of modestly priced site-built homes clustered around golf courses, pools, tennis courts, and clubhouses. Other developments are gated communities of sprawling homes built on multiacre lots. Affluent retirees interested in larger homes and more open space are finding these developments attractive. These communities and the beach towns are only minutes from nearby cities for shopping and entertainment.

When Grandkids Visit. There are few beaches in the northern part of this region, but the many springs and clear, spring-fed rivers for swimming, snorkeling, and diving more than make up for the lack. The *Homosassa Springs State Wildlife Park* features a museum, a children's center with educational programs, a nature trail, and an underwater viewing room from which you can watch manatees feed, swim, and care for their young. Behind the safety of a strong fence you can observe huge alligators in their native habitat. The entrance fee to the park is $7.95 for adults and $4.95 for children ages 4 to 12.

For the young baseball fan a visit to the *Ted Williams Baseball Museum and Hitters Hall of Fame* near Crystal River is a must. Admission is $3.00 for adults and $1.00 for kids. The *Crystal River State Archaeological Site and Museum* offers a fascinating look at 2,000 years of the region's history with ancient temple platforms, burial mounds, and a riverside earthen pyramid. Admission to the state park is $2.00 per vehicle with up to eight passengers with a charge of $1.00 per each additional passenger. *Weeki Wachee Springs and Buccaneer Bay* are adjoining commercial enterprises with an underwater "mermaid" show and a water park for the kids. Admission to all the Weeki Wachee Springs attractions—including the show, a jungle river cruise, an exotic bird show, and a birds of prey show—is $16.95 for adults, $15.25 for seniors, and $12.95 for kids ages 3 to 10. The admission to Buccaneer Bay, a huge water park, is $12.95 for adults, $11.65 for seniors, and $9.95 for kids 3 to 10.

In the middle and southern part of this region you have the excellent beaches of Clearwater, St. Petersburg, Bradenton, and Sarasota, but that's not all. The Greek community of *Tarpon Springs* is an interesting excursion, and a visit to the sponge fishing docks will show your grandkids what real sponges look like. At the tip of St. Petersburg is *Fort DeSoto Park* where you can explore a 100-year-old fort with an array of 12-inch cannons or swim at the more than three miles of beaches. The park's 235 campsites and well-equipped campground is popular with families.

Older kids and those interested in art will enjoy a visit to the *Salvador Dali Museum* in St. Petersburg. The museum contains the world's largest collection of art works by this famous Spaniard. Admission is $8.00 for adults, $7.00 for seniors, and $4.00 for students. Kids under 11 are free. A fun way for kids to spend a rainy day is the *St. Petersburg Beach Amusement Center* filled with video games, pool tables, and pinball machines. For $5.50 they can play for hours with no coins.

Tampa has *Busch Gardens*, a wildlife and amusement park with thousands of animals, a dizzying array of roller coasters, tamer rides, and live entertainment. Single-day tickets that include all the attractions in the park are $38.95 for adults and $32.95 for kids ages 3 to 9. Combination tickets can be purchased for Busch Gardens and Adventure Island water park in Tampa and for Busch Gardens and SeaWorld in Orlando. For more information on Busch Gardens try the park's Web site at www.buschgardens.com. The excellent *Florida Aquarium* in downtown Tampa will introduce your visitors to Florida's marine life. Admission is $10.95 for adults, $9.95 for seniors, and $5.95 for kids ages 3 to 12. The *Museum of Science and Industry*, with dozens of exhibits and more than 450 hands-on activities, is the largest science center in the Southeastern United States. It is home to MOSIMAX, a domed IMAX movie theater. Admission is $8.00 for adults, $7.00 for seniors, and $5.00 for kids.

In Bradenton you can take in a view of the heavens at the Bishop Planetarium. Admission is $7.50 for adults, $6.00 for seniors, and $3.50 for kids ages 5 to 12. Pre-schoolers are free.

Sarasota is home to the Mote Marine Aquarium, one of the nation's best-known marine laboratories and research facilities. The aquarium has several fish and turtle tanks and a 135,000-gallon shark tank. It is also a research and teaching center for ecology and environmental awareness. Admission is $8.00 for adults and $6.00 for students ages 4 to 17.

Finally, all the attractions at Walt Disney World, SeaWorld, and Universal Studios in Orlando are only an hour or two from most locations in this region. They are described more fully on p. 207.

CITRUS COUNTY: Crystal River and Inverness

The three northernmost counties in this region—Citrus, Hernando, and Pasco Counties—are alike in several respects. The low-lying coast of the Gulf of Mexico forms their western boundaries, but as you move toward their eastern boundaries 20 or 30 miles away, you quickly find yourself in the lakes and hills of central Florida. There are no large cities in these counties; instead you find many small towns and unincorporated communities. The Gulf Coast communities are clustered on or near U. S. Highway 19 and seem to have attracted a great many mobile-home parks and developments of small manufactured homes. The inland towns are typical of small Florida towns settled in the late nineteenth century. As I travel through the pleasant towns of Inverness, Brooksville, and Dade City, I find it difficult to tell them apart. Each has hills, brick streets beneath huge old oaks, a beautifully restored turn-of-the-century courthouse, and blocks of elegant nineteenth-century homes.

Citrus County (pop. 107,889) has several towns that are very popular with retirees. Crystal River is on the Gulf side of the county. Inverness is 15 miles away on the eastern side. The entire county is dotted with small unincorporated developments that draw mainly retirees. Citrus County, along with Levy and Sumter Counties, recently ranked twenty-fifth out of all U.S. counties in the number of retirees moving in from out of state.

Cost of Living. The cost of living in Citrus County is lower than in many other parts of Florida. Citrus County ranks fifty-sixth in the state with a cost of living 91.71 percent of the state average. The county does not have an additional sales tax. The cost of housing is 12.94 percent below the state average. The average purchase price for a home is $80,849. Citrus County ranks fifty-fifth in the state with an average monthly apartment rent of $345.

Climate. The climate on Citrus County's Gulf coast, moderated by its proximity to water, is more akin to that of Tampa. Its hilly eastern region has weather more like that of Gainesville.

Tampa–Western Citrus County Weather

| | In degrees Fahrenheit | | | | |
	Jan.	Apr.	July	Oct.	Annual Rainfall
DAILY HIGHS	69.8	81.7	90.2	84.3	43.92"
DAILY LOWS	50.0	60.8	74.5	65.2	

Gainesville–Eastern Citrus County Weather

| | In degrees Fahrenheit | | | | |
	Jan.	Apr.	July	Oct.	Annual Rainfall
DAILY HIGHS	65.6	80.7	90.7	81.0	51.81"
DAILY LOWS	42.5	55.8	70.9	59.7	

Medical Care. Two hospitals with a total of 299 beds serve Citrus County. The excellent Shands Teaching Hospital at the University of Florida in Gainesville is about an hour away.

Transportation. The Citrus County Transit operates a shared-ride bus service Monday through Friday, excluding holidays. This service is "on demand" and reservations must be made by noon one business day in advance. Pickups and drop-offs are made in order of location, so travel time may be longer than expected. Fare is $1.50 for inside a city and $3.00 for cross-county service. The nearest commercial airport with direct flights around the country is the Tampa International Airport.

Opportunities for Continuing Education. The Citrus County school system offers a full program of adult education including "Life Long" classes designed to assist the senior citizen with problems of health, safety, human relations, consumer economics, environment, government, and education. Central Florida Community College with a campus in Lecanto, only a few minutes from Crystal River and Homosassa Springs, offers a diversity of continuing-education courses designed for personal and professional enrichment. These courses range from one-day seminars to semester-length courses.

Crystal River

Crystal River, with a population of 4,072, is the largest town on the west coast of Citrus County. It is located on spring-fed Kings Bay at the northern end of the Central Gulf Coast region. Known as the Nature Coast, this area is famous for its huge freshwater springs and crystal-clear rivers that flow to the nearby Gulf of Mexico. These spring-spawned rivers—seven in Citrus County—are havens for manatees, waterbirds, and fish. The land they run through, mostly natural forest teeming with wildlife, becomes marshy wetlands as the rivers spread out and flow into the Gulf. Because of the delicate ecology of the area, much of the land between the springs and the Gulf is protected by the state as wilderness preserves. The springs and rivers attract divers, fishers, and tourists, and the communities attract retirees who like living in small towns with beautiful natural settings.

Housing. Citrus County's affordable housing costs are reflected in many wonderful options for apartments and homes in some of Florida's most interesting, lush landscape. Waterfront property in this area means riverfront, on a canal, or on a natural spring. There is little need for the man-made lakes developers pour into new communities in other parts of the state. Natural water and wooded lots are abundant and affordable. Touted as a fisherman's paradise, a two-bedroom stilt home with two docks, davits, boat ramp, crab farm, and waterfront views recently listed for $102,000. If you have simpler needs, a two-bedroom one-bath house with tongue-and-groove cedar ceilings in downtown Crystal River went on the market at $35,000. Large new homes on the Gulf, where you would expect to pay a premium for the accompanying docks, three-car garages, and sunset views, may go for $170,000. A huge five-bedroom home on a double lot with a 150-foot seawall, dock, two fireplaces, two porches, a grand entry foyer, and a two-car garage listed for $199,900. Waterfront homes inland offer great value and beautiful back-to-nature settings. Desirable two- or three-bedroom homes list from $60,000 to $130,000, depending on the acreage and the size of the home. Other recent listings included a charming home with hardwood floors, an open floor plan, and one-half acre of land in a quiet subdivision for $68,000. The county property tax rate, among the lowest in the state, is about $18 per $1,000 nonexempt valuation. Property taxes for homes within the city of Crystal River are about $24 per $1,000.

Culture and Entertainment. When it comes to culture and entertainment, Crystal River and its neighbors are small towns with simple pleasures. There are frequent art shows and festivals that bring entertainment to each of the towns. The Citrus County Art League's 400 members maintain a cultural center with monthly exhibits, theater presentations, and other special events throughout the year. Many cultural programs, including lectures, symphonies, dance performances, and plays, are presented by Central Florida Community College at its nearby Lecanto campus and on its main campus in Ocala, not quite an hour away. This area is rural but it is far from isolated, and for more sophisticated culture and entertainment its residents go to several nearby cities. Gainesville, Clearwater, St. Petersburg, and Tampa are a little more than an hour away. Many cultural and entertainment activities are offered on the campuses of the University of Florida in Gainesville and the University of South Florida in Tampa.

Sports and Recreation. For those who wish to take advantage of it, the Crystal River area has an abundance of outdoor activities. Fishing in the rivers and the Gulf is a major sport here, with four marinas and six charter boat companies available to enthusiasts. All water sports such as canoeing, snorkeling, scuba diving, and swimming in the many springs and amazingly clear rivers are very popular. A number of marinas, canoe rental shops, and dive shops provide equipment and instruction. For those who would prefer to stay dry there are several trails for hiking, running, and biking. There are thirteen golf courses in Citrus County. The Black Diamond course in Beverly Hills is considered one of the top golf courses in the state.

Law Enforcement and Safety. In 1996 there were 133 criminal offenses reported per 1,000 year-round residents in Crystal River.

Senior Centers. The nearest senior center is in Lecanto, 8 miles east of Crystal River.

Nearby Communities. **Homosassa Springs** (pop. 6,300) is an unincorporated community 7 miles south of Crystal River. The two towns have blended together so that now it is difficult to tell where one leaves off and the other begins. **Sugarmill Woods** is 12 miles south of Crystal River on Highway 19. Although more upscale than some, it is typical of unincorporated housing developments in this part of Florida. Sugarmill Woods isn't age restricted, but its location—somewhat isolated and away from many jobs and schools—makes it most attractive to nonworking seniors. There are currently 2,500 houses built with another 5,000 single-family and multifamily home sites available. Home sites are priced around $10,000, and the flyers I received indicated that homes would run from $92,900 to $163,900. With a stated emphasis on environmental protection, 30 percent of the land has been preserved in greenbelts. A prominent feature of Sugarmill Woods (and other developments like it) is its golf courses (forty-five holes in all) with all of the accompanying clubhouses, swimming pools, tennis courts, and dining facilities.

Walden Woods Mobile Home Park, a few miles south of Homosassa Springs, is also typical of certain retirement communities throughout Florida. It is a development of double-wide mobile homes restricted to age fifty-five and above. Residents own their homes but rent the land for a monthly fee "guaranteed to the year 2000" of $175 per month. For this the resident gets a swimming pool, a clubhouse, shuffleboard courts, sewer, property taxes, garbage pickup, water, and lawn mowing. There are eighty-seven units in the park. Forty percent of the residents live in Walden Woods year-round. The rest are snowbirds, some from as far away as Europe. Bob Pierce, the manager with whom I spoke, said that most people choose Walden Woods because it is "small, friendly, and away from the crowds." A community like this is a far cry from the old image of a "trailer park." Homes here are beautifully maintained and not inexpensive. The two very nice three-bedroom two-bath models I looked at were priced just above $50,000.

Beverly Hills (pop. 13,000) is an unincorporated community of site-built homes in a beautiful setting. Located 7 miles east of Crystal River in an area of rolling, wooded hills, Beverly Hills is another development with no age restrictions but so popular with retirees it earned the nick-name "Florida's Retirement Home Town." The community includes a twenty-two-acre park with a lake for fishing, a swim and tennis club, an eighteen-hole golf course, a library, and a recreation hall where many social and educational activities are held. More than 100 civic and social organizations have been formed by the residents. New homes are priced from the $70s to the $160s while homes up for resale are priced from the $30s to the $90s. I noted that older homes are built on much larger lots than newer ones. Police protection is provided by the Citrus County Sheriff and fire protection by a local fire department.

Inverness

Although still in Citrus County and less than 20 miles from the Gulf of Mexico, the countryside surrounding Inverness, with its rolling hills and many lakes, has more in common with the Central Florida area described more completely in Chapter Eight than with the coastal cities and towns in this chapter. Bordered on the north and east by the cluster of seven lakes known as the Tsala Apopka chain and spread over several hills, Inverness has one of the prettiest settings of any town in the state. Downtown Inverness, filled with Victorian houses and elegant public buildings dating from the town's founding in 1891, is one of the most pleasant community centers you may ever discover. The centerpiece of the town's restoration efforts and of the town itself is the beautiful turn-of-the-century courthouse with its silver dome. The cypress-bordered lakes with their coves and bayous almost surround Inverness so that you seem to come upon a view of one around every curve or over every hill as you wander through the little town. It is the county seat of Citrus County and has a population of 6,741.

Housing. The low price of housing in some of the most idyllic neighborhoods you could hope for makes Inverness a most appealing option in Florida. The median cost of housing here, excluding condos and mobile homes, is $74,000. At every turn on the winding hill and lakeside roads that traverse Inverness, you'll find beautiful and unique real estate bargains from the tiniest waterfront cottage to a sprawling executive home on a beautifully manicured city lot or a nineteenth-century multistory Victorian mansion. A towering, historic home occupying an entire city block was priced at $135,000. Small lakeside bungalows or stilt cottages nested among cypress and oak trees with lovely views may be found for as little as $30,000. A modest but very comfortable newer home with a pool may run $70,000. A three-bedroom ranch with a large, caged pool listed for $69,900. A large, new executive home in town will run around $120,000. And if you're an ambitious groundskeeper, you can find lots of land here. A twenty-acre "ranchette," including a 3,500-square-foot home, plus four assorted garages and barns, and a 1,400-square-foot guest apartment, listed for $209,900. Property taxes for homes within Inverness are about $26 per $1,000 of nonexempt valuation.

Culture and Entertainment. What has been said for Crystal River also applies to Inverness. There are many art and music festivals and a couple of art galleries, but Inverness is still a relatively small town. The local community college provides cultural activities and entertainment for the community, including lectures, theater, music, and touring performances, and you're not far from several larger cities.

Sports and Recreation. Fishing, boating, waterskiing, and canoeing are perhaps the most obvious sports in this lake-oriented community. The Tsala Apopka chain of lakes is justly famous for its bass fishing, and the calm, 23,000-acre interconnected lakes with their many coves and canals are ideal for canoeing. The Withlacoochee State Trail is a wonderful idea and a popular recreational facility for residents of Inverness. It is a 12-foot-wide asphalt-paved trail that replaced an abandoned railway. It begins about 15 miles north, touches Inverness, and then runs another 30 miles south. The right-of-way was purchased under the state's Rails-to-Trails program, and the trail is now managed by the Florida Park Service as a "linear state park." Originally intended for bikers, backpackers, and walkers (no motor vehicles are allowed), it is now equally popular with in-line skaters. This is horse country and a riding trail is located adjacent to the paved trail. Since the trail uses the old railway as its base, there are bridges over streams and either underpasses or overpasses at major highway intersections.

Law Enforcement and Safety. In 1996 fewer than 35 criminal offenses per 1,000 year-round residents were reported in Inverness.

Senior Centers. The nearest senior center is in Lecanto, 9 miles away.

Nearby Communities. **Citrus Springs** (pop. 2,300) is 17 miles north of Inverness. The largest planned urban development in Citrus County, its 32,000 home sites are spread over 15,000 acres of hilly woodlands. The community has an eighteen-hole semi-private golf course and country club, a branch clinic of Citrus Memorial Hospital, twelve churches, a library, dozens of civic and social organizations, and greenbelt access to the Withlacoochee River and Rainbow Springs. One advertisement I found listed 1,977-square-foot three-bedroom homes for $71,900 including the lot, and there were no closing costs.

Lecanto (pop. 3,686) and **Hernando** (pop. 9,496) are two more towns in Citrus County that are popular with retirees. In fact, the median age in Lecanto is sixty-five. Hernando has a somewhat younger population, with a median age of just under fifty. Both towns are in the hilly, wooded central part of the county.

Addresses and Connections

Chambers of Commerce: Citrus County Chamber of Commerce, 208 W. Main Street, Inverness, FL 34450; (352) 726–2801

Nature Coast Chamber of Commerce, 28 Northwest Highway 19, Crystal River, FL 34428, (352) 795–3149; Fax, (352) 795–4260

Newspapers: *The Citrus County Chronicle* (daily), 1624 Meadowcrest Boulevard, Crystal River, FL 34429; (352) 563–6363

The Citrus Times (daily), 1122 North Suncoast Boulevard, Crystal River, FL 34429; (352) 860–7333

HERNANDO COUNTY: Brooksville

Hernando County (pop. 119,931), bordered on the north and east by the Withlacoochee State Forest and by the Gulf of Mexico on the west, is one of the quietest and most beautiful counties in Florida. Its Gulf Coast area is growing rapidly as population expands northward from the densely populated Clearwater–St. Petersburg area. Hernando County's eastern area is growing more slowly and retains its quiet charm. In recent years, Hernando County ranked twenty-fourth among all U.S. counties in the number of retirees moving in from out of state.

Cost of Living. Hernando County ranks fortieth in the state with a cost of living 93.56 percent of the state average. The sales tax is 6 percent. The cost of housing is 11.06 percent below the state average. The average purchase price for a home is about $84,500. Hernando County ranks fortieth in the state with an average monthly apartment rent of $440.

Climate. The weather in Brooksville is typical of the central Florida highlands. Without the moderating influence of the Gulf of Mexico or Tampa Bay, Brooksville temperatures may be slightly cooler in winter and warmer in summer than those listed below, taken from the National Oceanic and Atmospheric Administration station in nearby Tampa. Spring Hill, on the other hand, has the benefit of its nearness to the Gulf.

Tampa–Hernando County Weather

| | In degrees Fahrenheit | | | | |
	Jan.	Apr.	July	Oct.	Annual Rainfall
DAILY HIGHS	69.8	81.7	90.2	84.3	43.92"
DAILY LOWS	50.0	60.8	74.5	65.2	

Medical Care. The Brooksville Regional Hospital has ninety-one beds. Three other hospitals in Hernando County bring the total to 370 beds.

Transportation. There is no local public transportation. The major airport serving Hernando County is Tampa International Airport about an hour away.

Opportunities for Continuing Education. Hernando public schools and Pasco-Hernando Community College's Brooksville campus provide classes and activities geared to the needs and interests of retirees.

Brooksville

Brooksville is the county seat of Hernando County, and with a population of 7,794, it is the largest municipality in the county. The area around Brooksville is typical central Florida lake and hill country. Brooksville is noted for its old brick streets lined with huge oak trees and for its many restored Victorian houses. One of the most beautiful examples is the ornate Victorian mansion that now houses the Hernando Heritage Museum. This four-story, seven-gable, pastel confection of a house was built in 1856. Any lover of small-town living will immediately want to put down roots in Brooksville.

Housing. Among the many options for housing in Brooksville are beautifully restored older homes. These homes reflect the historical setting and are a part of the tourist appeal of this area, and you may find them hard to resist. Restored gingerbread Victorians are available in the center of town for less than $120,000. I recently saw a three-bedroom, two-and-a-half-bath historic home in lovely condition just a short walk from the downtown courthouse on the market at $109,000. You may decide you don't need quite so much history, or quite so much house. Charming three-bedroom homes with fireplaces and other period touches often list for about $45,000. Recently a delightful four-bedroom two-story bungalow with a wood-burning fireplace and a two-car detached garage a short walk from downtown shopping was priced at $44,900. When I was there last, a unique three-story, three-bedroom, three-bath home with two fireplaces, three balconies, and four acres of land was available for $115,000. In Brooksville, if you want loads of interior space you can easily find five-bedroom homes nestled among mature oak trees for less than $150,000. There is an excellent selection of affordable contemporary housing. A custom-built four-bedroom ranch home with four baths, a formal sunken living room, an elevated dining room, an interior atrium, an in-ground pool and hot tub, plus a horse barn, stocked pond, and tennis courts was priced at $279,000. With costs 11 percent below the state average, you will probably find whichever type of home appeals to you a solid real estate investment. Real estate taxes in Brooksville will run about $27 per $1,000 nonexempt valuation.

Culture and Entertainment. Like Inverness and other small towns in this area, Brooksville does not offer as wide a selection of cultural and entertainment activities as you will find in several larger cities nearby. The seventy-member volunteer Hernando Symphony Orchestra performs at the Performing Arts Center and the Springstead Theater. Both touring Broadway shows and student productions are scheduled at the Hernando High School Center for the Performing Arts. The Stage West Community Playhouse is a nonprofit community theater. Pasco-Hernando Community College brings a variety of cultural activities to its Brooksville campus and to its main campus in nearby Dade City. Tampa, with many cultural activities, is less than an hour away.

Sports and Recreation. Golf is very popular here, and Brooksville and its neighboring communities have access to eighteen golf courses. Tennis is almost equally popular and there are many courts in and around Brooksville. The Gulf of Mexico (less than 20 miles away), several lakes, and the Withlacoochee River provide fishing and every kind of water sport. There are many trails for hiking and biking. The nearest point of access to the Withlacoochee Trail is about 12 miles from Brooksville.

Law Enforcement and Safety. In 1996 there were ninety-eight criminal offenses reported per 1,000 year-round residents in Brooksville. In unincorporated Hernando County the number was less than forty.

Senior Centers. There is a senior citizens club, but there are no senior centers in Brooksville.

Nearby Communities. For the last thirty or more years, as Pinellas County and the western portion of Pasco County have become more densely populated, there has been a steady growth northward along U.S. Highway 19. **Spring Hill**, founded in the 1960s by a development corporation, has now mushroomed into one of the largest unincorporated communities in this part of the state. It is surprising how quickly you find yourself in wooded hills after you leave the flat land along U.S. 19 and head east in Spring Hill. It is also surprising how far this community of attractive small homes extends. Unofficial population figures for Spring Hill itself are around 34,500, but it is agreed the general area exceeds 75,000 and there are no signs of the growth diminishing. And housing bargains abound in Spring Hill. A recent Gulf-access home with three bedrooms, a dock and sea wall, and a waterfront canal was for sale at $79,900, and a huge four-bedroom contemporary home on a quarter-acre corner lot with a pool and an oversize garage listed for $102,900. Several companies are building homes in the area now. I walked through models ranging in price from $74,900 for a three-bedroom two-bath home to $95,400 for four bedrooms and two baths, all to be built on your lot. Lots in this area sell for $5,000 to $10,000 depending on size and location.

Addresses and Connections

Chamber of Commerce: Greater Hernando County Chamber of Commerce, 101 East Fort Dade Avenue, Brooksville, FL 34601; (352) 796–0697; Fax: (352) 796–3704; http://www.hernandochamber.com

Newspaper: The Tampa Tribune (daily), P.O. Box 191, Tampa, FL 33601; (800) 282–5588

PASCO COUNTY: Dade City and New Port Richey

Pasco County (pop. 309,936) is another Gulf Coast county with mushrooming growth along its coast and slower development among its older inland towns. Dade City, on the eastern side of the county, dates back to the late nineteenth century, but its population still is less than 6,000. New Port Richey, on the other hand, has developed almost entirely in the last thirty years and its population has now reached 14,555. The county has a population of 276,401 in unincorporated areas; many of these are retirees living in mobile-home parks and in manufactured home developments. Increasingly popular with retirees, Pasco County recently ranked ninth out of all U.S. counties in the number of retirees moving in from out of state.

Cost of Living. Pasco County ranks thirty-fourth in the state with a cost of living 94.54 percent of the state average. The sales tax is 6 percent. The cost of housing is 11.97 percent below the state average. The average purchase price for a home is around $80,000. Pasco County ranks forty-seventh in the state with an average monthly apartment rent of $422.

Climate. Without the moderating influence of the Gulf of Mexico or Tampa Bay, Dade City temperatures may be slightly cooler in winter and warmer in summer than those listed below, which are taken from the National Oceanic and Atmospheric Administration station in nearby Tampa. New Port Richey, on the coast, will be more akin to Tampa.

Tampa–Pasco County Weather

	Jan.	Apr.	In degrees Fahrenheit July	Oct.	Annual Rainfall
DAILY HIGHS	69.8	81.7	90.2	84.3	43.92"
DAILY LOWS	50.0	60.8	74.5	65.2	

Medical Care. Pasco County is served by five hospitals with a total of 1,032 beds. All the medical facilities of Tampa, Clearwater, and St. Petersburg are nearby.

Transportation. The nearest airport with direct flights to many points in the United States is Tampa International Airport. There is no local public transportation system in Pasco County.

Opportunities for Continuing Education. Pasco County schools and Pasco-Hernando Community College, with campuses in Dade City and New Port Richey, offer courses, programs, and activities designed for seniors.

Dade City

Dade City, population 5,963 and the county seat of Pasco County, is yet another small town in this beautiful part of Florida that has been discovered by retirees. It is less than 20 miles southeast of Brooksville and has the same general terrain, climate, and history as other small towns nearby. Less than an hour from the major metropolitan area of Tampa, Dade City has the advantage of being so close that you may live in the peace and quiet of a rural community yet be in a big city in a matter of minutes.

Dade City has several claims to fame of which it is justifiably proud. The town was recognized in 1994 as "Florida's Outstanding Rural Community of the Year" by the state of Florida, and was named a "Tree City USA" by the National Arbor Day Foundation. Dade City is recognized as a Main Street community by the National Trust for Historic Preservation.

Housing. Finding a home in Dade City will be a most pleasant adventure, and since it is such a small town, you may explore every street and country road before making your decision. You will understand why when you see that a bungalow in town may sell for less than $35,000. A four-bedroom older home in town or a three-bedroom country home with a pool, a huge lot, workshops, and garages may list for less than $100,000. An extraordinary custom-designed 3,000-square-foot house that was the home of a nationally known artist came right out of *Architectural Digest.* Situated on a one-acre hillside in a pristine village setting, this unique home listed for $279,000. Just a few blocks away, a picture-perfect, three-bedroom two-bath one-story home with two additional half-baths and wood floors throughout listed for $89,000. An immaculately restored two-bedroom cottage in town was for sale at $49,900. All of this, and you are just a stone's throw from downtown Tampa with all its urban offerings. Real estate taxes in Dade City are about $28 per $1,000 nonexempt valuation.

Culture and Entertainment. Dade City has all the cultural and entertainment opportunities one could expect in a small town. There is a local theater group and an art association, and there are many community festivals. Pasco-Hernando Community College and Saint Leo College both offer annual cultural series. Tampa's cultural and entertainment possibilities are forty minutes away.

Sports and Recreation. With access to forests, lakes, rivers, and the Gulf (only 35 miles away), Dade City is a paradise for anyone interested in hunting, fishing, or boating. There are eight golf courses in the Dade City and Zephyrhills area and many tennis courts. The Withlacoochee Trail ends just north of Dade City.

Law Enforcement and Safety. In 1996 the Dade City Police Department reported 130 criminal offenses per 1,000 year-round residents. It should be kept in mind that in the winter the population of Dade City nearly doubles.

Senior Centers. There is no senior center in Dade City, but the Zephyrhills Senior Center 8 miles away offers a range of educational, health, social, and recreational services.

Nearby Communities. **Zephyrhills**, 9 miles south of Dade City, is extremely popular with winter-only residents. I was told that the 8,867 population of year-round residents swells to an astounding 90,000 during the winter months. Because there is an extraordinary number of mobile-home communities and RV parks serving these seasonal residents in and around Zephyrhills, one's first impression is that this area feels more transient than other nearby towns.

New Port Richey

New Port Richey (pop. 14,555) is a delightful small town on the Gulf Coast side of Pasco County. Located just off the U.S. 19 corridor only a few miles north of Tarpon Springs and Clearwater, it has shared the growth explosion of this part of Florida in the past thirty years, yet it has managed to retain a lot of small-town charm. I was amazed at how quickly (really just a few blocks) you leave the clutter of busy U.S. 19 and find yourself in a pretty country village—a bit reminiscent of an immaculate small European town. It helps that there is a lovely, quiet river running through the center of town. New Port Richey looks today as though its city leaders have done a lot recently to revitalize and beautify the downtown area with wide, tree-lined boulevards and many parks. A number of nicely landscaped neighborhoods have attracted many retirees.

Housing. Almost as delightful as the town itself is the low cost of homes here. A one-of-a-kind five-bedroom home with a great room, cathedral ceilings, a wood-burning fireplace, new appliances, and ceiling fans throughout was listed for $118,000. A two-bedroom home on a canal with gulf access was priced at $68,900. A modest, modern villa condominium in town was for sale at $39,899. On the "high end" of the scale in New Port Richey, you might look for something like a recent listing, a $229,000 "exquisite" custom-built four-bedroom three-bath brick Tudor home with an in-ground pool in a wooded setting. Property taxes in New Port Richey are about $25 per $1,000 nonexempt valuation.

Culture and Entertainment. For other than movies and the cultural presentations of Pasco-Hernando Community College, New Port Richey residents may take advantage of the offerings in Tarpon Springs, Clearwater, and Tampa.

Sports and Recreation. Fishing in the Gulf and Pasco County's many rivers and streams is a major attraction. Twenty-two golf courses in Pasco County keep golfers happy. Jogging trails and bike paths keep many residents active. Many of the spectator sports of Hillsborough and Pinellas Counties are nearby.

Law Enforcement and Safety. In 1996 there were eighty-three criminal offenses reported per 1,000 year-round residents in New Port Richey.

Senior Centers. The Claude Pepper Senior Center (named after Florida's beloved U.S. senator who championed the causes of seniors throughout the nation) is one of several in the area. In New Port Richey, the center shares its space with the Cares Senior Health Clinic and the local Alzheimer's organization. There is an emphasis on health and well-being, but there is also a full schedule of social, educational, and recreational activities. The friendly staff explained that the senior center in nearby Elfers had more room and was "much more social."

Nearby Communities. **Port Richey** (pop. 2,629) is only a few miles north on U.S. 19.

Addresses and Connections

Chambers of Commerce: Greater Dade City Chamber of Commerce, 38035 Meridian Avenue, Dade City, FL 33525; (352) 567–3769; Fax, (352) 567–3770; http://www.dadecity.org; E-mail chamber@dadecity.org

West Pasco Chamber of Commerce, 5443 Main Street, New Port Richey, FL 34652; (813) 842–7651; http://westpasco.com

Newspaper: *The Tampa Tribune* (daily), P.O. Box 191, Tampa, FL 33601; (800) 282–5588

PINELLAS COUNTY: Tarpon Springs, Clearwater, and St. Petersburg

That Pinellas County (pop. 881,383) is the most densely populated county in Florida should come as no surprise to anyone familiar with the area. The county is a rather narrow peninsula with the Gulf of Mexico on one side and Tampa Bay on the other. Compared to many other counties in Florida, Pinellas is quite small, and it has been very successful in attracting a great many new residents, many of them retirees. All in all, the county has managed its growth very well.

In recent years Pinellas County ranked fourth in the nation among counties attracting new retirees from other states. A large number of these 35,065 retirees came to St. Petersburg and its neighboring towns. A great many military retirees settle in Pinellas County because of the excellent medical facilities at the Veterans Administration's Bay Pines

Medical Center and all the amenities of the huge MacDill Air Force Base just across the bay in Tampa. But lest you think Pinellas County is only for older people, it should be noted that the median age is 42.1.

Cost of Living. While the cost of living, particularly housing, varies greatly from place to place here, Pinellas County ranks seventh in the state with a cost of living 100.91 percent of the state average. The sales tax is 7 percent. The cost of housing is 5.08 percent above the state average. The average purchase price of a home is about $105,780. Pinellas County ranks twelfth in the state with an average monthly apartment rent of $614.

Climate. All of Pinellas County has delightful weather. With water on three sides, there is almost always a breeze, and temperatures are moderated, slightly warmer in winter and cooler in summer, than those listed below.

Tampa–Pinellas County Weather

	\ In degrees Fahrenheit \ Jan.	Apr.	July	Oct.	Annual Rainfall
DAILY HIGHS	69.8	81.7	90.2	84.3	43.92"
DAILY LOWS	50.0	60.8	74.5	65.2	

Medical Care. There are seventeen hospitals in Pineallas County with a total of 4,615 beds. The 781-bed Bay Pines VA Medical Center provides care for veterans.

Transportation. Residents of Pinellas County have a choice of the St. Petersburg/Clearwater Airport with service to twenty-five cities in the United States, Canada, and the Bahamas, or the much larger Tampa International Airport less than thirty minutes from most locations. Local bus transportation is provided by the Pinellas Suncoast Transit Authority with 144 buses and more than forty routes. The Jolley Trolley, a San Francisco–style trolley car system, takes passengers around Clearwater Beach and into downtown for 50 cents.

Opportunities for Continuing Education. The Pinellas County school system provides an excellent and diverse program of adult education. St. Petersburg Junior College, with campuses in Tarpon Springs, Clearwater, Seminole, and two in St. Petersburg, offers many courses and activities for seniors. The University of South Florida's St. Petersburg campus offers an array of day and evening classes for area residents, and its

Learning in Retirement Institute provides a wide selection of courses and activities for seniors.

Tarpon Springs

Tarpon Springs is one of the most interesting, eclectic, and charming towns in Florida. Located where the Anclote River flows into the Gulf of Mexico, the area is a maze of bayous and tributaries creating more than fifty miles of waterfront property in this relatively small town. It was first settled in the 1870s and quickly became a winter resort. In 1890 prolific sponge beds were discovered in the Gulf waters nearby, and soon sponge fishermen from the islands of Greece arrived to create a thriving industry. These early settlers built beautiful homes on the water and throughout the town. Even though the town has grown to more than 20,000, their influence is still strongly felt. Greek language, religion, customs, and cuisine have been handed down from generation to generation. The sponge industry barely survived the creation of synthetic sponges, and although sponges are still harvested and sold, it is now primarily a tourist attraction.

The beautiful setting of Tarpon Springs and its proximity to Tampa, Clearwater, and St. Petersburg have made it a popular retirement destination. Its Old Main Street district is now included on the National Register of Historic Places. Despite its growth, the town has maintained a friendly small-town atmosphere. Tarpon Springs is a town of many wonderful restaurants, particularly for Greek cuisine. One, though, stands out in my memory. I recently ate breakfast in a tiny cafe in the center of town where many specialties were listed for ninety-nine cents and where every one of the customers (all over age sixty-five) knew each other and began their day with friendly banter.

Housing. Because of the eclectic profile of this community, you will find a luxurious waterfront mansion next door to a modest home or a ramshackle cottage. Whether you are looking for something at the high end, low end, or middle of the road in home prices, Tarpon Springs offers many interesting options. Homes in the busy downtown area or hidden away on a quiet peninsula of land in a neighborhood accessible by bridge can range from fixer-uppers to stately, luxurious mansions. Since weatherworn homes of every variety are scattered throughout the city, one of the challenges here will be finding the right home in a neighborhood you feel reflects your own pride of ownership This is one area where you will want to do a lot of exploring and where you will benefit from seeking expert real estate advice.

On a quiet downtown street ½ block from the Gulf, a stunning three-bedroom contemporary home with a large detached workshop was listed for $98,500. Also downtown, an attractive two-bedroom one-bath home listed for $52,000. If you can afford the prices most bayfront homes command, a spectacular recent listing was a three-bedroom three-bath home on the water with an all-glass Florida room, a heated spa, and a pool for $339,500. Of particular interest, and typical of the eclectic mix of architecture found here, an Art Nouveau home I spotted included an in-ground pool, tile floors, and a one-bedroom guest cottage, all for $124,900. There is an abundance of beautiful pool homes with three or four bedrooms for about $150,000. Costs in Tarpon Springs are slightly higher than you might expect because it is so close to the Clearwater, St. Petersburg, and Tampa metropolitan centers; however, a charming "Cracker" house in the town will run less than $70,000. The median home value in Tarpon Springs is $80,700. Property taxes in Tarpon Springs are about $23 per $1,000 nonexempt valuation.

Culture and Entertainment. The Tarpon Springs Cultural Center, the former City Hall, was built in 1915 and is now beautifully restored. In addition to two exhibit halls for art shows and historical exhibitions, there is an intimate eighty-four-seat theater for dramatic and musical performances. The Tarpon Springs Performing Arts Center, located in a 1925 schoolhouse, contains a 400-seat theater with a fully equipped stage. A full season of performances is scheduled January through May. Tarpon Springs is an easy drive from Clearwater, Tampa, and St. Petersburg for additional cultural and entertainment opportunities.

Sports and Recreation. Since Tarpon Springs is bordered on the east by Lake Tarpon and on the west by the Gulf of Mexico, fishermen have their choice of freshwater or saltwater fishing. Several parks provide opportunities for swimming, boating, diving, and sunning. The Pinellas Trail, another reclaimed railroad right-of-way purchased under the Rails-to-Trails program, begins at Tarpon Springs and runs nearly 34 miles south to St. Petersburg. The immensely popular asphalt-paved trail provides an excellent facility for running, walking, and biking. The only motor vehicles allowed on it are motorized wheelchairs. There are five city parks with tennis courts and softball diamonds.

Law Enforcement and Safety. In 1996 there were fifty criminal offenses reported per 1,000 year-round residents. Many winter residents and a great many tourists inflate the population.

Senior Centers. The Tarpon Springs Community Center is host to Neighborly Senior Services, an organization that offers a wide range of social, educational, and recreational services to seniors.

Nearby Communities. **Palm Harbor** is a 33-square-mile area of unincorporated neighborhoods with a population of more than 65,000. Here you will find new waterfront mansions, older bungalows, new communities of site-built homes in several price ranges, and several mobile-home developments.

Clearwater

Located in mid-Pinellas County and stretching from the Gulf of Mexico on the west to Old Tampa Bay on the east, Clearwater is a beautiful city of 101,867 year-round residents. Taking every advantage of its water orientation, Clearwater literally sparkles. With tourism its acknowledged major industry, the city has made certain that every nook and cranny is not only clean but attractive and well landscaped. Its famous beaches are beautifully maintained and the causeway connecting Clearwater Beach to the mainland city is one of the most attractive roads in the state. Clearwater and St. Petersburg (see page 76) are two excellent examples of Florida cities where the efforts to make the area attractive to tourists has been equally beneficial to year-round residents. Not only do Pinellas County residents enjoy a wide range of cultural and entertainment activities, sports, restaurants, and beautiful cities maintained by tourist business, but each year visitors pick up $67 million of the county's tax tab.

Housing. Clearwater is a rapidly growing city, and housing costs, reflecting the demand, are 5.08 percent above the state average. There is so much recent growth that more than 60 percent of all housing is less than twenty years old, yet Clearwater offers many charming neighborhoods of older homes, some affordable and some absolutely luxurious. As a newcomer, your first decision will be whether the amenities of a newer home are what you want or whether you would prefer to find an older home with character and great bones, but perhaps a bit dated in its style. Typically, newer homes might be beach condominiums or in recently developed inland neighborhoods. In the downtown area of Clearwater, small cottages and bungalows are often available for less than $60,000. Large homes from executive styles to gorgeous mansions can begin well over $200,000, particularly in the most desirable neighborhoods near the bay.

Elsewhere in Clearwater prices are more moderate. A three-bedroom two-bath home with a one-bedroom guest bungalow with its own kitchen listed for $105,000. A custom "dream home" with a gated entry, a domed kitchen, an in-ground pool, a luxurious master bath, and leaded French doors was priced at $129,900. For just $49,900 a very handsome two-bedroom two-bath house with an oversize garage on a pond was available. Single-family homes generally start at $75,000, and there is an endless supply of handsome, well-situated two- and three-bedroom homes with oversize garages available for less than $100,000. The median value of owner-occupied housing in Clearwater is $99,846. Property taxes in Pinellas County are about $22 per $1,000 nonexempt valuation. In the city of Clearwater, property taxes are about $27 per $1,000. The average rent for an apartment in Clearwater is $433.

Culture and Entertainment. Clearwater has its own full schedule of culture and entertainment, but its residents can also take advantage of activities in Tampa, 20 miles to the east, and St. Petersburg, the same distance to the south. The Florida Orchestra performs in all three cities. The 2,100-seat Ruth Eckerd Hall at the Richard B. Baumgardner Center for the Performing Arts is home for concerts and stage productions. The hall has legendary acoustics, and houses galleries for art shows and exhibits. A new cultural activity is known as "Sunset at Pier 60." Monday through Thursday local musicians and artists perform against the backdrop of a glorious Gulf sunset.

Sports and Recreation. Clearwater is justifiably proud of its miles of white sand beaches. Whether for swimming, walking, shell collecting, or just lying in the sun, the beach is this town's most popular spot for recreation. In 1997 *Condé Nast Traveler* named Clearwater Beach the best city beach on the Gulf of Mexico. The Clearwater Marina is home to the largest sport fishing fleet on Florida's west coast. Many charter boats are available for deep-sea fishing in the Gulf, and fishing from several piers and bridges is popular. Twenty-six public and semiprivate golf courses keep golfers busy. Avid baseball fans enjoy watching St. Petersburg's new baseball team, the Tampa Bay Devil Rays, and the Toronto Blue Jays and the Philadelphia Phillies during their spring training in the Clearwater area. There are more than 1,000 acres of parks and recreational facilities in Clearwater. The Pinellas Trail is a popular site for hiking, biking, and skating.

Law Enforcement and Safety. In 1996 the Clearwater Police Department reported seventy-four criminal offenses per 1,000 year-round residents. In 1996 *Money* magazine named Clearwater the safest of all Florida cities.

Senior Centers. The Senior Citizens Service, Inc., is a nonprofit operation founded in 1958 and dedicated to the "well-being and interests of the aging." It is wholly independent and self-sustaining, receiving no local, state, or federal funds. Among the services provided are adult education, employment assistance, hobbies and crafts, recreational activities, social activities, tax return assistance, tours, sickroom supplies, and wheelchairs and walkers. The center's services are free of charge to all seniors but membership is encouraged. Annual dues are $5.00 for an individual and $7.50 for a couple.

Nearby Communities. **Oldsmar,** a community of almost 10,000 people, was named for its founder, Ransom E. Olds, the creator of the Oldsmobile. Located at the top of the Pinellas County peninsula and almost on the Hillsborough County line, Oldsmar is closer to Tampa than to Clearwater or St. Petersburg. **Safety Harbor** is a community of 16,750 people, with many quiet neighborhoods that have been very attractive to retirees. **Dunedin** (pop. 35,104) is one of the most attractive communities near Clearwater. Described by the chamber of commerce as a "picturesque waterfront village," Dunedin is much more than that, and is worthy of a look by any retiree interested in this part of Florida.

St. Petersburg

St. Petersburg has been one of America's most popular and best-known retirement destinations for so many years its name is practically synonymous with retirement. Because it is almost a cliché, I am often asked if it is still a viable choice for retirement. My answer is a definite yes! St. Petersburg has remained so popular over the years because it has so many of the things retirees seek: wonderful weather, affordable housing, a rich cultural and entertainment scene, nearby beaches, and many friendly neighborhoods. Don't just take my word for it. The author of the latest edition of *Retirement Places Rated* ranked St. Petersburg second out of 183 of America's most popular retirement destinations.

With a population of 241,276, St. Petersburg is by far the largest municipality in Pinellas County and the fourth largest city in Florida. Bordered by Tampa Bay on its east and south and Boca Ciega Bay between it and the barrier island beaches on the west, St. Petersburg has grown in the only direction it could: to the north. Now as you go north from the southern tip of the city it is difficult to tell when you leave St. Petersburg proper and enter one of several suburban towns. Even though it is one of Florida's most densely populated cities, St. Petersburg doesn't seem crowded. The center of the city, with an expansive view of Tampa Bay and many tree-shaded parks, has an open feel to it.

It isn't realistic to look at St. Petersburg in isolation when it comes to culture, entertainment, sports, and recreation. Clearwater, St. Petersburg, and Tampa—the triangle of Tampa Bay cities—are only about 20 miles apart. All of the activities of the three cities are easily accessible to you wherever you may live in the area. A couple I met recently chose to live in a St. Petersburg beach community. They have season tickets to a series of Broadway shows and attend football games in Tampa, go to Clearwater for events at Ruth Eckerd Hall, attend baseball games and play golf in St. Petersburg, and spend their quiet hours on the beach across the street from their condominium.

Housing. St. Petersburg offers a housing environment somewhat like Clearwater, with one difference: St. Petersburg is a bigger city with bigger ambitions. The growing downtown area has an urban feel and there is constant renovation and construction along the major thoroughfares, particularly in areas near the sprawling Tropicana Stadium. Yet, as in Clearwater, newer beach condominiums, luxurious homes, and an ample supply of modest older homes in the downtown area are available. Because there is a great supply of smaller, older homes, prices are very affordable. A two- or three-bedroom home in the downtown area can be found for $45,000 to $60,000. A cozy little bungalow with high ceilings, two bedrooms, and a two-car garage, shaded by mature, tall oaks, recently listed for $56,500. Charming older homes, like a three-bedroom Victorian on a secluded lot for $144,500, are always available. Even beach living is affordable in St. Petersburg. When I was there last a very modern 2,400-square-foot home with a light, open plan, a large backyard entertainment area with a pool and heated spa, situated a few steps from the beach was priced at $137,000. On the upper end, sumptuous older and newer homes on the water in a luxurious bayfront area like Snell Isle will typically begin at over $500,000 and rocket up into the several million dollars. The average sale price of a home is about $95,000. Property is taxed at about $26 per $1,000 nonexempt valuation. The average monthly rent for an apartment in St. Petersburg is $531.

Culture and Entertainment. There is no shortage of cultural organizations and companies nor venues to house them in St. Petersburg When you add the offerings in Clearwater and Tampa, the list seems endless. One piece of promotional literature I saw listed forty-two music groups (from opera to barbershop) and eleven theater companies in the area. A full season of Broadway shows, opera, dance performances, and concerts, including the Tampa-based Florida Orchestra, is scheduled in the beautiful 2,000-seat Mahaffey Theater in the Bayfront Center. Artspace, Inc., a multipurpose art complex in downtown St. Petersburg, provides studio, classroom, and exhibit space. The spectacular Museum of Fine Arts has an excellent collection of paintings, sculpture, and decorative arts. Ballroom dancing—classes, demonstrations, and social-events—takes place in the historic Coliseum with its beloved all-wood dance floor.

Sports and Recreation. Once again, St. Petersburg seems to have it all. Whether you prefer to be a spectator at major-league baseball, football, and hockey games; actively participate in golf, tennis, racquetball, or shuffleboard; or simply do your own thing—in-line skating, swimming, snorkeling, fishing, running, or lying in the sun—you can do it all here. St. Petersburg's newest pride and joy is a major-league baseball team, the Tampa Bay Devil Rays. With its own team in town and a total of seven major-league baseball teams in the area for spring training, St. Petersburg has moved up to national sports status. The Pinellas Trail (see page 73) has caught on, with residents all over Pinellas County who walk, run, bike, and skate its length. More than forty public, semiprivate, and private golf courses are available in Pinellas County. Dog racing, horse racing, and jai alai, all with pari-mutuel betting, are popular with retirees here. As in so many of Florida's coastal cities and towns, it is water that provides the most attractive sports and recreation for St.

Petersburg's residents. In all, St. Petersburg has 236 miles of shoreline on Tampa Bay, Boca Ciega Bay, the Gulf of Mexico, and the Intracoastal Waterway. At last count there were forty-three public and private golf courses in Pinellas County.

Law Enforcement and Safety. In 1996 there were one hundred criminal offenses reported per 1,000 year-round residents in St. Petersburg.

Senior Centers. As you might expect in a city with so much experience in providing services for retirees, there are many centers and programs providing for a variety of interests and needs. St. Petersburg's Department of Leisure Services operates community centers open to senior citizens throughout the city. The Office on Aging at the Sunshine Center in downtown St. Petersburg provides information about local services and volunteer opportunities. The Senior Helpline is operated by Family Resources and offers free information to seniors about services available in the community. Finally, Neighborly Senior Services provides assistance to those over sixty who need help in order to continue living independently. Services include in-home care, transportation, adult day care, and meals.

Nearby Communities. The small town of **Gulfport** (pop. 11,871) is on the southwestern side of St. Petersburg. Gulfport is home to the Gulfport Arts Village, the largest organized art community in the Tampa Bay area. Gulfport has its own beach on Boca Ciega Bay. **Kenneth City** (pop. 4,334), on the northwestern border of St. Petersburg, is very popular with retirees. **Pinellas Park** (pop. 44,472) and **Seminole** (pop. 9,658) are two communities located in the area between St. Petersburg and Clearwater. Both are popular with younger residents, who work in several electronics and communication industries nearby, and with retirees who enjoy a little more open space but want to live near all the amenities of St. Petersburg.

A string of small beach communities runs the length of the barrier island from just south of Clearwater Beach to its southern tip. All are connected to the mainland by causeways or bridges over the Intracoastal Waterway or Boca Ciega Bay. In these communities you will find a range of housing including small beach cottages, Gulf-front mansions, high-rise condominiums, low-rise condominiums, and rental apartments. Some are more upscale than others, and some have more of a residential look and feel than others where tourist motels predominate. Unless you look very carefully, you will not know where one begins and another ends as you drive the length of the island. From north to south, these communities and their populations are **Belleair Beach** (2,138), **Belleair Bluffs** (2,221), **Indian Rocks Beach** (4,169), **Indian Shores** (1,473), **North Redington Beach** (1,147), **Redington Beach** (1,605), **Madeira Beach** (4,225), **Treasure Island** (7,347), and **St. Petersburg Beach** (9,589).

Addresses and Connections

Chambers of Commerce: Greater Clearwater Chamber of Commerce, P.O. Box 2457, Clearwater, FL 33757; (813) 461–0011; Fax, (813) 449–2889; http://www.clearwatercc.com

Dunedin Chamber of Commerce, 301 Main Street, Dunedin, FL 34698; (813) 736–5066; Fax, (813) 734–8942

Gulf Beaches of Tampa Bay Chamber of Commerce:

Indian Rocks Beach Office, 105 Fifth Avenue North, Indian Rocks Beach, FL 33708; (800) 944–1047 or (813) 595–4575

Madeira Beach Office, 501 150th Avenue, Madeira Beach, FL 33708; (813) 391–7373; Fax, (813) 539–4259

St. Petersburg Beach Office, 6990 Gulf Boulevard, St. Petersburg Beach, FL 33706; (813) 360–6957; Fax, (813) 360–2233; http://www.stpetebeach.com

Treasure Island Office, 152 108th Avenue, Treasure Island, FL 33706; (813) 367–4529; Fax, (813) 360–1853

Gulfport Chamber of Commerce, P.O. Box 5212, Gulfport, FL 33737-5023; (813) 327–2062

Greater Oldsmar Chamber of Commerce, 163 State Road 580, Oldsmar, FL 34677; (813) 855–4233; Fax, (813) 854–1237

Greater Palm Harbor Area Chamber of Commerce, 32845 U.S. Highway 19 North, Suite 210, Palm Harbor, FL 34684-3123; (813) 784–4287; Fax, (813) 786–2336

Pinellas Park/Mid-County Chamber of Commerce, 5851 Park Boulevard, Pinellas Park, FL 33780; (813) 544–4777; Fax, (813) 545–1678; http://www.infousa.com/PPMC/welcome.htm

Safety Harbor Chamber of Commerce, 200 Main Street, Safety Harbor, FL 34695; (813) 726–2890; Fax, (813) 726–2733

St. Petersburg Area Chamber of Commerce, P.O. Box 1371, St. Petersburg, FL 33731; (813) 821–4069; Fax, (813) 895–6326; http://www.stpete.com

Greater Seminole Area Chamber of Commerce, P.O. Box 3337, Seminole, FL 33772; (813) 392–3245; Fax, (813) 397–7753

Greater Tarpon Springs Chamber of Commerce, 11 East Orange Street, Tarpon Springs, FL 34689; (813) 937–6109

Newspaper: St. *Petersburg Times* (daily), P.O. Box 1121, St. Petersburg, FL 33731-9977

HILLSBOROUGH COUNTY: Tampa and Sun City Center

While Hillsborough County (pop. 910,855) draws its share of tourism and retirees, its economy and major concerns are far more diverse than most of its neighboring counties. The largest port in Florida is in Tampa and a high percentage of the state's exports pass through it. The eastern side of the county is home to a $500-million-a-year agricultural business. That said, the county is host to more than 4.5 million visitors each year, and it ranks seventeenth among counties in the United States as a retirement destination. Hillsborough County literally wraps itself around huge Tampa Bay.

Cost of Living. Hillsborough County ranks eighth in the state with a cost of living 100.82 percent of the state average. The chamber of commerce reports that the overall cost of living in Tampa averages about 5 percent lower than most other metropolitan areas in the nation. Hillsborough County residents have voted an additional ½ percent sales tax. The cost of housing is 2.85 percent above the state average. The average purchase price of a house is about $101,000. Hillsborough County ranks thirteenth in the state with an average monthly apartment rent of $607.

Climate. With the moderating influences of the Gulf of Mexico, Tampa Bay, and the Hillsborough River, Hillsborough County has delightful weather year-round.

Tampa–Hillsborough County Weather

| | In degrees Fahrenheit | | | | |
	Jan.	Apr.	July	Oct.	Annual Rainfall
DAILY HIGHS	69.8	81.7	90.2	84.3	43.92"
DAILY LOWS	50.0	60.8	74.5	65.2	

Medical Care. Ten hospitals with 3,454 beds serve the people of Hillsborough County.

Transportation. Tampa International Airport is undoubtedly one of the best in the nation. For several years it has received the number one rating from the Airline Passengers Association. Local bus service is provided by Hillsborough Area Regional Transit.

Opportunities for Continuing Education. Hillsborough County public schools; Hillsborough Community College with campuses in Tampa, Ybor City, Brandon, and Plant City, and the University of South Florida offer many courses and activities geared to the continuing-education needs of retirees in the area.

Tampa

Tampa (pop. 289,337) is the largest of the Tampa Bay cities, and it is by far the most urban of the three. Tampa is a major seaport and an industrial center, but that does not make it any less desirable as a retirement destination. There are almost one million people in Hillsborough County, many of them in Tampa's very livable and attractive suburban communities. Tampa has no beaches, but it has one of the most beautiful and user-friendly waterfronts anywhere. Bayshore Boulevard is a lovely winding street along Tampa Bay with what is supposed to be the longest continuous sidewalk in the world. As stated earlier, whether you choose to live in Tampa, St. Petersburg, Clearwater, or any of the nearby towns, you have the amenities of all the Tampa Bay cities close at hand. In exchange for the beautiful beaches of the other two cities, Tampa brings more professional sports and the most varied entertainment and cultural opportunities to the mix. Tampa's MacDill Air Force Base is an important draw for military retirees throughout central Florida.

Housing. Although the cost of housing in Hillsborough County is slightly above the state average, there is no shortage of wonderful bargains to be found here. Tampa's popularity as a center of business and industry as well as a retirement destination has caused builders to develop a large inventory of single-family homes, high-rise condominiums, town houses, golf course communities, and waterfront homes in a wide range of prices. Currently the median value of an existing home is $75,300. In most neighborhoods and nearby communities you will find an excellent mix of housing as well as prices. There are older homes

(Craftsman bungalows from the 1920s abound), new condominiums, homes on the city's many golf courses, and homes fronting Tampa Bay, the Hillsborough River, or any one of the many lakes in the area. Tampa's oldest existing neighborhoods dating from the early 1900s coexist comfortably with a host of brand-new subdivisions throughout the city. Carrollwood, for example, is a community in north Tampa with homes ranging in price from $90,000 to $700,000. In that neighborhood a four-bedroom two-and-a-half-bath home listed for $149,900. A small, immaculate three-bedroom home on a cul-de-sac adjoining a greenbelt, professionally decorated and landscaped, was listed for $84,900. Along Bayshore Boulevard beautifully restored mansions sell for well over $1 million; condominium units may be found for $75,000. Tampa's contrasts are very evident in two properties that were listed at the same time. A 1925 bungalow with three bedrooms in a quiet, middle-class neighborhood was priced at $64,800, while a similar 1925 bungalow with an in-ground pool in fashionable Hyde Park was selling for $153,900. The *1997 Tampa Bay Community Resource, Relocation, and Newcomers Guide*, published by the Tampa Chamber of Commerce, lists thirty-two neighborhoods with housing prices ranging from $60,000 to $2 million. Property taxes in Hillsborough County are $19.26 per $1,000 of nonexempt valuation. In the city of Tampa, they range from $26.82 to $29.46.

Culture and Entertainment. With the exception of Miami, Tampa probably has the richest mixture of culture and entertainment in Florida. The Hispanic (Cuban and Spanish) and Italian origins of the city are still visible in the music and dance one finds here. The anchor of Tampa's cultural life is the Tampa Bay Performing Arts Center, now the largest performing arts venue in the southeast. With four theaters ranging from small and intimate to the 2,493-seat Festival Hall with facilities capable of staging the biggest Broadway shows, the center is home to concerts, opera, theater, and dance. The Florida Orchestra presents a full season of concerts there. The Loft Production Company presents innovative theater in the Off Center Theater of the Tampa Bay Performing Arts Center. The Ballet Folklorico of Ybor is dedicated to the presentation of native Spanish, Cuban, and Italian dance. The Tampa Museum of Art, the University of South Florida's Contemporary Art Museum, and many commercial galleries present the visual arts to the community. Of particular note is the Tampa Theater, a 1926 movie theater restored to its original grandeur. The interior, a wondrous rendering of a starlit night in a Renaissance Venetian courtyard, will bring back memories of all the bygone glories of such theaters. The Tampa Theater now specializes in classic and foreign films, and before most showings you are treated to a live performance on the 868-pipe organ. The University of South Florida brings many cultural events to the community each year.

Sports and Recreation. Tampa's best-known contribution to professional sports in the area is the Tampa Bay Buccaneers football team. But that's not all! Tampa now has professional soccer, arena football, and hockey. For baseball fans, Tampa is the spring home of the New York Yankees, and in 1998 St. Petersburg's own Tampa Bay Devil Rays played their inaugural season. In 1997 the University of South Florida fielded a football team that has become a local favorite. For active sports participants, the list is almost endless. The Hillsborough River, Tampa Bay, and the nearby Gulf of Mexico provide venues for just about every water sport imaginable. Eight public and six private golf courses and nearly one hundred public tennis courts keep those players busy. Tampa has a popular dog racing track and a jai alai fronton with pari-mutuel wagering.

Law Enforcement and Safety. In 1996 there were 148 criminal offenses reported per 1,000 year-round residents in the city of Tampa. In unincorporated Hillsborough County the rate was sixty-six.

Senior Centers. One privately funded and two publicly funded programs serve senior needs in Tampa. The Hillsborough County Department of Aging Services, Inc. provides social, physical, and emotional support for local citizens over age sixty. The North Boulevard Senior Center, supported by the city of Tampa, provides a range of services and activities for seniors. The Life Enrichment Center is a private, nonprofit corporation whose services and activities are open to all seniors on a space-available basis. The center offers educational, social, and recreational programs, classes, and activities. It is supported through contributions from private citizens, foundations, churches, and fundraising events.

Nearby Communities. **Brandon** is a fast-growing unincorporated community east of Tampa that has become popular with retirees as well as with young families. The population of the area exceeds 100,000 when you include the many little towns generally referred to as Brandon. The area is east of I–75, but an easy drive to the city center via the

Crosstown Expressway. Homes in Brandon and its surrounding neighborhoods—some are modest single-family homes while others are luxury homes on golf courses or lakefront estates—sell for between $60,000 and $500,000. **Temple Terrace** is an incorporated town on the Hillsborough River about 10 miles from downtown Tampa. This municipality, now the home of the University of South Florida, also boasts the Temple Terrace Golf and Country Club with one of the state's largest and oldest golf courses. Almost 20,000 people now live in Temple Terrace, where houses range in price from $80,000 to $350,000.

Sun City Center

Forget every preconceived notion you might have had about retirement communities when you think about Sun City Center. Think instead of a nearly perfect community where just about everything a retiree could want has been provided. If you wish to retire to a place where a home, resident services, recreation, entertainment, and a flawless environment have all been planned with retirees in mind, then you should learn about Sun City Center before you decide on a retirement destination. The only thing you might question about this community (and it is a negative or a positive, depending on your preference) is that it has a very firm age restriction. At least one member of a couple must be over age fifty-five and no one under age eighteen may reside in the community. Younger guests may stay no longer than thirty days.

From the time you leave I-75 and begin the 2-mile drive to Sun City Center you begin to experience the charm of the community, for even the public highway is beautifully landscaped. By the time you enter the gates of the development, you feel you are in a park. The parkways and public spaces are landscaped with flowers, trees, natural areas, and lakes. One thing you notice quickly is that within the confines of Sun City Center most of the residents get around in golf carts.

Sun City Center was founded by the Del Webb Corporation in 1961, and is now under development by Florida Design Communities. The community is 25 miles from Tampa on I-75 and 8 miles (as the crow flies) from the Gulf of Mexico. It consists of 5,000 acres, of which 3,000 have been developed. At present there are 7,500 households with more than 13,000 residents. There are two developments within Sun City Center. Kings Point is a controlled-access development in which the

homes are in condominium organizations that provide outside maintenance. The Sun City Center segment consists largely of individually
owned and privately maintained homes.

Since Sun City Center is an unincorporated community in the larger
Tampa–Hillsborough County metropolitan area, it could have been
treated as a nearby community in the profile of Tampa; however, its
development is such an outstanding example of a planned retirement
community it deserves special treatment

Housing. In spite of all its unique qualities and in spite of design considerations developed to serve the special needs of its retired citizenry,
housing in Sun City is available for every budget. Roomy villa residences
start in the $50,000 range, attractive modern smaller homes start around
$110,000, and new homes with pools and spas are available for
$130,000. Larger homes also abound in the high $100,000 range. If you
don't need the amenities of recent construction, you can really econo-
mize by buying a resale, some of which may be just a few years old. On
the high end of the Sun City scale, "Signature Series" homes on premium lots, with 3,000 to 4,000 square feet of living space, range from
$200,000 to more than $340,000.

Culture and Entertainment. The Town Hall Complex within the
community includes facilities for entertainment, shows, and social
events. In addition, Sun City Center is less than an hour's drive from all
the cultural and entertainment opportunities in Tampa, Clearwater, and
Sarasota. St. Petersburg is only a short distance farther.

Sports and Recreation. Other than for the many spectator sports
events in nearby Tampa Bay cities, you would never need leave the envi-
rons of Sun City Center for all the recreation and sports you could pos-
sibly want. There are Olympic-size indoor and outdoor swimming pools,
complete exercise facilities, lawn bowling greens, a softball diamond,
shuffleboard, volleyball, and tennis courts. There are six golf courses
with a total of 126 holes, including two executive-length courses.

Law Enforcement and Safety. In addition to the protection of the
Hillsborough County Sheriff's Department, there is a 1,500-member Sun
City Center resident volunteer security patrol, five security patrol cars,
and a 24-hour neighborhood watch program. A fire station within Sun
City Center provides fire protection.

Medical Care. A 112-bed hospital is located within Sun City Center.
Other hospital facilities are located in Tampa and at the University of

South Florida. MacDill Air Force Base in Tampa provides services for military retirees.

Transportation. Sun City Center is served by the Hillsborough Area Rapid Transit with buses into Tampa.

Senior Centers. With its single-minded dedication to the needs of retirees and those over age fifty-five, the entire community of Sun City Center could be considered a senior center.

Opportunities for Continuing Education. Many courses, programs, and activities are planned by and for the residents of the community.

Addresses and Connections

Chambers of Commerce: Greater Tampa Chamber of Commerce, P.O. Box 420, Tampa, FL 33601; (813) 228–7777; Fax, (813) 223–7899

Sun City Center Chamber of Commerce, 1651 Sun City Center Plaza, Sun City Center, FL 33573; (813) 634–8437; Fax, (813) 634–8438

Newspaper: The Tampa Tribune, P.O. Box 191, Tampa, FL 33601; (813) 282–5588

Other Resources: Sun City Center Information Office, 2020 Clubhouse Drive, Sun City Center, FL 33573; (800) 237–8200; http://www.suncityctr.com

MANATEE COUNTY: Bradenton

Manatee County (pop. 236,778) is the first county south of Tampa Bay, and it seems nearly surrounded by water. Part of its coastline faces Tampa Bay; the rest looks out over its barrier islands to the Gulf of Mexico. The county is bisected by the broad Manatee River. Like the rest of the counties from Tampa Bay south to the tip of Florida, most of the residents of Manatee County live on a fairly narrow strip of land along the coast. Much of the land east of that strip comprises farms, groves, ranch land, or a marshy floodplain for the Manatee and Myakka Rivers. Recently Manatee County was twentieth among all counties in the United States in the number of retirees moving in from other states.

The spectacular 4-mile-long Sunshine Skyway Bridge spans the mouth of Tampa Bay, connecting Manatee County to the southern tip of St. Petersburg, giving Manatee residents direct access to all the activities and amenities of St. Petersburg and Clearwater. A surprising number of people commute daily over the bridge to work in Pinellas County.

Cost of Living. Manatee County ranks eleventh in the state with a cost of living 98.88 percent of the state average. To the state's 6 percent sales tax, Manatee County has added a 1 percent sales tax on the first $5,000 of a purchase. The cost of housing is 1.10 percent below the state average. The average purchase price of a home is about $95,300. Manatee County ranks twenty-ninth in the state with an average monthly apartment rent of $536.

Climate. Mostly surrounded by water, Bradenton's climate is always moderate and very often breezy.

Tampa–Manatee County Weather

| | In degrees Fahrenheit | | | | |
	Jan.	Apr.	July	Oct.	Annual Rainfall
DAILY HIGHS	69.8	81.7	90.2	84.3	43.92"
DAILY LOWS	50.0	60.8	74.5	65.2	

Medical Care. Two hospitals with a total of 895 beds serve the residents of Manatee County. In addition, all of the medical facilities of Sarasota County are only a few minutes away.

Transportation. Local bus transportation is provided by Manatee County Area Transit with routes from neighboring Palmetto on the north to the Ringling Museum in northern Sarasota.

Opportunities for Continuing Education. Manatee Community College and the Manatee County school system provide many courses and activities designed to meet the continuing-education needs of the area's retired population.

Bradenton

Bradenton (pop. 48,031) is a pleasant town located where the Manatee River (so wide at this point it resembles a broad bay) flows into Tampa Bay and the Gulf of Mexico. This part of Manatee County is really a peninsula with the river to the north, Palm Sola Bay to the west, and Sarasota Bay to the south. The latter two separate Bradenton from its nearby beach communities. All combine to give the city 150 miles of shoreline and a beautiful water orientation. Bradenton is only a few miles north of Sarasota. It is an easy drive from Tampa via I–75 and from St.

Petersburg via the Sunshine Skyway Bridge. Bradenton is an easy-going beach-oriented town whose residents may enjoy an afternoon at the beach or take advantage of all the cultural, entertainment, and recreational amenities of the much larger cities nearby.

Housing. Housing options here are as diverse as any location in the state, but offer somewhat more reasonable prices. Considering the beautiful beaches and proximity to Sarasota, St. Petersburg, and Tampa, you can find real bargains in Bradenton. Deluxe two-bedroom condominium units overlooking a lake list for around $50,000. At the very lowest end, modest but attractive small homes in an adult community sometimes list for around $25,000—prices that would afford you only a small trailer home in other areas. While there are very expensive homes on the islands, now and then an absolute bargain is offered—a modern duplex for less than $180,000, for example. Inland, a three-bedroom historic home on a creek in a convenient country setting may run just over $100,000. In the large areas of quiet neighborhoods (Bradenton residents are proud of their small-town ambience), tidy three-bedroom two bath homes proliferate in the $60,000 price range. A new four-bedroom three-bath home with an in-ground pool and oversize two-car garage came on the market at $127,500. Beach living is not out of the question for many retirees here. An Old Florida–style cottage duplex comprising a two-bedroom and a one-bedroom unit with a tropical backyard near the beach was priced at $117,900. For the extremely price-sensitive, a pleasant one-bedroom condominium in a very attractive historic landmark complex listed for $17,900, and a two-bedroom unit in the same building listed for $24,900. Property taxes in Bradenton are about $18.50 per $1,000 nonexempt valuation.

Culture and Entertainment. The Art League of Manatee County, a comprehensive center for the visual arts, provides gallery space, classrooms, and regular exhibitions. Live theater is presented by the Manatee Players at the Riverfront Theater and by the Island Playhouse on nearby Anna Maria Island. The Neel Auditorium on the campus of Manatee Community College is the site of many concerts and other cultural events. In addition to the cultural and entertainment offerings in Bradenton, residents here attend events scheduled in Sarasota, St. Petersburg, and Tampa.

Sports and Recreation. Fishing is a major recreational activity in Bradenton. Thirty marinas and eight boat ramps provide access to the rivers, bays, bayous, and the Gulf of Mexico. Several fishing piers eliminate the need for a boat to pursue this popular pastime. The approaches to an old Skyway Bridge have been converted to fishing piers on both the Pinellas County and Manatee County sides. The 1.59-mile Manatee County portion is thought to be the longest fishing pier in the world. There are twenty-nine public and private golf courses in Manatee County and another 200 in nearby counties. The Pittsburgh Pirates train in Bradenton.

Law Enforcement and Safety. In 1996 there were seventy-eight criminal offenses reported per 1,000 year-round residents in Bradenton.

Senior Centers. Neighborly Senior Services of Manatee provides a range of services and activities for seniors including adult day care, health care, computer classes, home assistance, volunteer coordination, telephone reassurance, and assistance with health insurance problems. The Manatee Aging Network is a not-for-profit voluntary coalition of profit and not-for-profit organizations concerned with the needs of seniors. The Network publishes an excellent senior services directory annually.

Nearby Communities. **Palmetto** (pop. 9,860) lies on the northern shore of the Manatee River. Connected to Bradenton by convenient bridges, Palmetto has become a popular residential community for retirees and for many who work in Bradenton. A unique new unincorporated development north of Palmetto is **The Palms of Manasota.** To my knowledge it is the first retirement community in Florida designed and marketed for "alternative lifestyles."

Four beach communities run the length of Bradenton's two barrier islands, Anna Maria Island and the northern half of Longboat Key. **Anna Maria** (pop. 1,843), at the northern tip of Anna Maria Island, is surrounded on three sides by beaches. **Holmes Beach** (pop. 5,043) has many condominiums and cottages. It is the site of Manatee Public Beach and is known for its flock of free-roaming peacocks. **Bradenton Beach** (pop. 1,682), at the southern tip of Anna Maria Island, is the site of Coquina Beach, a 96-acre public recreational park. **Longboat Key** is both an island off the coast of Manatee and Sarasota Counties and a town that crosses the county lines. The northern portion of the town in Manatee County has a population of 2,649.

Addresses and Connections

Chamber of Commerce: Manatee Chamber of Commerce, P.O. Box 321, Bradenton, FL 34206-0321; (941) 748–3411; Fax, (941) 745–1877; http://www.manatee-cc.com; E-mail: chamber@manatee-cc.com

Newspapers: Bradenton Herald (daily), 102 Manatee Avenue West, Bradenton, FL 34205; (941) 748–0411; http://www.bhip.com

Sarasota Herald-Tribune (daily) 801 South Tamiami Trail, Sarasota, FL 34236; (941) 365–6060; http://www.newscoast.com

Senior Connection (monthly); 220 West Brandon Boulevard, Suite 108, Brandon, FL 33511; (813) 653–1988; Fax, (813) 651–1989; http://www.seniornews.com/senior-connection; E-mail: srconnect @aol.com/

SARASOTA COUNTY: Sarasota and Venice

Sarasota County (pop. 305,848) has nearly 40 miles of the most beautiful beaches in this part of the state. Its barrier islands are separated from the mainland by broad Sarasota Bay. A snowbird mecca, its year-round population grows by more than a third during the winter when these seasonal residents return from their summer homes. Sarasota County ranks eighth in the nation among counties attracting new retirees from other states. In *Retirement Places Rated* Sarasota ranked thirty-first among the 183 most popular retirement locations in the United States.

Cost of Living. Sarasota County's high average cost of living reflects its high concentration of affluent residents: it ranks fifth in the state with a cost of living 102.98 percent of the state average. Sarasota County has added a 1 percent local sales tax to the state's 6 percent. The cost of housing is 4.57 percent above the state average. The average purchase price of a house is around $101,400. Sarasota County ranks sixth in the state with an average monthly apartment rent of $714.

Climate. Sarasota shares in the delightful weather of the entire Tampa Bay area. Gulf breezes keep the air clean and moderate summer temperatures and humidity.

Tampa–Sarasota County Weather

	Jan.	In degrees Fahrenheit Apr. July		Oct.	Annual Rainfall
DAILY HIGHS	69.8	81.7	90.2	84.3	43.92"
DAILY LOWS	50.0	60.8	74.5	65.2	

Medical Care. Medical care in Sarasota and its surrounding communities is as good as you will find anywhere. Four hospitals with 1,562 beds serve the residents of Sarasota County. In addition, there are a total of sixty-nine hospitals in the general Tampa Bay area.

Transportation. For air travel Sarasotans have a choice of commercial jet service out of the convenient Sarasota/Bradenton International Airport or the huge Tampa International Airport an hour away. Bus transportation inside Sarasota County is handled by the Sarasota County Area Transit. SCAT's buses are comfortable and service is frequent and reliable.

Opportunities for Continuing Education. Manatee Community College with campuses in nearby Bradenton and Venice and the very active adult education division of Sarasota County schools provide a great many opportunities for continuing education. Programs for adults and seniors with artistic ambitions are offered throughout the year at the Ringling School of Art and Design, a studio-based school for the creative visual arts.

Sarasota

Quite proud of its reputation as the "Culture Capital" of Florida, Sarasota's art, music, film, dance, and theater offerings far exceed what you would expect from a city of 53,700, prompting *Southern Living* magazine to declare it "the nation's per capita arts capital." However, with miles of extraordinarily beautiful beaches, revitalized downtown districts, and access to almost every type of sport and recreational activity, culture isn't the only reason Sarasota is one of Florida's most popular retirement destinations: It seems to have just about everything a great many retirees want in a community. As one transplanted Bostonian told me when I asked him why he had chosen Sarasota, "It's simple. Not too big, not too small, and lots of personality!"

Put all of the above together with a wonderful climate, and you have the reasons *Money* magazine ranked Sarasota among its "Top Twenty

Places to Retire" and fourteenth on its "Best Places to Live in the U.S." list. Sarasota is a great place to live, work, and raise a family, and for tens of thousands it's a great place to retire.

Housing. In spite of its ranking among Florida's most expensive areas, housing costs here range from the astronomical to modest, and you will find affordable homes of every kind. Naturally, you will pay the customary premium for beach property; property with views of broad, scenic Sarasota Bay; or homes in the central and southern areas of the city situated on winding, quiet bayous with deepwater access to the bayou. Even in the prime areas, however, by shopping wisely you may find an exceptional home at a price you can afford. For example, a renovated two-bedroom two-bath waterfront condo with an optional dock listed recently for $74,000. And a beach duplex in mint condition with a two-bedroom two-bath unit and a one-bedroom one-bath unit listed for just $137,000. A "unique and romantic" 1924 Ringling era Spanish-style home with three bedrooms and two baths, in a lush, tropical setting near the bay, listed for $139,500.

At the same time luxury abounds for those who can afford it. A typical, modestly luxurious beach property on Longboat Key offered a Key West–style tropical home on deep water, with soaring ceilings and separate guest quarters for $369,000. High-rise condominiums in the beach areas of Sarasota have always commanded a premium price; at the same time, ultraluxury, high-rise condominium buildings now dominate the city's bayfront marina. Two- and three-bedroom condos priced from several hundred thousand to well over a million dollars are sold as quickly as they can be built.

If you look a bit inland, your options are unlimited, and you can trade proximity to the water for lake views, spacious floor plans, and the latest home amenities. Neighborhoods of two- and three-bedroom pool homes priced from $100,000 to $120,000 cover large areas of the city. A centrally located four-bedroom home with wooden floors listed for $89,900. While condominiums in all price ranges abound throughout the city, two-bedroom condominium units for less than $60,000 are easy to find. Scattered throughout the city and especially appealing are renovated homes with unique character. A completely remodeled home on Phillippi Creek with three bedrooms and a separate artist studio was priced at $155,000. In dozens of inland gated communities, popular three-bedroom homes in the $130,000 to $160,000 range are being built. Property taxes in Sarasota County are about $13.90 per $1,000 nonexempt valuation. In the city of Sarasota the rate is about $20.40.

Culture and Entertainment. The most visible anchor of the Sarasota cultural scene is the John and Mable Ringling Museum of Art, which includes spacious galleries in the former Ringling residence, the Circus Gallery, and the eighteenth-century Asolo Theater, imported in pieces from Italy and reassembled on the thirty-eight-acre Ringling estate. All are now owned and operated by the state of Florida. Adding a modern voice to the Ringling's old-world atmosphere is Sarasota's diverse, independent, but very determined group of contemporary artists. To serve the tastes of tourists and residents, the city has several commercial galleries. Two "artsy" neighborhoods, Burns Court and Towles Court, offer pleasant shopping diversions in their boutiques, galleries, studios, and restaurants. Burns Court is also the home of the city's impressive foreign, avant-garde, and art film complex, the Burns Court Cinema.

The city boasts a number of professional performing ensembles: the Florida West Coast Symphony, the Gloria Musicaea (a professional chamber choir), the Sarasota Ballet, the Player's Theater, the Florida Studio Theater, and the Sarasota Opera, which enjoys sold-out seasons every year at its historic opera house. Topnotch amateur groups like the 125-voice Key Chorale and the Florida Symphonic Band showcase the combined talents of accomplished amateurs and retired professional musicians. The city's primary venue for performances, the bayfront Van Wezel Performing Arts Hall, will close March 31, 1999 for a massive expansion and refurbishing and will reopen in January 2000.

Sports and Recreation. Along with all this culture, residents of Sarasota enjoy swimming, snorkeling, fishing, and boating on Sarasota Bay and the Gulf of Mexico. Hunters and freshwater fishermen take to the rivers, lakes, and nearby woodlands. Sixty-five public and private golf courses, dozens of tennis courts, and miles of bike and running trails meet the needs of Sarasota's physically active population.

Law Enforcement and Safety. In 1996 there were 113 criminal offenses reported per 1,000 year-round residents in the city of Sarasota.

Senior Services. One very important senior service in Sarasota is First Call for Help, an information and referral center sponsored by the United Way of Sarasota County. Trained personnel provide advice, counseling, and confidential referrals to appropriate agencies. Another service is The Friendship Center, operated by Senior Friendship Centers, Inc., a private, nonprofit corporation offering services to people over sixty years of age. The center, close to downtown Sarasota, is host to a multitude of senior services including The Living Room, an adult day-care program; the Elder Hotline, a statewide information and referral service sponsored by the Florida Department of Elder Affairs; Candlelight Dining–Home Delivered Meals, a service providing well-balanced meals at local sites or through home delivery to seniors whose nutritional needs are not being met; a variety of health services; and door-to-door transportation for seniors needing assistance. This very active senior center even maintains a welcome center at the Sarasota/Bradenton Airport. Another food service is provided by Community Mobile Meals of Sarasota, a nonprofit organization staffed primarily by more than 400 volunteers. This group provides more than 500 meals each day to seniors who are unable to shop for food or prepare their own meals. The cost for a meal is $2.00, but there is no charge for recipients who are unable to pay.

Nearby Communities. Two communities on Sarasota County's barrier islands provide unique living possibilities in close proximity to all the advantages offered by Sarasota. **Longboat Key** is a long, narrow island and a town that is half in Sarasota County and half in Manatee County. The Sarasota half is a very upscale community of 3,907 year-round residents. The population nearly triples in the winter season. Here condominiums and houses on the Gulf or on Sarasota Bay may sell for several million dollars. Most of the beaches on Longboat Key are not easily accessible to the public. **Siesta Key** (population 12,000 year-round residents and another 12,000 winter-only residents) is more of a typical Florida beach community, with many areas of affordable housing, several interesting shopping districts, and a wonderful public beach with extensive parking and visitor facilities.

Venice

Venice is a delightful small city on the southern edge of Sarasota County. Its current population is nearly 19,000 with 32 percent over age sixty-five. Named after the Italian city because of its many canals and waterways, Florida's counterpart has followed a tradition of architecture that is Italian Renaissance in style, particularly in its charming downtown area. With the completion of the Intracoastal Waterway in the 1960s, Venice became an island community worthy of its Italian namesake. Several bridges connect the beach side of Venice with its mainland neighborhoods and its several eastern suburbs.

Housing. What distinguishes this small city is the affordability of beach real estate—a rarity among Florida's Gulf Coast cities. Venice offers a wide range of homes from modest to luxurious, all within a short drive or walk to the Gulf beaches. Two-bedroom condominiums are often listed for less than $50,000 and three-bedroom two-bath homes with a pool can be found for $150,000. And there are unusual and interesting small condominium complexes located in the downtown shopping area for less than $60,000. The metropolitan area offers a diverse selection of manufactured home parks, new site-built homes, older homes, and inland condominium and villa developments. It is not uncommon to locate a three-bedroom single-story home with an in-ground pool for around $110,000, and huge "family" homes with four or five bedrooms and two-car garages are still available for less than $150,000. A three-bedroom home built in 1987 with beach access in South Venice listed for $113,900. A renovated two-bedroom two-bath home on Venice Island was for sale at $89,900. A modest three-bedroom home with a caged pool was recently remodeled and put on the market at $109,900. In addition to the many luxurious housing developments in this area there are a great number of manufactured and mobile-home communities. In 1996 there were 20,827 mobile homes occupied either by owners or renters. Property taxes in the county of Sarasota are about $13.90 per $1,000 of nonexempt valuation. In the city of Venice the rate is about $17.30.

Culture and Entertainment. Theater is alive and well at the Venice Little Theater, a 500-volunteer organization. Classical music is presented by the Venice Symphony. The Venice Art Center presents exhibitions year-round and offers classes in the visual arts. The Golden Apple Dinner Theater is popular with retiree residents. Residents in Venice find themselves in the enviable position of being between Sarasota and Fort Myers, two larger cities with full cultural and entertainment calendars.

Sports and Recreation. Easy access to wonderful beaches is a major reason why so many people choose Venice. There are natural beaches and beaches developed with parking, food concessions, and all the other public amenities one could want. As a result of a commendable civic effort, Venice's beaches have been "renourished" and are now among the widest in Florida. Ten public and private golf courses meet the needs of the area's golfers. Eight tennis courts, well lit for evening play, are operated by the city.

Law Enforcement and Safety. In 1996 there were thirty-one criminal offenses reported per 1,000 year-round residents in the city of Venice.

Senior Centers. Venice's Senior Friendship Center is an active organization providing many services for residents age fifty-five and older.

Nearby Communities. **Englewood** (pop. 15,000) and **North Port** (pop. 15,905) are on Sarasota County's southern boundary. With much open land for housing, yet easily accessible to Sarasota's amenities, these towns provide affordable housing and are among the area's fastest-growing retirement communities.

Addresses and Connections

Chambers of Commerce: Greater Sarasota Chamber of Commerce, 1819 Main Street, #240, Sarasota, FL 34236; (941) 955–8187; Fax, (941) 366–5621; http://www.sarasota-online.com/chamber; E-mail: saracham@ix.netcom.com

The Venice Area Chamber of Commerce, 257 Tamiami Trail North, Venice, FL 34285-1908; (941) 488–2236; Fax, (941) 484–5903

Newspapers and Magazines: Sarasota Herald Tribune (daily), 801 South Tamiami Trail, Sarasota, FL 34236; (941) 365–6060; http://www.newscoast.com

Sarasota Magazine, 601 South Osprey Avenue, Sarasota, FL 34236; (941) 366–7272; http://www.sarasotamagazine.com; E-mail: saramag@earthlink.net

City Tempo (quarterly), Trafalgar Communications, Inc., 2621 Mall Drive, Sarasota, FL 34231; (941) 921–7005, http://www.citytempo.com; E-mail: ct@citytempo.com

THE SOUTHWEST GULF COAST

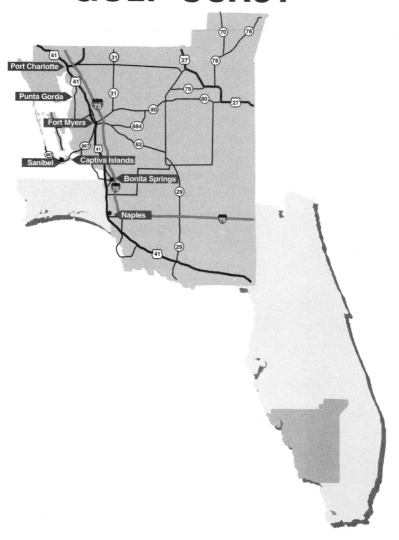

THE SOUTHWEST GULF COAST

The Southwest Gulf Coast region begins south of the Tampa Bay area and runs more than one hundred miles to the southern tip of Florida, where dry land gives way to the watery prairie known as the Everglades. It includes from north to south the following counties and their major cities and towns: Charlotte County (Punta Gorda and Port Charlotte), Lee County (Fort Myers, Sanibel and Captiva Islands, and Bonita Springs), and Collier County (Naples). These three counties were recently among the top twenty U.S. counties in attracting new retirees.

As you go south from Tampa Bay you immediately begin to notice a difference in the scenery. The roadside forests and the landscaping in towns become greener and more lush, and even in midwinter there is a profusion of flowers. Before you know it, gracefully curving coconut palms have replaced hardier trees, and by the time you reach Fort Myers it is clear that you are in tropical Florida.

This part of Florida is unsurpassed in scenic beauty, both natural and man-made. Natural areas are often junglelike with cypress trees and wild orchids lining wide, slow-moving rivers. Cities and towns, vying for tourists, have made the most of their tropical climate and rich soil. Parks, city streets, and housing developments are often a palette of shades of green and a mix of bright flowering plants. And everywhere you look you see a vista of a river, a bay, or the Gulf itself. The west coast of Florida is justifiably proud of its wonderful sunsets. There are almost always clouds here. White and fluffy during the day, they turn violet, pink, and gold as the sun disappears into the Gulf.

A distinguishing characteristic of this part of Florida's Gulf Coast is the succession of broad bays formed where some of the state's most scenic rivers join and flow into the Gulf of Mexico. Some of the towns we will visit in this chapter were established on these harbors. Others are on the string of barrier islands that continues just off the coast.

When Grandkids Visit. The *Florida Adventure Museum* in Punta Gorda has four galleries featuring traveling exhibits from other museums and excellent displays of the history of Florida and the region. Many exhibits are hands-on for the kids. Admission is $1.00 per person. An unusual and exciting outing can be found at *Babcock Wilderness Adventures*, a nature tour on a 90,000-acre ranch in eastern Charlotte County about 40 minutes from Punta Gorda. You can ride a swamp buggy into the 8,000-acre Telegraph Cypress Swamp, home to the rare Florida panther, deer, wild turkeys, alligators, and many other native animals. The cost of the tour is $17.95 for adults and $9.95 for kids ages 3 to 12.

Your budding scientists will insist on a visit to the *Edison-Ford Winter Estates* in Fort Myers where the winter home and laboratories of Thomas Edison and Henry Ford are open for tours. Admission is $10.00 for adults, $5.00 for kids ages 6 to 12 and includes a tour of both homes, the botanical gardens, and the Edison museum.

Shelling on *Sanibel Island* is an interesting excursion and the only charge is the $3.00 toll on the bridge to the island. If seashells are of real interest to your visitors, you can cap off your day with a visit to the *Bailey–Matthews Shell Museum*. The only one of its kind in the United States, this museum exhibits nearly a third of the world's shell specimens. Admission is $5.00 for ages 17 and older, $3.00 for kids ages 8 to 16, and no charge for those under age 8. The *J.N. "Ding" Darling Wildlife Refuge*, a 5,000-acre wildlife sanctuary on Sanibel Island, provides a wonderful opportunity to view southwest Florida nature. The Refuge includes an observation tower and several hiking, biking, and canoe trails. More than 200 species of birds—many of them endangered—nest here, and alligators are plentiful. Admission to the 5-mile wildlife drive is $5.00 for cars and $1.00 for bikers and hikers.

In this part of Florida a visit to the Everglades is a must. Tours range from the luxurious with cruises and airboat rides as well as lunch and transportation for upwards of $90.00 to walking tours on boardwalks in public nature parks. Air boat and swamp buggy tours are offered on the Seminole Indian reservation about 25 miles east of Naples. All will give you and your visitors a better understanding of the plants and animals living precariously in this endangered ecosystem. The local chamber of commerce has flyers with information on costs for many such tours.

If, after all that wildlife, your grandkids would like something a little tamer, take them to the *Teddy Bear Museum of Naples*. More than 3,000 bears live here, from antique to animated and from tiny to gigantic. Admission is $6.00 for adults, $4.00 for seniors, and $2.00 for kids ages 4 to 12.

CHARLOTTE COUNTY: Punta Gorda and Port Charlotte

Charlotte County (pop. 129,468) wraps around impressive Charlotte Harbor, a slightly smaller twin of Tampa Bay. Here the Peace River joins other rivers and streams to form the several-miles-wide bay. Like Tampa to the north and Fort Myers to the south, Punta Gorda was first established because the harbor, deep and well protected by barrier islands, encouraged Spanish exploration and settlement in the sixteenth and seventeenth centuries. Later, Charlotte Harbor provided the safe port needed by ships that plied the entire Gulf Coast of Florida from Pensacola to the Florida Keys and all the way down to Cuba in the nineteenth century. Those ships brought settlers and supplies to the fledgling American communities being established in southwest Florida in the late 1800s.

Today Charlotte Harbor and the rivers and canals that flow into it not only provide a safe anchorage for countless pleasure boats of all sizes, they provide the beauty and the recreational opportunities that have created a haven for thousands of new citizens, many of them retirees from northern climes. According to the U.S. Census Bureau, Charlotte County was the fastest-growing county in the nation during 1989–90. Charlotte County ranks nineteenth among all U.S. counties in the number of new retirees from other states. In 1997 *Money* magazine rated the Punta Gorda Metropolitan Statistical Area (all of Charlotte County) the fourth best place to live in the nation, and for the second year in a row, the best place to live in the South.

Cost of Living. Charlotte County ranks twenty-third in the state with a cost of living 96.59 percent of the state average. The sales tax here is 7 percent. The cost of housing is 9.34 percent below the state average. The average purchase price of a house is around $85,400. Charlotte County ranks fifty-seventh in the state with an average monthly apartment rent of $329.

Climate. Breezes from the Gulf and Charlotte Harbor give Punta Gorda and Port Charlotte clean air and moderate temperatures.

Fort Myers–Charlotte County Weather

| | In degrees Fahrenheit | | | | |
	Jan.	Apr.	July	Oct.	Annual Rainfall
DAILY HIGHS	74.3	84.2	91.1	85.8	53.37"
DAILY LOWS	53.2	62.0	74.5	68.6	

Medical Care. Two hospitals in Port Charlotte and one in Punta Gorda with a total of 669 beds serve Charlotte County.

Transportation. The Charlotte County Airport provides limited air service. Southwest Florida International Airport in Fort Myers and Sarasota/Bradenton International Airport provide more extensive service. There is no local bus service at this time.

Opportunities for Continuing Education. In addition to the Port Charlotte Cultural Center, described more fully below, adult and continuing education are provided by Charlotte County schools, the Charlotte County campus of Edison Community College, and Florida's newest state university, Florida Gulf Coast University in nearby Fort Myers.

Punta Gorda and Port Charlotte

Punta Gorda and Port Charlotte share beautiful Charlotte Harbor. Punta Gorda is a very old south Florida town rejuvenated in recent years by a flood of new residents, many of them retirees. In fact, with 35 percent of its population of retirement age, Punta Gorda has Florida's highest percentage of retirees. Punta Gorda sits on the Peace River and the south side of Charlotte Harbor. Port Charlotte is a rather new (dating from the 1950s) unincorporated community growing rapidly on a peninsula between the Myakka and Peace Rivers on the north side of Charlotte Harbor. Punta Gorda's population is 12,308. The population of unincorporated Charlotte County, many of whom live in or near Port Charlotte, is 117,160. The two communities combine to make a very pleasant place to live. Port Charlotte, with new public buildings and shopping malls, has all the modern amenities you could want. Punta Gorda, with a quaint waterfront and many nineteenth-century houses, has the charm of a historic Florida town. Both have made the most of their stunning waterfronts.

Housing. Your first impression of Punta Gorda's breathtaking older mansions on the esplanade facing the harbor is that you are seeing the most beautiful and historic waterfront homes this side of Charleston, South Carolina. The more than 130 homes in the most desirable sections of Punta Gorda's historic district carry hefty price tags. An extraordinary home near the harbor may cost $300,000 or $400,000, but they would be dollars well spent. A couple of blocks away, however, a handsome but modest two- or three-bedroom bungalow or newer home may run well under $100,000. Recently a quaint, historic Punta Gorda home with five downtown lots on a brick street was priced at $159,900. A newer four-bedroom executive home with caged pool and three baths listed for $178,000. A small waterfront home with a large lanai and in-ground spa, but in need of some cosmetic repairs, was put on the market at $84,000.

Port Charlotte, on the north side of Charlotte Harbor, offers even more affordable alternatives. In these neighborhoods a spacious executive home with a pool may cost $130,000 to $140,000. With miles of shoreline on the two rivers and the harbor, with many bayous and creeks, and with 165 miles of man-made waterways, you are always close to water in Port Charlotte. Since waterfront lots abound, they are a very good value. You can easily find 2,000-square-foot homes with a boat lift and in-ground pool for less than $160,000. Recently a three-bedroom home with two lots, professional landscaping, a heated pool and spa, and central vacuum, was for sale for $129,900. A large, elegant "Georgia Saltbox" home with a large pool, situated on a canal with Gulf access listed for $165,000. Pool homes for less than $90,000 are in great supply. Appealing condominiums come on the market at even more modest prices, like a recent listing for a two-bedroom two-bath remodeled unit priced at $39,900. Property taxes vary throughout the county and the city. An average of $17.50 per $1,000 nonexempt valuation is a safe approximation for the city of Punta Gorda.

Culture and Entertainment. The Visual Arts Center in Punta Gorda has more than 700 members and brings the visual arts to the area with its exhibitions, classes, and workshops. From November through March the Performing Arts Series is presented in the 1,500-seat Charlotte County Memorial Auditorium. The Charlotte Players Theater Group presents five plays annually at the Port Charlotte Cultural Center.

Sports and Recreation. Like most of Florida's coastal areas, sports and recreation in Charlotte County focus on the abundance of water. Saltwater fishing in the Gulf and freshwater fishing in the many rivers and streams are major activities and the reason many retirees have chosen to relocate here. Others prefer sailing, canoeing, swimming, water-skiing, or diving. Twenty-eight marinas and thirteen boat ramps allow easy access to the rivers and to Charlotte Harbor. The 840-acre Charlotte Harbor Environmental Center provides nature trails and picnic areas. Miles of canals within residential subdivisions provide additional access to open water. There are more than 12 miles of beaches with fifteen public-access sites. There are eighteen golf courses in Charlotte County. Much of the county is still rural woodlands where camping and hunting are major attractions. The Texas Rangers hold spring training in Port Charlotte.

Law Enforcement and Safety. In 1996 there were thirty-five criminal offenses reported per 1,000 year-round residents in Punta Gorda. In unincorporated Charlotte County, including Port Charlotte, the rate was just under thirty-one.

Senior Centers. The Port Charlotte Cultural Center began as "Port Charlotte U," an adult education activity. It has grown into a unique enterprise that includes a public library, a 418-seat theater, a craft center, several classrooms, and a 25,000-square-foot "Senior Lounge" with a dining room, music room, gift shop, nurses' station, meeting rooms, and offices. The center is staffed by more than 1,000 volunteers, most of them seniors. Continuing-education courses are provided by Charlotte County schools. The Center is open to residents of all ages, but there is a clear emphasis on the needs and interests of retirees. All charges are modest.

Nearby Communities. **Englewood** is an unincorporated community of about 40,000 that straddles the line between Sarasota and Charlotte Counties. It is more laid-back than most of the cities and towns in either county. There is definitely a small-town atmosphere and prices for housing are low for a Gulfside community. If you do not require big-city amenities and a full cultural agenda, but love fishing, gardening, or sunning on a white sand beach, Englewood is an undiscovered gem. **Boca Grande** is a beautiful little community sitting on the very tip of a tiny island jutting into the Gulf of Mexico at the mouth of Charlotte Harbor. Accessible only by a series of bridges and very isolated from the rest of Charlotte County, it reminds one of a quieter, more elegant Key West with its quaint old houses and buildings. Boca Grande, however, has an aura of chic priceyness that Key West lacks. The newer emphasis is on huge, luxury winter homes and condominiums.

Addresses and Connections

Chambers of Commerce: Charlotte County Chamber of Commerce, 326 West Marion Avenue, Punta Gorda, FL 33950; (941) 639–2222; http://www.charlotte-florida.com/chamber; E-mail: chamber@sunline.net

Englewood Area Chamber of Commerce, 601 South Indiana Avenue, Englewood, FL 34223; (941) 474–5511

Boca Grande Chamber of Commerce, P.O. Box 704, Boca Grande, FL 33921; (941) 964–0568

Newspaper: *Charlotte Sun Herald* (daily), P.O. Box 2390, Port Charlotte, FL 33949; (941) 629–2855

LEE COUNTY: Fort Myers, Sanibel and Captiva Islands, and Bonita Springs

Lee County (pop. 383,706) begins at the southern tip of Charlotte Harbor and wraps around the last and smallest of the bays that mark the southwest Florida coast. This bay is the mouth of the Caloosahatchee River, almost 2 miles wide where it flows into the Gulf of Mexico. The Intracoastal Waterway that has been between barrier islands and the mainland southward along the coast turns eastward here and via a series of locks crosses the state by way of the Caloosahatchee River, Lake Okeechobee, and the St. Lucie Canal to connect with the east coast Intracoastal Waterway near Stuart.

Lee County continues the pattern of a sparsely populated, agricultural eastern portion and a densely-populated, urban area along the Gulf Coast. Coconut palms, royal palms, and jungles of lush vegetation tell you that Lee County is in tropical Florida. Lured by mild, sunny weather, winter residents and tourists increase Lee County's population by more than 100 percent between January and March. In the island communities the increase is closer to 200 percent. In a recent study of retirement migration, Lee County was sixth among all U.S. counties in attracting retirees from other states. In *Retirement Places Rated* the Fort Myers/Cape Coral area ranked thirteenth out of the 183 most popular retirement locations in the United States.

Cost of Living. Lee County ranks fifteenth in the state with a cost of living 97.49 percent of the state average. The sales tax is 6 percent. The cost of housing is 2.99 percent below the state average. The average purchase price of a home is around $101,500. Lee County ranks ninth in the state with an average monthly apartment rent of $641.

Climate. Lee county's tropical climate is mild year-round. The following figures are from the NOAA station in Fort Myers.

Fort Myers–Lee County Weather

| | In degrees Fahrenheit | | | | |
	Jan.	Apr.	July	Oct.	Annual Rainfall
DAILY HIGHS	73.4	84.2	91.1	85.8	53.37"
DAILY LOWS	53.2	62.0	74.5	68.6	

Medical Care. Five hospitals with 1,536 beds serve the residents of Lee County.

Transportation. Southwest Florida International Airport provides jet service to many cities in the Southeast and connecting service to others. Local bus service is provided by Lee County Transit.

Opportunities for Continuing Education. Lee County schools and Edison Community College combine to provide a rich array of classes and life-enrichment programs to retirees in the area.

Fort Myers

Fort Myers, located on the broad Caloosahatchee River 12 miles inland from where the river flows into the Gulf, is another Florida city established many years ago when transportation was primarily by boat and the most important factor was a safe harbor. Barrier islands not only protect the harbor here but provide wonderful beaches. Several well-known beach communities have developed on these islands. As soon as you enter Fort Myers from any one of several highways lined with tall, stately royal palms, you know why it calls itself "The City of Palms." The original palms—many of them still standing—were brought over from Cuba on the boats that ran between Fort Myers and Havana trading in cattle, fish, fruits, and all the commerce needed to keep an isolated town alive in the late nineteenth century. A rustic winter resort for the adventurous at the time, Fort Myers gained its most famous fan and promoter when Thomas Edison honeymooned here in 1886 and decided to build his winter retreat in the small town. His friend Henry Ford followed, and Fort Myers soon became a fashionable winter resort. Today Fort Myers is a lovely tropical Florida city of 46,328 year-round citizens that, along with its neighboring communities of Cape Coral and Sanibel and Captiva Islands, has become a magnet for tourists, snowbirds, and retirees.

Housing. You can be certain about one thing when you choose a home in Fort Myers: It is going to have palm trees! Whether you choose a brand-new home designed for retirees in Cape Coral (where many lovely three-bedroom models with all the latest amenities cost around $90,000) or the most luxurious million-dollar estate in Fort Myers, you will never be far from the city's famous palm trees. And in this city of bays, rivers, canals, bayous, and islands, you will also never be far from the water. Affordable housing options in the $90,000 to $130,000 range are spread throughout Fort Myers, North Fort Myers, and Cape Coral. A Spanish-style, three-bedroom home with a one-bedroom guest cottage and three remodeled baths was for sale at $124,900. For an ambitious retiree, a five-unit Art Deco apartment building with wood floors and fireplaces in a desirable location listed for $239,900. An Old-Florida home on a large lot with four bedrooms and two baths listed for $78,000. For those who prefer condominium living, typical two-bedroom two-bath condo units in well-landscaped pool complexes regularly go for around $40,000. Property taxes in Fort Myers range from $16.52 to $19.74 per $1,000 nonexempt valuation, depending on location.

Culture and Entertainment. Fort Myers has an array of venues for the performing and the visual arts. Harborside, a downtown convention center, has facilities to house large theatrical events and touring Broadway shows. The Barbara Mann Performing Arts Hall on the campus of Edison Community College has excellent acoustics and hosts concerts and touring shows. It is home to the Southwest Florida Symphony Orchestra and Chorus. Seven playhouses in Lee County bring live theater to the area. The Lee County Alliance of the Arts presents classes, performances, art shows and exhibitions, festivals, and concerts in the William R. Frizzell Cultural Center's 150-seat theater, outdoor amphitheater, and three galleries.

Sports and Recreation. Fishing and all the water sports of a town located on a major river and the Gulf of Mexico keep Fort Myers residents happy and busy. Beaches on all the area's barrier islands attract swimmers and sun lovers. Southwest Florida has been dubbed the "Golf Course Capital of the World" with more golf holes per capita in Fort Myers and Naples than anywhere else in the United States. There are fourteen golf courses in Lee County. The Boston Red Sox and the Minnesota Twins hold spring training in Fort Myers.

Law Enforcement and Safety. In 1996 there were 153 criminal offenses reported per 1,000 year-round residents in the city of Fort Myers. In Cape Coral the rate was forty-two.

Senior Centers. The Fort Myers Senior Center provides services and activities for residents of Fort Myers and nearby communities.

Nearby Communities. **Cape Coral** is the city's closest neighbor. The second largest incorporated area in Florida and now home to 87,632 citizens, Cape Coral is a little sister who has quickly outgrown her older sibling. With coral-colored sidewalks, broad avenues, seemingly endless acres of land, and 400 miles of canals, Cape Coral is a developer's dream. Since Cape Coral is primarily a residential community, its citizens go to Fort Myers for much of their entertainment and shopping. A new Midpoint Memorial Bridge connects the center of Cape Coral to central Fort Myers. **North Fort Myers** is a large unincorporated community on the north side of the Caloosahatchee River that has seen tremendous growth in the last twenty years. Many of the 237,869 people who live in unincorporated Lee County are in neighborhoods in and around North Fort Myers. There are many neighborhoods of attractive, affordable homes here as well as several communities of manufactured homes. **Fort Myers Beach** (pop. 6,039) is mainly a beach resort with many motels and other tourist accommodations, but there is a good number of beach cottages for rent and for sale. The white sand beaches are among the best in the state.

Sanibel and Captiva Islands

Two connected barrier islands, Sanibel and Captiva (with a combined population of about 7,000 year-round residents), are among Florida's most famous island communities. Sanibel Island is perhaps the best-known shelling locale in the nation, and both islands are famous for their beaches, tropical vegetation, and rare animal life. Fifteen miles southwest of Fort Myers and connected to the mainland by a 3-mile toll causeway, the islands are popular with tourists and residents, a great many of them retirees. Sanibel and Captiva are models of community concern for a fragile ecology. The islands are not large (Sanibel Island is about 12 miles long and 5 miles across, and Captiva is about 5 miles long and only ½ mile wide), but more than 40 percent of the land has been protected in wildlife preserves. Much has been done to preserve an island look and feel here. Public buildings such as the library look like old island shelters.

Housing. Living on the island communities of Sanibel and Captiva is now mainly for the very well-to-do. Tiny, modest homes there start near $200,000, but you may find an occasional condominium resale affordable. A recent listing for a two-bedroom two-bath villa condominium on Sanibel with a den, studio, and decks on a quiet cul-de-sac near the beach was listed at $189,555—a very reasonable price for this area. And a three-bedroom stilt home overlooking the Sanibel River was put on the market at $189,000. Most listings on Sanibel or Captiva are well above $300,000 or $400,000, and many run into the millions. Property taxes in Sanibel are about $18.80 per $1,000 nonexempt valuation. In Captiva the rate is about $18.40.

Culture and Entertainment. Island residents have a choice of a great many cultural and entertainment activities right on their own turf, or all of those in nearby Fort Myers. The Barrier Island Group for the Arts (known locally as BIG Arts) coordinates the many arts organizations on the islands and sponsors art exhibits, lectures, films, and performance art events. More than twenty galleries show the work of local and nationally known artists. Every March the Sanibel Music Festival presents a season of seven performances of classical music including chamber music and opera. The Pirate Playhouse presents a season of theater from October through April each year.

Sports and Recreation. The beaches are the main reason most people visit and live on Sanibel and Captiva. Shelling, beach walking, swimming, snorkeling, and just lazing in the sun are the islands' most popular pastimes. More than 20 miles of paved trails encourage biking, running, walking, and in-line skating, allowing residents and visitors to exercise as well as get around the islands safely. Of course, with all the water around, fishing and boating are also very popular. Bridges and piers allow those without boats to test their angling skills. Canoes are available for rent and are the best way to get around the huge wildlife sanctuaries.

Law Enforcement and Safety. In 1996 there were forty-four criminal offenses reported per 1,000 year-round residents of the islands.

Senior Centers. Many services are provided by Island Seniors, the senior center operated by the city of Sanibel.

Bonita Springs

Bonita Springs is an attractive unincorporated community of about 25,000 year-round residents and another 30,000 winter residents. Since it sits on the line between Lee and Collier Counties, its residents enjoy the benefits of both Fort Myers and Naples. Bonita Springs has an interesting old downtown and miles of beautiful white sand beaches. The area around the original small town developed rapidly with two very different kinds of planned communities. Several nicely landscaped communities of manufactured homes with pools, clubhouses, and recreational facilities are scattered throughout the area. More recently, huge gated developments of very luxurious homes with every community facility one could imagine, from the very best in golf courses to private gourmet restaurants, have begun to appear. In Bonita Springs the resident in the $35,000 mobile home shares the same sunshine and wonderful community ambience with the resident of the $2 million home on the bay.

Housing. With its central location between Naples and Fort Myers, Bonita Springs offers an extreme range of real-estate alternatives in a relatively small town. Site-built three-bedroom homes in new communities may cost only $100,000, with many more in the $125,000 to $135,000 range. At the same time, luxuriously appointed modern homes proliferate in the new and very upscale developments on the Gulf such as Bonita Bay, for example. Bonita Bay carries a high price tag, but it is a pioneer among a new breed of communities. It is a planned development that balances golf and recreational amenities with luxurious native landscaping and a basic commitment to preserving the environment. Its 2,400-acre site has become one of the most idyllic and unusual housing areas in the country. Here three-bedroom condominiums may start at $170,000. And palatial homes on its rivers, bays or Gulf front can range well over $500,000. But more modest real estate abounds in the quiet neighborhoods of manufactured homes that surround Bonita Springs. In recent years the median price for a two-bedroom home was $64,500; for a three-bedroom home the price was $159,000, and for a condominium the median price was $125,000. Property taxes in Bonita Springs are $18.53 per $1,000 nonexempt valuation.

Culture and Entertainment. Twenty miles south of Fort Myers and the same distance north of Naples, the residents of Bonita Springs have all the benefits of both towns when it comes to entertainment and cultural activities. Please see the profiles of Fort Myers above and Naples below for details of these cities' offerings.

Sports and Recreation. The same is true for sports and recreation. Bonita Springs does have lovely beaches and no shortage of water for every type of water sport. Just a few miles inland from the coast you will find forests and freshwater streams for hunting and fishing. Bonita Springs residents can also find activities in Fort Myers and Naples, both 20 miles away.

Law Enforcement and Safety. In 1996 there were thirty-six criminal offenses reported per 1,000 year-round residents in Lee County.

Senior Centers. The Bonita Senior Recreation Program run by the Bonita Spring Parks and Recreation Department offers many services to the area's seniors.

Addresses and Connections

Chambers of Commerce: Greater Fort Myers Chamber of Commerce, 2310 Edwards Drive, Fort Myers, FL 33901, (941) 332–3624, (800) 366–3622; Fax, (941) 332–7276; http://www.fortmyers.org; E-mail: fortmyers@fortmyers.org

Cape Coral Chamber of Commerce, 2501 Cape Coral Parkway East, Cape Coral, FL 33910; (941) 549-6900

Sanibel-Captiva Chamber of Commerce, 1159 Causeway Road, Sanibel, FL 33957; (941) 472–1080; E-mail: Island@ sanibel-captiva.org; http://www.sanibel-captiva.org

Bonita Springs Area Chamber of Commerce, 25071 Chamber of Commerce Drive, Bonita Springs, FL 34135; (941) 992–2943, (800) 226–29430; Fax, (941) 992–5011; E-mail: info@bonitaspringschamber. com; http://www.bonitaspringschamber.com

Newspapers: News-Press (daily), 2442 Dr. Martin L. King Jr. Boulevard, Fort Myers, FL 33901; (941) 335–0303

Naples Daily News (daily), 1075 Central Avenue, Naples, FL 34102; (941) 262–3161

COLLIER COUNTY: Naples

Collier County (pop. 193,036) is one of Florida's most interesting counties. It makes up the very southwestern tip of Florida, and it is a land of extreme contrasts. The majority of its 193,000 citizens live in an area of high ground along the Gulf Coast in sophisticated communities like Naples. Go just a few miles east and south of the coast, however, and you are in as desolate and primitive a land as you will find anywhere in the United States—the Big Cypress Swamp. Much of the Big Cypress Swamp is protected in the 729,000-acre Big Cypress National Preserve. North of the swamp is rich muck land that has been seized from the Everglades, drained, and turned into truck farms. Here you find small villages of migrant farm workers. Throughout this area an ongoing battle is being fought among environmentalists, developers, and farmers over the protection of the ecology of one of this country's rarest national treasures, the Everglades, and its endangered plant and animal life. A powerful environmental group, the Nature Conservancy, is at the vanguard of efforts to preserve the wild beauty of Collier County's natural setting. It fights alongside Federal programs to restore and preserve the Everglades and Collier County's wilderness areas. Alligator Alley (I–75) goes across this land in almost a straight line between Naples and Fort Lauderdale. Other than Marco Island, an isolated and expensive enclave for tourists and winter residents, Naples is the southernmost center of population on Florida's Gulf Coast. In recent years Collier and Monroe Counties together were ranked sixteenth among all U.S. counties in attracting retirees from other states.

Cost of Living. Collier County ranks sixth in the state with a cost of living 101 percent of the state average. The sales tax is 6 percent. The cost of housing is 4.76 percent above the state average. The average purchase price of a house is $116,658. Collier County ranks eighth in the state with an average apartment rent of $644.

Climate. Collier County is about as tropical as you can get in the United States. Temperatures in the coastal areas are moderated by Gulf breezes, but inland the heat and humidity can be sweltering for much of the year.

Fort Myers–Collier County Weather

| | In degrees Fahrenheit | | | | |
	Jan.	Apr.	July	Oct.	Annual Rainfall
DAILY HIGHS	74.3	84.2	91.1	85.8	53.37"
DAILY LOWS	53.2	62.0	74.5	68.6	

Medical Care. One hospital with 434 beds serves the residents of Collier County.

Transportation. Naples Municipal Airport provides limited service. The nearest airports of any size are Southwest Florida International Airport in Fort Myers, about forty-five minutes away, and Fort Lauderdale International Airport, about two hours away. There is no local bus transportation in Collier County.

Opportunities for Continuing Education. Collier County schools and the Collier County campus of Edison Community College sponsor programs, courses, and activities geared to the continuing-education needs of the senior community. It is too soon to measure the impact of Florida's tenth and newest four-year university, Florida Gulf Coast University, which opened its doors in 1998 on a site in southern Lee County between Fort Myers and Naples.

Naples

Naples is a most elegant community, a sparkling gem set amid the lushest tropical landscape you can imagine. With a population of 21,127, it is not a big city, but there is about as much wealth per capita here as in any city in Florida. And it shows! The town is immaculate, beautifully landscaped, and every street, public building, and park seems to reflect the quiet, good taste of Naples residents. The low-rise downtown shopping area will remind you of Las Olas Boulevard in Fort Lauderdale or Worth Avenue in Palm Beach with its unique shops, lovely arcades, palms, and flowers. If money were no object and you wanted to design a perfect community for retirees, you might come up with Naples. It is a city designed and managed to attract and keep happy its wealthy retirees, both year-round and winter-only. That does not mean that ordinary people cannot or do not live in this pleasant small city. Actually, it is a very nice place for middle-income people to live because so many amenities—the new performing arts center is just one example—are heavily endowed by residents with very deep pockets, but appreciated by all. The atmosphere created by and for very wealthy retirees is shared and enjoyed by all who call Naples home. *Money* magazine named Naples to its 1996 list of "Five Best Small Places to Live in America," and Naples was number fifteen on that magazine's list of "Best Places to Live in America."

Housing. When looking for housing in Naples the first time, you might be intimidated by the number of Rolls Royces, Jaguars, vintage cars, and other luxury vehicles parked along its quaint streets. And the fashionable citizens do lend the area an air right out of "Lifestyles of the Rich and Famous." However, once you steer past the jaw-dropping million-dollar estates on the Gulf of Mexico and the many bayous, you'll learn there are many beautiful and affordable homes in Naples, some only a few blocks away from those mansions. Within a short drive of downtown Naples are countless golf and gated communities you'll want to consider. Striking golf course residences can be found for less than $150,000. And unique homes in all areas of the city are available for less than $120,000. Some of these are within walking distance of the Gulf beaches or on rivers or bayous. A large two-bedroom home with two living rooms and two baths, located just seven blocks from the beach was priced at $123,900. And a unique cedar home with four bedrooms, three baths, and a 200-foot walking deck in a secluded river setting was recently offered for $119,900. Naples has an unusually large supply of courtyard condominium residences with pools and tennis courts, where a three-bedroom three-bath condominium might list for less than $120,000, and two-bedroom two-bath units in the same complex might cost just under $70,000. In the oldest part of Naples a three-bedroom two-bath unit in a courtyard complex was recently priced at $119,500, and in another downtown complex a first-floor two-bedroom two-bath condo with covered parking listed for $61,000. In the countryside near Naples, mini-estates proliferate. A three-bedroom home on ten acres of land with a horse barn was priced at $145,900. A nearby two-story Victorian home with three bedrooms and two and a half baths on five acres but in need of some remodeling listed for $96,000. For a small city that offers the luxury and amenities one would only expect in a larger city, the housing here is diverse and, all things considered, a very good value. Property taxes in Naples vary from $13.76 to $16.85 per $1,000 nonexempt valuation, depending on the exact location. Countywide the average is about $15 per $1,000 nonexempt valuation.

Culture and Entertainment. It isn't just a cliché to say that Naples has the best cultural activities and entertainment money can buy. The elegant new centerpiece of Naples' cultural life is the nine-year-old Philharmonic Center for the Arts. Costing $43.4 million at last count, 80 percent of which was raised from private and corporate sources, the "Phil" is perfection for those who love the performing and visual arts. However, just giving money for bricks and mortar wasn't the end of the support for the arts in this culturally minded city. Ongoing support and endowments allow the Center to hire nationally known conductors and directors. The Center is home to the Naples Philharmonic, an eighty-member professional symphony, and the 110-voice Philharmonic Center Chorale. It is the west coast home for the Miami City Ballet. An enthusiastic public supports 400 audience events each year—most scheduled for Naples' busy fall and winter season—ranging from symphonies to Broadway shows. With 5,000 square feet of gallery space and two sculpture gardens, the Phil is almost as much a venue for the visual arts as it is for the performing arts. Exhibitions of paintings and sculpture are presented October through May. Many of the world's most important contemporary artists have placed their works in the spectacular lobby and in alcoves and niches throughout the building. The Center's Lifelong Learning Program includes recitals, book reviews, and lectures on music and art history.

Elsewhere in Naples, an active United Arts Council of Collier County coordinates the activities of museums, galleries, theater groups, and music organizations. The visual arts are well represented by an ever-growing number of art galleries on Fifth Avenue South, Naples' popular downtown walking and shopping street, on Broad Avenue, and on Third Street South, another downtown street of interesting shops, galleries, and restaurants. A new downtown Visual Arts Center will provide studios, classrooms, and exhibition spaces to showcase the work of many local, national, and international painters and sculptors. The Naples Players present comedies, dramas, and musicals throughout the year. The Naples Historical Society maintains and sponsors tours of historic houses and sites, and the Collier County Museum exhibits interesting artifacts pertaining to local history. If a small town saturated in culture is your cup of tea, Naples may be your best bet for a fascinating retirement.

Sports and Recreation. Culture isn't all Naples has to offer. Its wonderful climate and Gulfside location make the city a sports paradise too. The Naples area is proud of being part of what has been recognized as the "Golf Capital of the World." Eight public and three semiprivate courses (most designed by well-known golf course architects) and a great many private courses in Collier County alone make this area a haven for golfers. Each year major golfing events take place here. Fishing and boating in the Gulf or in the many freshwater rivers and streams is a popular pastime in Naples.

Law Enforcement and Safety. In 1996 there were sixty-eight criminal offenses reported in Naples per 1,000 year-round residents.

Senior Centers. The East Naples Seniors Club and Our Place Senior Center provide many social, educational, and recreational services. During the winter season several city parks schedule activities for seniors.

Nearby Communities. **Naples Park** and **Vanderbilt Beach** are small unincorporated communities a few miles north of Naples. **Marco Island** (estimated population 11,000) is an off-shore unincorporated resort community about 15 miles south of Naples.

Addresses and Connections

Chamber of Commerce: Naples Area Chamber of Commerce, 3620 Tamiami Trail North, Naples, FL 34103; (941) 262–6376; Fax, (941) 262–8374

Chamber Visitor Center, 895 Fifth Avenue South, Naples, FL 34102; (941) 262–6141; Fax, (941) 435–9910; http://www.naples-online.com; E-mail: chamber@naples-online.com

Newspaper: Naples Daily News (daily), 1075 Central Avenue, Naples, FL 34102; (941) 262–3161

THE SOUTHEAST ATLANTIC COAST

To understand the generations-old appeal of southeast Florida's "Gold Coast," just drive a few blocks along Fort Lauderdale's magnificently landscaped beach or along the dunes high above Juno Beach's natural oceanfront. Winter or summer, the sun seems always bright, the sand is golden, the air is fresh off the ocean, and the Atlantic is a beautiful shade of turquoise. As a native Floridian living here year-round, I took all this for granted, and it wasn't until I was living in the north and flew to Fort Lauderdale one January that I fully appreciated the impact south Florida can have on a visitor from the north in midwinter. No wonder my great grandparents and others equally adventurous braved an untamed jungle to live in so beautiful a place!

As you travel through this amazing region, however, you begin to realize that the sun, sand, coconut palms, and Atlantic Ocean are about the only things the very different communities of southeast Florida have in common. Key West, Coral Gables, and Sunrise might be in different states, for they are so dissimilar in the ways they have evolved, the lifestyles they foster, and the people they attract. Once again, we are reminded that Florida seems to have a place for everyone.

With the exception of the Florida Keys, tiny coral islands off the southern tip of Florida, the geography here is similar to other coastal areas in Florida. The coast and the barrier islands are the most heavily populated and attract the most retirees. The Intracoastal Waterway is continuous throughout the region. In the Keys it is a channel on the more protected Gulf side of the islands. North of the Keys it separates the barrier islands from the mainland—islands with such well-known names as Key Biscayne, Miami Beach, and Palm Beach. Just a few miles inland, you find either the Everglades or—where extensive and controversial drainage has made the swampland usable for farming—vast sugar cane fields, truck farms that supply much of the north's winter vegetables, and acres of gladiolus for the cut-flower market. All along this area, however, you can see a movement westward of housing developments as more and more land is drained to accommodate the ever-increasing number of people seeking their place in the southeast Florida sun.

SOUTHEAST ATLANTIC COAST

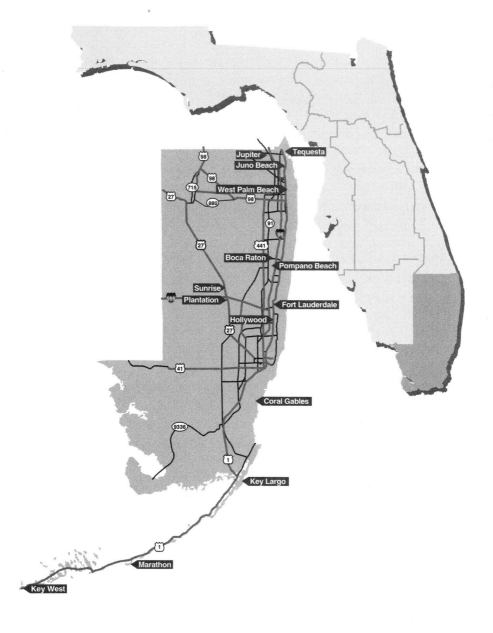

This region begins with Key West, the southernmost point in the continental United States, and reaches 240 miles north to beyond the Palm Beaches. It includes, from south to north, the following counties and their cities and towns most popular with retirees: Monroe County (Key West, Marathon, and Key Largo), Dade County (Coral Gables), Broward County (Fort Lauderdale, Hollywood, Plantation, Sunrise, and Pompano Beach), and Palm Beach County (Boca Raton, West Palm Beach, Juno Beach, Jupiter, and Tequesta). All of the counties in this region rank high among U.S. counties in attracting retirees from other states.

When Grandkids Visit. From Key West through Palm Beach County, the beaches in this region are spectacular, accessible, inexpensive, and great for your grandkids. All of Key West will be fun for you and your grandkids. Both the *Old Town Trolley* (fare $16.00 for adults and $7.00 for kids ages 7 to 12) and little *Conch Train* (fare $15.00 for adults and $7.00 for kids ages 4 to 12) will take you on a ninety-minute narrated tour of the sights of Key West, a good way to get an overview of this interesting place. Both will give you discount coupons for many other sights. At last count twenty-seven museums on this tiny island are dedicated to showing you the interesting history, geography, flora, and fauna of the Keys. One of the most interesting is the *Oldest House Museum.* Also known as the Wreckers' Museum, it is the 1829 house of a sea captain and wrecker. The museum tells the fascinating story of wreckers and their prey during the early days of Key West. Admission is $4.00 for adults and 50 cents for kids ages 5 to 12. You can spend a lot showing the grandkids the sights of Key West, but sunset at *Mallory Square*, the most fun of all, is free, except for your refreshments and what pocket change you might put in the hats of mimes, acrobats, musicians, and other entertainers who make sunset here a gala celebration every night.

Neither you nor your grandkids will want to miss the opportunity to go for a swim in Coral Gables' opulent *Venetian Pool.* Built in and around an abandoned rock quarry, the 820,000-gallon, spring-fed pool has grottoes, waterfalls, and caves. It is surrounded by buildings made to look like a Renaissance Venetian courtyard. Admission for Coral Gables residents is $3.00 for adults, $2.50 for teens ages 13–17, and $2.00 for kids 12 and under; nonresidents pay $5.00, $4.00, and $2.00.

The *Museum of Discovery and Science/Blockbuster IMAX Theater* in Fort Lauderdale will bring you back to today and the future in a hurry. A five-story-high new IMAX 3-D theater and a building full of hands-on science exhibits will keep grandkids happy while they learn. Admission is $6.00 for adults, $5.00 for students, seniors, and kids ages 3 to 12.

Blockbuster Golf and Games in Sunrise is an entertainment park with miniature golf, a driving range, bumper boats, batting cages, video games, and a climbing, sliding, crawling mazelike play area for the very young. Each activity is priced separately, ranging from $2.00 to $5.00.

The International Museum of Cartoon Art in Boca Raton boasts the world's largest collection of cartoons. Admission to the museum is $6.00 for adults, $5.00 for seniors, $4.00 for students, and $3.00 for kids 6 to 12.

The Arthur R. Marshall Loxahatchee National Wildlife Refuge near Boynton Beach is a 145,665-acre sanctuary for Everglades wildlife. There are nature trails, a variety of educational programs, and no admission charge.

MONROE COUNTY: Key West, Marathon, and Key Largo

The 150-mile-long string of small islands we know as the Florida Keys is one of the truly unique places in the United States. From the air, they look like an ivory-and-jade necklace spread out on a cloth of iridescent blue and green. The culture of the Keys is as unique as their geography. Isolated for generations and tempered by the sea and hurricanes, a strange mixture of people made the Keys their own. For more than three centuries the islands were a refuge for pirates and men who preyed on ships for salvage. Immigrants from the Bahamas, Cuba, and islands of the Caribbean found a home in the Keys. In this century the Keys have been a haven for artists, writers, and others wanting to escape the rigid confines of "normal" society. In the 1960s and '70s the Keys were popular with the generation of "flower children," and their legacy lives on in the culture of Key West. Now, adding to that culture are hordes of tourists and sports enthusiasts seeking sun and surf, and retirees from other climes who find the Keys exciting and wildly hospitable. Not only are the Florida Keys unique, the people of the Keys revel in this uniqueness! There is simply no other place like it in the world. Where else is sunset an event worthy of a daily celebration?

The transition from the mundane to the magical begins when U.S. Highway 1 leaves the mainland and becomes the Overseas Highway. Like a stone skipping over water, it hops from island to island, barely above the waves, for 110 miles on its way toward its southern terminus in Key West. Following the path of Henry Flagler's railroad that traversed the Keys from 1912 until it was destroyed by a hurricane in 1935, the Overseas Highway connects the islands with forty-two bridges, one 7 miles long. The Highway briefly expands to four lanes on a couple of the larger islands, but all the rest, including the bridges, is a two-lane road, making getting to and from the lower keys slow when traffic is moving and nearly impossible when it comes to a stop on busy weekends. It is, however, one of the most beautiful drives you can take. If you must be stuck in traffic, where better than under a coconut palm on a small coral isle with the crystal-clear waters of both the Gulf of Mexico and the Atlantic Ocean almost within your reach? While you wait, schools of dolphins play tag, pelicans dive for their dinner, and just a short distance from shore divers explore the third largest living coral reef in the world.

There are hundreds of islands and islets in the Florida Keys. Most, barely above water, are uninhabitable. Many are only islands being born—small mud flats with a growth of mangroves. Most of these islands are in an area between the southern edge of the Everglades on the mainland and the upper half of the better-known Keys, a corner of the Gulf of Mexico called Florida Bay. This area is an important marine environment with shallow warm waters providing a nursery for sea and bird life. While all of these islands large enough to be named are called keys, the islands generally referred to as the Florida Keys are those accessible via the Overseas Highway.

The Florida Keys are divided into three regions. The Lower Keys region begins with Key West and includes all the islands up to the Seven Mile Bridge, about 36 miles north. Most of the small islands in the Lower Keys are inhabited only by the very small and endangered key deer. The Middle Keys region begins at the Seven Mile Bridge and goes to Long Key Channel, about 32 miles north. It includes the town of Marathon. The Upper Keys region begins with Long Key Channel and ends 42 miles north, just beyond Key Largo. This is where the Overseas Highway turns west toward the mainland and, like Cinderella after the ball, turns back into plain old U.S. 1 again. Locations in the Keys are given in terms of distances along the Overseas Highway, indicated by mile marker signs with the symbol MM and the mileage from Key West, which is zero. Addresses often use the MM number plus either "oceanside" or "bayside," indicating whether the location is on the Atlantic or the Gulf side of the Overseas Highway. For example, the address of the Key Largo Chamber of Commerce is MM106 bayside.

Monroe County (pop. 83,789) covers the Florida Keys and a southwestern section of the Everglades on the mainland. Monroe County (lumped together with Collier County) ranks sixteenth among all U.S. counties in the number of retirees attracted from other states.

Cost of Living. Monroe County is the most expensive county in the state with a cost of living 108.4 percent of the state average. The sales tax is 7 percent. The cost of housing is 21.67 percent above the state average. The average purchase price of a house is $145,610. Monroe County ranks first in the state with an average monthly apartment rent of $888.

Climate. Washed by the warm Gulf of Mexico and the Atlantic's Gulf Stream and stretching farther south than any other part of the continental United States, the Florida Keys have the mildest weather anywhere in Florida. Constant breezes from the Gulf or the Atlantic further moderate temperatures year-round.

Key West–Monroe County Weather

| | In degrees Fahrenheit | | | | |
	Jan.	Apr.	July	Oct.	Annual Rainfall
DAILY HIGHS	74.8	81.7	89.1	84.4	39.59"
DAILY LOWS	65.0	72.2	79.6	75.5	

Medical Care. Three hospitals with 269 beds serve the residents of Monroe County.

Transportation. Only Key West has a public bus system. Key West International Airport provides limited service. The nearest major airport is Miami International.

Opportunities for Continuing Education. Monroe County schools and Florida Keys Community College with its main campus in Key West and centers in the middle and upper Keys provide adult and continuing education.

Key West, Marathon, and Key Largo

The Florida Keys curve southwest and then almost due west as they leave the mainland and thrust themselves into the Gulf of Mexico. Key West is not south of Miami, as is often thought, but almost directly south of Tampa and almost due north of Havana. This location made Key West an important port when transportation of people and goods was mainly by ship, and it was a natural stopping off point between New Orleans, Tampa, Havana, and ports on the east coast of the United States. Ships traveling between ports on the Gulf and those on the Atlantic had to negotiate the Florida Straits between Key West and Cuba, a narrow passage lined with treacherous reefs. Storms and unpredictable currents drove many ships onto the reefs while others were lured there by unscrupulous wreckers for the right to salvage the ships and all their goods. Its fortunate geographic position and the wealth enjoyed by its "wreckers" made Key West the largest city in Florida and the richest city per capita in the United States in the early 1800s.

Today, Key West (pop. 27,009) is an intriguing and popular tourist town. It is literally the end of the road in the continental United States. A sign at the southernmost point indicates that Havana, only 90 miles away, is the next stop. Key West is entertaining, historic, and picturesque. Its narrow streets are shaded by mango, poinciana, and jacaranda trees, and its yards are overflowing with banana trees and flowering vines and shrubs. Many old houses and buildings have survived. In fact, there are more than 3,000 buildings on the National Register of Historic Places in Key West, more than in any other city in the United States. Of particular interest are the many colorful little conch houses, many built from the wood of wrecked ships. Natives of the Keys call themselves "conchs," a reference to the crab whose abandoned shell makes the Key's most popular souvenir and whose meat (as tough and chewy as a piece of old inner tube but heavenly when pounded and diced to make conch fritters and conch chowder) was a staple of the islanders' diet long before it became a gourmet delicacy. Conch houses, once the simple wooden houses of fishermen but now "restored" to a glory their builders could not have imagined, are often featured in design and architecture magazines. These houses, with their deep porches and tin roofs, and larger homes with gingerbread trim and widow's walks have given their motifs to a style of architecture known as "Key West."

Key West is also an attractive destination for active retirees who want to dive—literally—into the sun and fun of a small town surrounded by open sea. The Navy always had a presence in Key West, and the Key West Naval Air Station is on nearby Boca Chica Key. Many military retirees remember the Keys fondly and choose to retire here.

Marathon (population estimated at about 12,500 year-round residents) is an unincorporated community in the Middle Keys and the second largest town in the Keys. Commercial and recreational fishing are important here. More than 10 miles of former bridges have been closed to traffic and turned into fishing piers.

Key Largo (population about 12,000 year-round residents) is an incorporated community at the top of the Upper Keys. Located at the beginning of the Overseas Highway, Key Largo is considered the gateway to the Keys, and it is very popular with fishermen, divers, and snorkelers. With extensive reefs rich in marine life, hundreds of wrecked ships, an underwater state park, and a national marine sanctuary, the Florida Keys have become one of the most popular places for snorkeling and scuba diving in the world. One of the state's largest charter fishing fleets is found in the Upper Keys.

In most of the cities and towns of Florida it isn't easy to sort through all of the amenities and qualities of life that determine which retirees will be happiest in which town. In the Keys it is very simple: To be happy here you must love the sea! Why else would you choose to live where the land is so limited (the island of Key West is only 3 miles long and 1½ miles wide) and the sea so omnipresent that it is never out of your sight? Why else would you live on an island where almost all recreation and entertainment have something to do with water? The sea is truly the *raison d'être* for life in the Florida Keys.

Housing. When you look at housing prices in the Keys, particularly in Key West, you may think piracy is still rampant in these far reaches of Florida. In their Mardi Gras meets *Gilligan's Island* setting, Key West homes are small, outrageously expensive, and often display a quirky, alternative-lifestyle personality. With space at such a premium, garages and covered parking are a real luxury here. After looking at the following examples, you will probably agree with me that Key West must have the fewest per capita bathrooms in the continental United States. It seems the basic formula must be one bathroom per $100,000 in price. When you read a property description that includes the words, *quaint,* *charming,* or *cozy,* that simply means "one bathroom." Keep this in mind when the grandchildren come to spend a few weeks! For around $150,000 you may find a small condominium in a mid-rise building. One listing I saw was for a 1,050-square-foot three-bedroom two-bath condo priced at $151,000. Though tiny, this represents a real bargain in Key West. More typically, you might find a quaint (now you know what that means!) "shotgun style" house nestled in a small compound of free-standing cottage units surrounding a small community pool for $159,000. You would seem more like a Key West native, however, if you purchased a very eclectic recent $139,000 offering. It was a small mobile home situated on a deepwater canal with an enclosed spiral staircase leading to a strange addition—a wooden rooftop veranda. If you've brought your tool kit, you may be interested in a two-bedroom one-bath "fixer-upper" at around $200,000. To find a comfortable small home that is in move-in condition, you'll have to look in the mid-$200,000 range or higher. An attractive 952-square-foot cottage in a tree-lined neighborhood of old town Key West recently listed for $249,000. And a tiny but very stylish, bedroomless one-bath home in Old Town offered a spiral stair to a sleeping loft and a backyard cistern converted to a "dip pool" for $345,000. If you want a modest, updated home to house the Brady Bunch in Key West, you will have to look in the $500,000-plus range. Eclectic and expensive real estate is one more reason Key West appeals to a small, individualistic, and well-off group of retirees. Property taxes in Key West are about $17.30 per $1,000 nonexempt valuation.

Although certainly popular with both year-round residents and tourists alike, Marathon does not suffer the extreme demand that has driven Key West's property so high. Still, property here tends to be small, and prices do climb rapidly for those who demand water views or ocean access. Of course, on these small islands you're never more than a few blocks from the water. So " inland" two-bedroom condos well under $100,000 are plentiful, and bathrooms are somewhat more abundant in Marathon than in its bohemian cousin to the southwest. A two-bedroom one-bath condo in a pleasant complex of small three-story buildings with more than 700 square feet of living space recently listed for $74,900. And an attractive two-bedroom two-bath 1,100-square-foot condo with tile floors and optional dock access was priced at $99,500. You may find that in Marathon even a waterside home is within reach. A second-floor two-bedroom two-bath waterfront condo with two porches, a view of the harbor, and a heated community pool was priced at $139,500. For more space and privacy, a completely furnished two-bedroom town home with two and a half baths, wraparound balconies, community pool and tennis courts, and boat dockage was situated on the water and priced at $195,000. Property taxes in Marathon are about $14.55 per $1,000 nonexempt valuation.

Not only is Key Largo the beginning steppingstone to all the Florida Keys, it is also the first rung on the real estate ladder that climbs to the high prices of Key West. With land a tad more available in this largest of the Florida Keys, you might afford a real home here at a price that won't keep you awake nights. In Key Largo, you get genuine Florida Keys scenery, climate, ambience, and a Keys address, and yet you can still afford a second or third bathroom and some elbow room. I recently saw a listing for a three-bedroom three-bath single-family home on a canal with bay views, tiled floors, a separate laundry room, and covered parking for $159,000. A small but appealing two-bedroom one-bath home here was priced at $87,000. For much more space at a still-modest price, I saw a two-bedroom home with a separate one-bedroom ground-floor apartment on a double lot, which included a detached garage—a rarity in the Keys—for $139,000. For those with deeper pockets, there are some wonderful homes priced at a level unthinkable anywhere else in this part of Florida. A contemporary two-bedroom stilt home with two and a half baths, a huge expanse of decks, a large-screen entertainment area, wood floors, an open loft overlooking the living area, and a deep-water location with a 60-foot dock was priced at $239,000. Property taxes in Key Largo are about $15 per $1,000 nonexempt valuation.

Culture and Entertainment. Cultural activities and entertainment are more limited in the Keys than in most other Florida cities and towns. Quite simply, communities here are isolated and their size precludes activities that need the support of a larger public. In Key West there are a few art galleries, four history museums including the Hemingway House, and two playhouses. Florida Keys Community College brings live theater, concerts, and other cultural activities to the community. Marathon has two museums of history and a community theater. Key Largo has an art gallery and the Maritime Museum. All three towns have movie theaters.

Sports and Recreation. You may assume that those who choose to live in the Florida Keys have willingly traded extensive cultural and entertainment opportunities for a singular style of living and wonderful sports and recreation activities. With land so precious, golf and tennis are somewhat limited, but if it can be done in, under, or on water, it will be plentiful in the Keys. In all of the Keys you may fish from piers, from small boats in nearby waters, or from charter boats far out in the Atlantic or the Gulf. Sailing among the Keys is a popular sport. Diving and snorkeling are outstanding in the Keys, with several schools providing lessons and any number of dive shops providing equipment. One of the best-known spots for diving is the unique John Pennekamp Coral Reef State Park, a 120-square-mile underwater park protecting a huge living coral reef. Key West, Marathon, and Key Largo each have a public golf course and several tennis courts.

Law Enforcement and Safety. In 1996 there were 102 criminal offenses reported per 1,000 year-round residents in Key West. Since they are not incorporated municipalities, no figures are given for Marathon or Key Largo. In 1996 the rate for all of unincorporated Monroe County was sixty-eight.

Senior Centers. Monroe County Social Services provides a variety of activities and programs for seniors including counseling, meals, and transportation.

Addresses and Connections

Chambers of Commerce: Greater Marathon Chamber of Commerce, MM53 bayside, 12222 U.S. Highway 1, Marathon, FL 33050; (800) 262-7284

Key Largo Chamber of Commerce, MM106 bayside, 106000 Overseas Highway, Key Largo, FL 33037; (800) 822-1088, Fax, (305) 451-4726

Key West Chamber of Commerce, 402 Wall Street, Key West, FL 33040; (305) 294-2587; Fax, (305) 294-7806

Newspaper: The Key West Citizen (daily), 3420 Northside Drive, Key West, FL 33040; (305) 294-6641, Fax, (305) 294-0768

Internet: http://www.flkeysmag.com

DADE COUNTY: Coral Gables

Dade County (pop. 2,043,316) is by far the most populous of Florida's counties. It is the second in geographic size, and its major city is one of the best-known in the nation. The only other Florida county with a population of more than one million is Broward County, our next stop north, and Palm Beach County is larger than Dade by only 29 square miles. For many years, Miami and Miami Beach were Florida's number one tourist destination. They drew large numbers of winter residents and vied with St. Petersburg as Florida's most popular retirement spot long before the rest of the state began to attract retirees.

No county in Florida, however, is more diverse or has overcome greater obstacles in its history. Established in the mid-1800s, Miami was an isolated fishing village accessible only by boat until Flagler's railroad reached the city in 1896. Mail was carried to Miami by "barefoot mailmen" who walked the beach from Juno and Palm Beach. It is hard to believe that bustling Miami and glittering Miami Beach were carved out of a mosquito- and snake-infested jungle less than a hundred years ago. Theodore Pratt's novel *The Barefoot Mailman* is an interesting and accurate description of life in south Florida at that time. It is based on an actual incident that happened in 1887. Knowing that my grandparents were among them, I have always found it fascinating to see photographs of pioneers in south Florida in the late 1800s. Ladies in long, ornate Victorian dresses, gloves, and huge hats, and gentlemen in high starched collars and bowlers pose incongruously beside an unpainted primitive house in a palmetto thicket or stand stiffly and stoically beside a large alligator. These early settlers were farmers seeking rich soil and good weather, developers seeking cheap virgin land, and adventurous speculators ready to gamble on the risky future of a wilderness area with only the sea, sun, and warm winters to recommend it. With the coming of the railroad to Miami, all began to see their dreams come true and the Miami we know began to develop.

The development of south Florida was not a smooth one. The early 1920s were a decade of hype and hope when every stick put in the ground grew and every shovel of earth broken turned magically into a community. During these years, Dade County was touted by the mayors of Miami, Miami Beach, Hialeah, and Coral Gables in a joint statement as "the most Richly Blessed Community of the most Bountifully Endowed State of the most Highly Enterprising People of the Universe."

It may seem odd to us today, but in the heady days of south Florida's adolescence, they actually believed it! It was in this atmosphere that Coral Gables was designed as a Mediterranean fantasy and its neighbor, Opa-Locka, as a scene from *The Arabian Nights*.

Of course, the Florida land boom did not last, and by the end of the 1920s elation had turned into depression as all of the United States sank to its lowest economic depths. Some new communities survived, mostly those well planned and built on solid ground, not merely staked out on uncleared land. For every Coral Gables, however, dozens of communities that had been heralded and sold were left as nothing more than fanciful and ornate stucco gates crumbling in a Florida hammock. It would not be until the postwar boom of the 1950s that south Florida would again feel such optimism.

Since the early 1960s, Dade County and Miami have assimilated a massive influx of immigrants, primarily Cubans and Haitians escaping oppression in their countries, and in 1992 survived one of the worst natural disasters in our nation's history, Hurricane Andrew. Miami, along with its suburban communities, is unquestionably the most international of all cities in Florida and perhaps in the United States. In some parts of the city it is not unusual to see signs in store windows indicating that English is spoken within. Like other metropolitan areas its size, Dade County has pockets of extreme poverty and islands of unimaginable wealth. Because of the image of Miami as a crowded urban center, it isn't well known that the Everglades still comprise vast areas—perhaps as much as two-thirds—of Dade County, and that quite a bit of the rest is farm and grove land.

A tourist destination since its inception, Miami is known throughout the country, and few are neutral in their opinions of it. Miami is viewed either as a city sinking under the weight of its urban problems or an exciting city of the future, the only truly international city in the United States. Since most retirees are not looking for major challenges in their retirement years and prefer safety and peace of mind to excitement, I have chosen to profile only one community in Dade County, Coral Gables. There are several nearby communities that are popular with retirees; in recent years Dade County ranked tenth among all U.S. counties in the number of retirees moving here from out of state.

Cost of Living. Dade County is the second most expensive county in the state with a cost of living 107.13 percent of the state average. The sales tax is 6 or 6.5 percent, depending on municipality. The cost of housing is 11.71 percent above the state average. The average purchase price of a house in Dade County is about $117,500. Dade County ranks fourth in the state with an average monthly apartment rent of $764.

Climate. Thanks to the cooling effects of the Atlantic Ocean in the summer and the warming power of the Gulf Stream in winter, Dade County has a pleasant climate year-round.

Miami–Dade County Weather

| | In degrees Fahrenheit | | | | |
	Jan.	Apr.	July	Oct.	Annual Rainfall
DAILY HIGHS	75.2	82.4	89.0	84.5	55.91"
DAILY LOWS	59.2	67.8	76.2	72.1	

Medical Care. Twenty-six hospitals with 10,132 beds serve the residents of Dade County.

Transportation. All of Dade County, including Coral Gables, is served by the Metro-Dade Transit Agency bus system. Dade County has a well-developed Metrorail system with two stations in Coral Gables. The Tri-Rail commuter train runs from Miami International Airport to West Palm Beach and connects with the Metrorail system. Miami International Airport, among the busiest in the nation, is 4 miles from Coral Gables.

Opportunities for Continuing Education. Dade County schools, Miami-Dade Community College (one of the largest in the United States, with several campuses and many centers throughout Dade County), Florida International University, the University of Miami, and several other colleges and universities provide a great many programs of continuing education for Dade County's senior population.

Coral Gables

Coral Gables (pop. 41,205) was established in 1921 as one of the first planned communities in the United States, a community to be built in the architectural styles of Spain and Italy with parks, neighborhoods, winding streets, waterways, areas for business, and even a university. Coral Gables survived all the boom and bust years and is now one of the most beautiful cities in this or any state. The entire community plan has been realized right down to the University of Miami, which brings an important element of culture to the city. The plan to bring business to Coral Gables is one of the most successful parts of the plan. The city is home to 140 multinational corporations and has earned the title "Corporate Capital of the Americas." The city has continued the original concept of Mediterranean architecture, which might look contrived elsewhere but seems perfectly at home in the tropical environment of Coral Gables. With its many historic buildings, the scenery in Coral Gables is magnificent. For example, there is the historic Biltmore Hotel with a tower that's a replica of the Giralda in Seville, Spain, the City Hall's Spanish Renaissance architecture, city gates modeled on those in Madrid, Moorish fountains, and the Venetian Pool, a huge spring-fed swimming pool transformed from a coral rock quarry into a grotto with waterfalls, surrounded by Venetian-style loggias and buildings. This unique landmark is the only swimming pool on the National Registry of Historic Places.

Housing. Because it is something of a contained, idyllic enclave in the middle of urban Miami, housing in Coral Gables is in great demand. Homes here have appreciated seven-fold in the past twenty-five years, and currently the median cost of a house is $275,000. One look around and you will feel these are Florida homes at California prices. To live in the singular beauty of Coral Gables you will have to accept the dearth of homes under $300,000. One of the least expensive properties recently listed was a tiny 565-square-foot one-bedroom poolview condominium priced at $72,900. In a high-rise building a more livable alternative was a small two-bedroom two-bath condo listed at $119,900. This seemed a very good value in Coral Gables. More typically priced were the dozens upon dozens of older, tiny two-bedroom, one-bath one-story homes on small lots for around $150,000. For $160,000 you could get a 1923 vintage two-bedroom two-bath stucco home with a fireplace and a small outdoor spa. A simple three-bedroom two-bath home with a one-car garage and 1,610 square feet of living space was listed for $173,900. I found a rare, attractive home priced under $300,000 on a lovely lot. It was built in 1925 and had four bedrooms, three baths, and a separate dining area, all squeezed into 1,900 square feet. Included in its $249,000 price tag was a one-car detached garage. Homes that might cost less than $200,000 in most other parts of Florida run in the mid-$300,000s in Coral Gables. You will either have to live in an extremely modest home or expect to spend between $300,000 and $500,000 for a nice family home with a Coral Gables address. Property taxes in Coral Gables are about $25 per $1,000 nonexempt valuation.

Culture and Entertainment. Coral Gables has long promoted itself as the cultural center of the Miami area and in the process has attracted residents who support the city's many activities. The Lowe Art Museum is a nationally recognized museum with more than 36,000 square feet of gallery and exhibit space. Up to 40 percent of the museum's collection of 8,000 art objects are on display at any given time. The collection includes Old Masters, pre-Columbian art, Native American art, American and European art from the seventeenth to the twentieth century, as well as art from Asia and Africa. Thirty-two commercial art galleries in Coral Gables present the visual arts to the community. Many of these galleries participate in Gallery Night, the first Friday of each month when galleries are open and the public is encouraged to come and look. Minibuses run throughout the community, taking viewers from one gallery to the next. Two cinema theaters, the Astor and the Bill Cosford, show foreign, avant-garde, and art films.

The performing arts are equally strong in Coral Gables. The Miami Symphony Orchestra performs in the University of Miami's Gusman Hall as well as in other venues in Miami and Miami Beach. The Miracle Theatre, an old 1940s movie theater in downtown Coral Gables, has undergone a $6 million restoration and is now where the Actors' Playhouse presents a full season of comedy, drama, and musicals. The New Theatre, an intimate space with fewer than one hundred seats, is a company that specializes in innovative and off-Broadway plays and musicals. The Ring Theater at the University of Miami has been a center of the performing arts in south Florida since 1929. The Florida Shakespeare Theatre presents classical and contemporary plays in a new 154-seat theater at the Biltmore Hotel. The Ballet Academy of Miami, the Civic Chorale of Greater Miami, the Coral Gables Chamber Symphony, the Coral Gables Opera, and the Greater Miami Community Concert Band all make their home in Coral Gables.

It should be pointed out that the above list, as ample as it is, includes only those activities and venues located in Coral Gables. Miami and Miami Beach have many cultural and entertainment programs and activities only a few minutes from Coral Gables. The Miami Opera is nationally known and respected, and some of the most exciting art galleries in Florida are in Miami, Miami Beach, and Coconut Grove.

Sports and Recreation. Coral Gables has three golf courses, two of which are run by the city, thirty-three public tennis courts, bike paths, and a total of thirty-one parks. The Venetian Pool, described earlier, is the main public swimming pool in the community. Matheson Hammock is a wonderful 600-acre park on the shore of Biscayne Bay where the public may walk through a preserved Florida hammock of hardwoods and a mangrove wilderness, as well as picnic, swim, fish, and launch boats from the public boat ramp. The War Memorial Youth Center is an excellent but misnamed athletic center—it isn't only for the young. Both indoor and outdoor recreation are the focus of the Center, and programs for all ages, including seniors, are ongoing. Coral Gables is only minutes from the Atlantic beaches and all of the water sports and activities found there. The Florida Marlins professional baseball team, the Miami Heat professional basketball team, the Miami Dolphins professional football team, as well as the University of Miami athletic teams keep sports spectators busy.

Law Enforcement and Safety. In 1996 there were 117 criminal offenses reported per 1,000 year-round residents in Coral Gables.

Senior Centers. There is no senior center in Coral Cables; however, the War Memorial Youth Center described above offers many social and recreational services to seniors. Several senior centers in Miami offer a broader range of services.

Nearby Communities. **Hialeah** (pop. 206,500) is a sprawling community a few miles north of Coral Gables. **Opa-Locka** (pop. 15,790) neighbors Hialeah on the north. **Key Biscayne** (pop. 8,886) is an expensive island community east of Coral Gables.

Addresses and Connections

Chambers of Commerce: Coral Gables Chamber of Commerce, 50 Aragon Avenue, Coral Gables, FL 33134; (305) 446–1657

Hialeah/Miami Springs Chamber of Commerce, 59 West Fifth Street, Hialeah, FL 33030; (305) 887–1515

Miami Chamber of Commerce, 1601 Biscayne Boulevard, Omni Complex, Miami, FL 33132; (305) 350–7700

Miami Beach Chamber of Commerce, 1920 Meridian Avenue, Miami Beach, FL 33139; (305) 672–1270

Newspapers: The Miami Herald (daily), One Herald Plaza, Miami, FL 33132

Miami Metro Magazine, P.O. Box 019068, Miami, FL 33101; (305) 445–4500; Fax, (305) 445–4600; http://www.miamimetro.com; E-mail: miamimetro@bellsouth.com

Internet: http://www.coralgables.net

Other Resources: City of Coral Gables, Development Department, P.O. Box 141549, Coral Gables, FL 33114; (305) 460–5311; Fax, (305) 445–9623

BROWARD COUNTY: Fort Lauderdale, Hollywood, Plantation, Sunrise, and Pompano Beach

Probably no county in Florida is more popular with tourists, winter residents, and retirees than Broward County (population 1,392,252). Fort Lauderdale, by far the largest and best-known city in the county, is an energetic and bustling beach-oriented community more interested in its tourists and cruise ships than in its retirees. However, Fort Lauderdale is surrounded by a cluster of very livable smaller cities and towns that have been extremely successful in their efforts to attract retirees. Residents of these communities have all of the advantages of Fort Lauderdale's cultural and recreational amenities but at a far lower cost and in appealing small-town settings. Fort Lauderdale's many high-rise beach condominiums are filled with winter residents who often make them their year-round homes when they retire. Because of these condominiums and its many small towns, Broward County ranks third among all U.S. counties in attracting retirees from out of state.

Like Dade County, Broward is a large county, but well over half of its area is in the Everglades and uninhabited. Even with so much vacant land, Broward County is second only to Pinellas County (St. Petersburg) in population density. Most of the county's population is either on the barrier islands or on a strip of land within 10 miles of the coast. The population is moving west, however, and every time I approach Fort Lauderdale from the west via Alligator Alley, it seems that housing developments have moved another couple of miles into what was Everglades. Throughout Broward County, the Intracoastal Waterway separates the beaches from the mainland. The barrier island that begins with Miami Beach is broken by the Port Everglades Inlet, which gives ocean access to one of Florida's major ports. The island resumes on the other side of the inlet and continues—except for inlets, which all have bridges—to north of Palm Beach. Broward County's barrier islands have some of the most beautiful and accessible beaches in the state.

Cost of Living. A saying you hear often in these parts is "Paradise doesn't come cheap!" Broward County is third in expensiveness, behind Dade and Monroe, with a cost of living 105.42 percent of the state average. The sales tax is 6 percent. The cost of housing is 8.5 percent above the state average. The average purchase price of a house is $107,500. Broward County ranks second in the state with an average monthly apartment rent of $809.

Climate. The climate is pleasant throughout Broward County. Ocean breezes moderate temperatures and bring a delightful freshness to the air.

Miami–Broward County Weather

	In degrees Fahrenheit				
	Jan.	Apr.	July	Oct.	Annual Rainfall
DAILY HIGHS	75.2	82.4	89.0	84.5	55.91"
DAILY LOWS	59.2	67.8	76.2	72.1	

Medical Care. Eighteen hospitals with 5,889 beds serve the residents of Broward County.

Transportation. Broward County Mass Transit provides bus service throughout the county. When I asked a group of retirees in Sunrise what they liked best about living there, the answer was the ability to get around via the excellent bus system. The Tri-Rail system that runs from Miami International Airport to West Palm Beach has several stops in Broward County. Fort Lauderdale International Airport is an excellent, relatively new airport providing domestic and international jet service.

Opportunities for Continuing Education. Broward County schools, Broward Community College with four campuses and several centers, and Florida Atlantic University all have programs, courses, and services to meet the continuing-education needs of the senior population. Nondegree courses in the visual arts are offered at the Art Institute of Fort Lauderdale.

Fort Lauderdale, Hollywood, Plantation, Sunrise, and Pompano Beach

Fort Lauderdale (population 150,150) is an interesting city. Perhaps because so much effort has been devoted to attracting tourists, the city has unsurpassed amenities: the most beautifully landscaped beach anywhere, a people-friendly Riverwalk, a great performing arts center, an outstanding art museum, one of the best public libraries in the state, lovely neighborhoods on canals, and an elegant street of interesting shops and restaurants. But there seems to be no recognizable center to the city. It is more like a theme park for tourists than a true community. The towns described below, however, are only minutes from any of Fort Lauderdale's attractions, and many retirees have found they can live nearby and take advantage of all Fort Lauderdale has to offer.

Hollywood (population 125,689) is in south Broward County and almost contiguous with Fort Lauderdale. Hollywood feels like a small town, but it really is a sizable community with a lovely downtown area, attractively landscaped streets and traffic circles, and a pleasant beach. There are many pretty residential neighborhoods, several near the town center with older Spanish-style homes from the 1920s and '30s, and many developments of new homes in a wide range of prices. Of the communities surrounding Fort Lauderdale, Hollywood is the most self-contained, with its own cultural and recreational venues and activities. Many of Hollywood's winter residents and visitors are Canadian.

Plantation (population 76,223) is a carefully planned and zoned city covering 22 square miles on the western side of Fort Lauderdale. Plantation has many neighborhoods with houses, villas, and apartments in all price ranges.

Sunrise (population 74,766) is a community on the western edge of Fort Lauderdale and one of the fastest-growing towns in Broward County. Sawgrass Mills, the world's largest outlet mall, is here. Spread out over several acres and 1 mile in length, the mall has become a popular all-weather walking site for seniors.

Pompano Beach (population 74,271) is a community just north of Fort Lauderdale that has all the advantages of Fort Lauderdale at a far lower price. Primarily a residential community, the city of Pompano Beach includes both the beach and the mainland communities.

Housing. Fort Lauderdale is a real challenge for the serious house hunter. Since it lacks a true downtown community, you may want to explore everything from condominiums on the beach or Intracoastal Waterway to condo, town house, and golf course communities reaching several miles inland. Other than in a narrow stretch of poor, rundown housing that divides the city along a north-south axis, you will find a wide range of prices in a wide range of interesting neighborhoods and enclaves in Fort Lauderdale. As in all of Florida, location dictates much of the pricing structure. On my last visit I saw a listing for a home on a large lot in Victoria Park, a very desirable older neighborhood, that offered three bedrooms, one bath, and a small cottage that could be renovated to become a guest apartment, an artist studio, or a workshop. It was a very modest home, but because of its Victoria Park location it was priced at $169,000. In contrast, in a less-prestigious neighborhood, a three-bedroom two-bath home with an updated Eurokitchen, a Florida room, fireplace, garage, and in-ground pool listed for just $129,000. Near the beaches, these prices would only get you a one- or two-bedroom condo in a typical modern high-rise building. In all beach condominiums, better views, more luxurious amenities, and higher floors command a higher price. But if you're looking for a lower-priced home, there are possibilities here too. A canal-front two-bedroom two-bath condominium with ocean access in a small complex was priced at $72,000. Small condos away from the water are available for even less.

Prices in Hollywood are generally lower than in the beach areas of Fort Lauderdale, and this lovely community offers a number of choices in nice neighborhoods. Many three-bedroom homes a short drive from the beach are available from around $100,000. A two-bedroom two-bath condo with a heated community pool recently listed for $57,600. A lovely custom ranch home in the Hollywood Hills neighborhood listed a lush, professionally landscaped yard surrounding an in-ground pool, three bedrooms and two and a half new bathrooms for $146,000. If you need a lot more home, an inland listing for an executive home included four bedrooms, three baths, a screened in-ground pool, and a private studio on a one-half acre lot for $229,900. A midsize two-bedroom villa with two patios and a garage in a complex with a community pool and tennis courts went on the market for $103,000.

Plantation is one of the inland communities of Greater Fort Lauderdale that offers value for home buyers and a bit of distance from the lively hubbub of the beaches. Here, new four-bedroom homes with two- or three-car garages abound in the $140,000 to $180,000 price range. And affordable smaller town houses and condominiums are being built at prices that seem very reasonable compared to the real estate near the Atlantic. A mint-condition newer three-bedroom home with more than 2,200 square feet of living space was put on the market at $129,000. At the low end of the scale, a very nice one-bedroom condo with a separate dining room and a community pool and gardens listed for only $23,000.

A few minutes farther inland you will find even lower-priced housing. In the little town of Sunrise a two-bedroom two-bath condo in an "over fifty-five" community was put on the market for $26,500. And three- and four-bedroom homes are plentiful in the $120,000 range. A four-bedroom two-bath home with a family room, entry hall, tile floors throughout, split bedroom plan, and in-ground pool was recently sold for $129,900.

Pompano Beach, on the coast and just north of Fort Lauderdale, offers a more reasonable housing environment and a slightly quieter profile than many of its neighboring communities. A second-floor corner unit condo with two bedrooms, two baths, and ocean access listed for $74,900. For the same price, a charming, older three-bedroom home near the beach in "Old Pompano" was also listed. I even spotted a one-bedroom unit in a tidy, smaller building listed for $22,900. A modern, luxurious two-bedroom condominium, in a "fifty-five plus" building very close to the beach and fronting on the Intracoastal Waterway was put on the market for $99,900. This unit had all new appliances, new Berber carpet, silk wallpaper, a large community pool, and access to a marina. And real luxury living near the water is far more affordable in Pompano than in neighboring communities. Property taxes in Broward County's cities range from $26.64 to $27.71 per $1,000 nonexempt valuation, depending on the municipality and the neighborhood.

Culture and Entertainment. Cultural activities in Broward County are coordinated by the Broward Cultural Affairs Council. The Council publishes the *Cultural Quarterly*, a calendar and a bimonthly newsletter. The impressive Fort Lauderdale Museum of Art has a fine permanent collection of more than 5,250 works and is host to outstanding touring shows. The Art and Culture Center of Hollywood, housed in one of the oldest homes in the city, presents changing exhibits, lectures, and a weekly series of jazz concerts. The Broward Art Guild offers classes and presents monthly juried exhibitions. The magnificent new Broward

Center for the Performing Arts in Fort Lauderdale presents a full season of concerts, touring Broadway shows, local productions, ballet, and opera in its two theaters. Brian C. Smith's Off Broadway is a 300-seat theater offering local productions of plays. Florida Grand Opera presents an annual season of opera from November through May. The Florida Philharmonic Orchestra performs a regular season from September through May and a summer season in July. The Gold Coast Opera, the county's oldest opera company, presents three productions each season. The Parker Playhouse in Fort Lauderdale presents touring Broadway shows and plays. The Pompano Amphitheater is an open-air theater where musical performances are scheduled throughout the year.

Sports and Recreation. Most people probably think of the beach when they think of Fort Lauderdale. That is good and bad for the city. It is good that the beach draws tourists, but the image that comes to many people's minds is that of college kids going wild on the beach during spring break. A few years ago the city leaders decided it was time to reclaim the image of a family vacation spot and the college young people were politely asked not to return. Since that time the city has spent millions "redoing" the beach, the beachfront road, and those buildings and businesses that front on it. The time, effort, and money spent on the project have paid off. Fort Lauderdale's beach is now among the most beautiful and inviting in the world. A low serpentine wall separates the beach from the new broad walkway, and hundreds of coconut palms have been planted. There are showers and passenger unloading spots. Parking, just a few blocks away from the beach, has been expanded. While most of this was done to attract tourists, residents probably enjoy it most.

Fishing and boating are major sports in this area. There are 300 miles of inland waterways and 23 miles of Atlantic coast in Broward County, and there are more than 42,000 privately owned boats. In addition, there are many charter boats for hire to take anglers far out into the ocean. Many piers offer good fishing for the landlubber, including one 875 feet long in Pompano Beach. Diving is also a popular pastime here with more than eighty dive sites, including eighteen major shipwrecks. Pompano Beach has seven reefs including the largest artificial reef on the eastern seaboard. There are more than 550 tennis courts and more than fifty-five public, private, and resort golf courses in Broward County.

Sports spectators have a full agenda with Miami's professional football, basketball, and baseball teams playing in nearby Dade County. The

Baltimore Orioles hold spring practice in Fort Lauderdale. There is horse racing, dog racing, and jai alai with pari-mutuel betting in Broward County.

Law Enforcement and Safety. In 1996 there were 170 criminal offenses reported per 1,000 year-round residents in Fort Lauderdale. The great number of tourists and winter residents makes this statistic somewhat misleading. The rates for other communities in Broward County per 1,000 year-round residents were: Hollywood, 100; Plantation, 80; Sunrise, 85; Pompano Beach, 128. The rate for unincorporated Broward County was 69 per 1,000.

Senior Centers. There are senior centers throughout Broward County, but the one in Sunrise deserves special mention. The new $2 million, 14,000-square-foot center is operated by the city of Sunrise through its Leisure Services Department. It is a spectacular building that includes an elegant room with a dance floor, classrooms, an arts and crafts room, a game room with four billiard tables, a reading room, and a screened atrium overlooking a lake where you can play cards, read, or just relax. Sports activities and trips are organized frequently.

Nearby Communities. There are a number of small cities and towns surrounding Fort Lauderdale. The following are just a few that are particularly popular with retirees. **Coral Springs** (pop. 98,553) is a 20-square-mile planned community northwest of Fort Lauderdale. **Dania** (pop. 17,320), located on U.S. 1 just south of Fort Lauderdale, is one of the oldest communities in Broward County. **Davie** (pop. 59,393) is Broward County's "Cowboy Town." Located west of Fort Lauderdale, it is a major center for livestock and horse breeding and delights in its western theme. With 42 square miles, Davie is the largest city in the county. **Hallandale** (pop. 31,458) is primarily a retirement community with bungalows and duplexes on the mainland and many high-rise condominiums on the beach side. **Deerfield Beach** (pop. 48,974) is a delightful community on the northern edge of Broward County with one of the prettiest, most user-friendly beaches in the area.

Addresses and Connections

Chambers of Commerce: Greater Deerfield Beach Chamber of Commerce, 1601 East Hillsboro Boulevard, Deerfield Beach, FL 33441-4389; (954) 427–1050; Fax, (954) 427–1056; http://www. deerfieldbeach.com; E-mail: dbchamber@worldnet.att.net

Greater Fort Lauderdale Chamber of Commerce, 512 Northeast Third Avenue, Fort Lauderdale, FL 33301; (954) 462–6000; Fax, (954) 527–8766

Greater Plantation Chamber of Commerce, 7401 Northwest Fourth Street, Plantation, FL 33317; (954) 587–1410; Fax, (954) 587–1886

Greater Pompano Beach Chamber of Commerce, 2200 East Atlantic Boulevard, Pompano Beach, FL 33062; (954) 941–2940; Fax, (954) 785–8358; http://www.pompanobeachchamber.com; E-mail: pompano@pompanobeachchamber.com

Sunrise Chamber of Commerce, 4237 Northwest Eighty-eighth Avenue, Sunrise, FL 33351; (954) 741–3300; Fax, (954) 741–8170; E-mail: suncc@sunrisechamber.org

Newspapers: Sun-Sentinel (daily), 200 East Las Olas Boulevard, Fort Lauderdale, FL 33301; (954) 761–4000

Senior Life and Boomer Times (monthly), 1515 North Federal Highway, #300, Boca Raton, FL 33432; (800) 230–1904; Fax, (561) 369–1476; http://www.gate.net/~srlife/; E-mail: srlife@gate.net

PALM BEACH COUNTY: Boca Raton, West Palm Beach, Juno Beach, Jupiter, and Tequesta

No name in Florida is more glamorous than Palm Beach. In this book, however, we will discuss Palm Beach County (pop. 981,793), and there is a very big difference. While Palm Beach County may have taken its name from its famous city, there is much more to it than an enclave of the very rich. The city of Palm Beach is not profiled in this book for two reasons. One, it is not a place where very many retirees can afford to live, and two, those retirees who will choose Palm Beach more than likely have been wintering there all along and know the city very well. Palm Beach County, however, is very attractive to retirees. Palm Beach County recently ranked second among all U.S. counties in attracting retirees from out of state. In *Retirement Places Rated* the Boca Raton–Delray Beach area ranked twenty-third out of the 183 most popular retirement locations in the United States.

Palm Beach County is north of Broward County, stretching from the Atlantic coast to Lake Okeechobee. It is the largest county in Florida and the ninth in terms of population density. By far the greatest percentage of its population is centered along the coastal area. The Intracoastal Waterway separates the barrier island from the mainland throughout Palm Beach County, becoming broad Lake Worth between Palm Beach and West Palm Beach. There are some areas of swampland, and the huge Loxahatchee National Wildlife Refuge covers the central part of the county, but most of Palm Beach County's interior is rich farmland. Sugar cane, winter vegetables, and other crops that grow in the rich black muck and tropical climate of the "Glades" comprise a half-billion-dollar business, second only to the $1.5 billion tourist industry.

Cost of Living. Palm Beach County ranks fourth in the state with a cost of living 104 percent of the state average. The sales tax is 6 percent. The cost of housing is 5.84 percent above the state average. The average purchase price for a house is around $104,000. Palm Beach County ranks third in the state with an average monthly apartment rent of $773.

Climate. Palm Beach County is farther north than other counties along the "Gold Coast," but the Gulf Stream is closer to land here than in any other part of the state. Its moderating influence keeps the weather mild.

Palm Beach County Weather

| | Jan. | In degrees Fahrenheit | | | Annual Rainfall |
		Apr.	July	Oct.	
DAILY HIGHS	74.5	82.0	89.9	74.5	60.75"
DAILY LOWS	55.7	64.7	74.5	70.7	

Medical Care. Fifteen hospitals with 3,478 beds serve the residents of Palm Beach County.

Transportation. PalmTran provides bus service throughout Palm Beach County. Depending on where you live, either Palm Beach International Airport or Fort Lauderdale International Airport will be convenient. The TriRail system runs from West Palm Beach to Miami with several stops in Palm Beach County.

Opportunities for Continuing Education. Palm Beach County schools, Palm Beach Community College with three campuses and several centers, and Florida Atlantic University provide for the continuing-education needs of the county.

Boca Raton

Like Fort Lauderdale, Boca Raton (pop. 67,754) also has an image problem. In this case it is an image of a community for only the wealthy. In fact, Boca Raton is a pleasant community with housing and amenities for a wide range of pocketbooks. Granted, on the Intracoastal Waterway or near the ocean there are million-dollar mansions and very expensive condominiums, but away from the coast there are many neighborhoods of affordable housing. Wherever you live in "Boca" you enjoy the beauty of this small city.

With careful zoning and building requirements, Boca Raton has created a unified community image. Public buildings, shopping malls, churches, and businesses all follow the pattern of pink Mediterranean-style architecture with tile roofs, wrought-iron work, arches, and columns. Everyone seems to participate in an effort to keep the community covered in flowers. It is one of the prettiest towns in Florida!

Housing. Of course, Boca Raton offers lots of high-end alternatives for those who can afford them. A recent real estate publication offered homes for sale in Boca Raton in ascending price order. The first thirty pages listed homes under $200,000, but the next thirty pages ranged from $200,000 up. The last several pages offered dozens of recent listings from $1 million to more than $4 million dollars! But there is a lot here for the cost-conscious, and if you search carefully, there are many choices in price, lifestyle, and location. Inland, golf communities offer countless one- and two-bedroom condominiums in the $50,000 range. A "light and bright" top-floor apartment near the beach was priced at $57,000. And on the beach, a 985-square-foot unit with sunset views from its large balcony was for sale for $74,900. Inland, a town house with an office/loft, exposed beam ceilings, two bedrooms, two and a half baths, a one-car garage, and an ample community pool and Jacuzzi was listed at $98,500. On a higher scale, the $236,000 price tag for a newer home in a good location may seem reasonable when you consider that it provides four bedrooms, four baths, a large pool/patio area, a tile roof, and a privacy fence surrounding a large landscaped lot. In the middle range, a three-bedroom town house in a family neighborhood, with three and a half baths, tile floors, and a huge screened lanai listed for $125,000. Property taxes in Boca Raton are about $21.80 per $1,000 nonexempt valuation.

Culture and Entertainment. While Boca Raton has its own ample cultural identity, it should be pointed out that residents here are only 20 miles from all the cultural activities of Fort Lauderdale and 26 miles from those in Palm Beach and West Palm Beach. The Boca Raton Museum of Art has a fine permanent collection, brings touring art shows to the community, offers classes and workshops, and schedules lectures. The Morikami Museum and Japanese Gardens bring exhibitions of Japanese culture to Boca Raton. The museum has a 224-seat theater, classrooms, a library, a teahouse and cafe, and lovely Japanese gardens. The Boca Pops presents ten concerts each year in the 2,400-seat auditorium at Florida Atlantic University. The Caldwell Theatre Company stages plays and musicals in its 305-seat theater. The Boca Ballet Company provides training and experience for dancers through a season of full-length classical ballets.

Sports and Recreation. There are more than twenty golf courses in Boca Raton and many more in Palm Beach County. There are public tennis courts in many of Boca Raton's parks. By purchasing oceanfront property over the years and developing parks with picnic facilities and parking, the city has ensured public access to its fine beaches.

Law Enforcement and Safety. In 1996 there were forty-three criminal offenses reported per 1,000 year-round residents in Boca Raton.

Senior Centers. The Mae Volen Senior Center in Boca Raton is typical of the many excellent centers and programs developed for Florida's senior population. At this center seniors enjoy meal programs, social and recreational activities, transportation to needed services, adult education programs and health screenings. Social workers assist with age-related problems. An adult day-care center helps families care for adults who need supervision and assistance.

Nearby Communities. **Delray Beach** (pop. 52,039) is a lovely little town 13 miles north of Boca Raton. There is an appealing, renovated downtown with sidewalk cafes, art galleries, and interesting shops. The town's beach has won several awards, and Delray Beach itself was named an All-America City in 1993.

West Palm Beach

Created in the late 1800s as a place for Palm Beach's "hired help" to live, West Palm Beach (pop. 78,370) is not the ugly stepsister, but Cinderella herself. Having been to the ball and married the prince, she now outshines her sister city in every way but old money. While not many retirees choose Palm Beach, they flock to West Palm Beach and the many smaller towns and communities nearby, enjoying the same sun and sea as their wealthier neighbors but probably better shopping and certainly more reasonable restaurants.

Housing. It will probably amaze you that only a short drive from legendary Palm Beach affordable housing is easy to find. You may shop, dine, and spend your leisure hours among society's richest, tannest, and oldest elite, then quickly return to the safe normalcy of your leafy little neighborhood just a few miles inland. A recent property for sale offered an interesting possibility: a two-story duplex with a pair of two-bedroom apartments for only $78,900. An older 1,700-square-foot three-bedroom home in great condition with mature landscaping and a heated in-ground pool was for sale for $99,900. A more contemporary offering was a six-year-old three-bedroom three-bath Mediterranean-style lakefront home with a large two-car garage and all appliances included for $149,900. A gorgeously landscaped three-bedroom two-bath home in a gated community with a split bedroom plan, vaulted ceilings, a tile roof, and a large formal dining room was put on the market at $155,900. For condominium living a lot is available in the low $100,000 price range. A two-bedroom two-bath high-rise condo unit with an open plan and 12-foot ceilings was listed for $124,900. Property taxes in West Palm Beach range from $27.35 to $29.35 per $1,000 nonexempt valuation ,depending on the neighborhood.

Culture and Entertainment. The arts, both visual and performing, are alive and well in West Palm Beach. The Palm Beach County Cultural Council coordinates art activities in the county and provides Artsline, a telephone service giving information about cultural activities twenty-four hours a day. The Armory Art Center is a venue for the visual arts, with gallery space for rotating shows of works by living Florida artists. It is located in a historic, art deco building that was once a National Guard armory. The Norton Gallery and School of Art has been designated a major cultural institution by the state of Florida. The Norton Gallery has an excellent permanent collection of French, American, and Chinese art and sculpture, extensive gallery space for rotating shows, classrooms, and facilities for lectures and concerts. The Palm Beach Community College Museum of Art presents works of contemporary art in the historic district in downtown Lake Worth. The Society of the Four Arts in

Palm Beach presents exhibitions, lectures, concerts, and a film series. The Professional Arts Building is an old building in downtown West Palm Beach that has been turned into studios, living quarters, and gallery spaces for artists.

The anchor of the performing arts in West Palm Beach is the magnificent new Raymond F. Kravis Center for the Performing Arts. The $55 million, 2,200-seat facility has one of the best-equipped and largest stages in the state. It is home to the Palm Beach Opera, Ballet Florida, the Symphony Pops of Boca Raton, and the Philharmonic Orchestra of Florida. The Coral Sky Amphitheater, located at the South Florida Fairgrounds in West Palm Beach, is the largest outdoor performing arts center in the state. The facility includes 7,000 theater-style seats and capacity for 13,000 on the lawn. The Masterworks Chorus of the Palm Beaches is a community chorus that performs classical choral works and a pops concert. The Palm Beach Opera presents four grand opera productions a year. Live theater is presented by the Duncan Theatre, the Delray Beach Playhouse, Florida Atlantic University, the Lake Worth Playhouse, the Florida Stage, and the Royal Poinciana Playhouse in Palm Beach.

Sports and Recreation. The Atlantic Ocean, the Intracoastal Waterway, Lake Okeechobee and several other lakes, as well as the Everglades provide for every kind of water sport one could imagine. No one is quite sure how many golf courses there are in Palm Beach County, but most estimates exceed 150. Another estimate is that there are about 1,100 tennis courts in the Palm Beaches; many are lighted and most are open to the public. For spectator sports the area is hard to beat. There are two polo clubs with regular games, dog racing, and jai alai. The Montreal Expos and the St. Louis Cardinals hold spring training in West Palm Beach, and all the spectator sports activities in Miami are only an hour away.

Law Enforcement and Safety. In 1996 there were 157 criminal offenses reported per 1,000 year-round residents in West Palm Beach. The rate for unincorporated Palm Beach County was sixty-nine.

Senior Centers. The Palm Beach County Division of Senior Services coordinates activities and services for seniors in the county.

Nearby Communities. **Lake Worth** (pop. 29,844) is one of the older communities in Palm Beach County. It is just south of and contiguous with West Palm Beach. Lake Worth has a fine, accessible beach. **Boynton Beach** (pop. 50,940) is a popular retirement community 10 miles south of Lake Worth. **Palm Beach Gardens** (pop. 31,909) is one of the fastest-growing communities in the county. Primarily a bedroom community for the Palm Beaches, it has excellent golf facilities and a wide range of housing opportunities. Located away from the coast, Palm Beach Gardens has almost unlimited land on which to grow.

Juno Beach, Jupiter, and Tequesta

Three towns on the northern edge of Palm Beach County, Juno Beach (population 2,659), Jupiter (population 30,599), and Tequesta (population 4,673), represent the newest and the oldest in southeast Florida towns. Settled as a fort in 1838 during the Seminole Indian War, Jupiter is the area's oldest community. The Jupiter lighthouse, built in 1860 to warn ships of one of the most protruding points of land on the eastern seaboard, is one of the oldest structures in southeast Florida. Juno, later renamed Juno Beach, was a main point on the Celestial Railway, which connected it to Venus, Mars, and Jupiter until the little railroad was sold at auction in 1896. From 1890 to 1900 Juno served as the county seat of Dade County, providing governmental services for all of southeast Florida. Tequesta is one of the newest towns in the state. Located where the branches of the Loxahatchee River, the Intracoastal Waterway, and the Jupiter Inlet converge to flow into the Atlantic Ocean, no communities on Florida's east coast are more beautifully situated than Juno Beach, Jupiter, and Tequesta. Wherever you look you see a beautiful body of water.

In Juno Beach, Jupiter, and Tequesta wonderful housing is in great supply and no matter which area you prefer, you're never far from the Intracoastal Waterway, the Loxahatchee River, the Jupiter Inlet, or the Atlantic Ocean with its beautiful beaches. In Jupiter a newer pool home nestled among mature pine trees on a one-acre lot with three bedrooms, two baths, and a two-car garage was recently on the market for $129,900. A chalet-style three-bedroom home with an in-ground pool and gazebo on more than an acre of land was listed for $139,500. For those with a desire to outshine the neighbors or host a lot of out-of-town guests, absolute luxury in the form of a five-bedroom four-bath custom-built Mediterranean home with more than 3,000 square feet of living space, a double-sided fireplace, and a three-car garage approached by an impressive circular driveway was on the market in Tequesta for

$280,000. Property taxes in Juno Beach are $24.05 per $1,000 nonexempt valuation. In Jupiter and Tequesta they range from $22.15 to $23.50 per $1,000 nonexempt valuation, depending on municipality and neighborhood.

Thanks to native son Burt Reynolds, who was born a few miles south in Riviera Beach but maintains a home here, this area has become known for its theaters. The Burt Reynolds Institute Theatre in Tequesta, a training ground for aspiring actors, presents classical and contemporary plays. The Carousel Jupiter Theatre brings Broadway shows to town in a dinner-theater setting. The annual Shakespeare-by-the-Sea Festival is held in the Carlin Park Amphitheater in Jupiter. Palm Beach Community College's Eissey Campus Theatre in Palm Beach Gardens contains a 750-seat theater and a 2,500-square-foot lobby for art exhibitions. The college brings in international artists with its "Arts in the Gardens" series as well as regular performances by local companies such as Ballet Florida, Palm Beach Opera, and the Choral Society of the Palm Beaches. The college's own theater department presents a season of plays. All of the cultural opportunities of Palm Beach and West Palm Beach are only a few miles away.

With 100 miles of shoreline on the Atlantic Ocean, Jupiter Inlet, the Intracoastal Waterway, and the Loxahatchee River, boating, fishing, swimming, surfing, and every other water sport are major activities here and the main reason many retirees have chosen to settle in the area. The underwater scene here lures divers with its spectacular reefs, underwater ledges and trenches, sunken ships, a statue of Neptune, and a 1965 vintage Rolls Royce. Several golf courses and many tennis courts round out the sports opportunities in this northernmost corner of Palm Beach County.

Addresses and Connections

Chambers of Commerce: Boca Raton Chamber of Commerce, 1800 North Dixie Highway, Boca Raton, FL 33432-1892; (561) 395–4433; Fax, (561) 392–3780; http://bocaraton.com; E-mail: chamber@ bocaraton.com

The Greater Boynton Beach Chamber of Commerce, 639 East Ocean Avenue, Suite 108, Boynton Beach, FL 33435, (561) 732–9501; E-mail: commerce@boyntonbeach.org

Greater Delray Beach Chamber of Commerce, 64 Southeast Fifth Avenue, Delray Beach, FL 33483; (561) 278–0424

Jupiter/Tequesta/Juno Beach Chamber of Commerce, 800 North U.S. Highway 1, Jupiter, FL 33477; (561) 746–7111; http://www.jupiter-inlet.com/; E-mail: chamber@jupiterfl.org

The Greater Lake Worth Chamber of Commerce, 1702 Lake Worth Road, Lake Worth, FL 33460; (561) 582–4401; E-mail: admin@glwcoc.org/

The Greater Lake Worth Chamber of Commerce, 1702 Lake Worth Road, Lake Worth, FL 33460; (561) 582–4401; E-mail: admin@glwcoc.org/

Northern Palm Beaches Chamber of Commerce, 1983 PGA Boulevard, Suite 104, Palm Beach Gardens, FL 33408; (561) 694–2300; Fax, (561) 694–0126; http://www.npbchamber.com; E-mail· info@npb-chamber.com

Chamber of Commerce of the Palm Beaches, 401 North Flagler Drive, West Palm Beach, FL 33401; (561) 833–3711; http://palmbeaches.com; E-mail: chamber@palmbeaches.com

Newspaper: *The Palm Beach Post* (daily), P.O. Box 24700, West Palm Beach, FL 33416; (561) 820–4100

Internet: http://www.GoPBI.com

MID-ATLANTIC
COAST

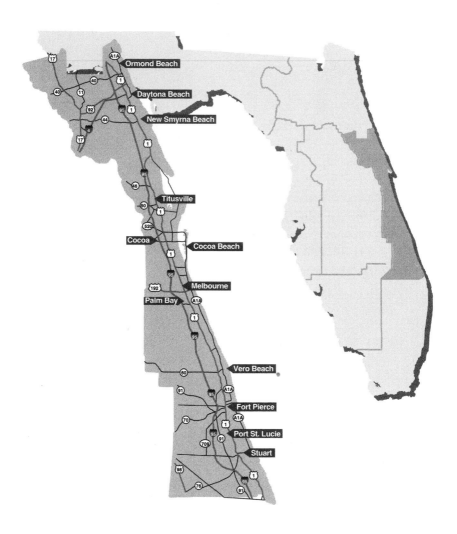

Ormond Beach

Daytona Beach

New Smyrna Beach

Titusville

Cocoa

Cocoa Beach

Melbourne

Palm Bay

Vero Beach

Fort Pierce

Port St. Lucie

Stuart

THE MID-ATLANTIC COAST

The Mid-Atlantic Coast region runs for about 175 miles north from the Palm Beach County line. It includes from south to north the following counties and their cities and towns most popular with retirees: Martin County (Stuart), St. Lucie County (Fort Pierce and Port St. Lucie), Indian River County (Vero Beach), Brevard County (Melbourne and Palm Bay, Cocoa and Cocoa Beach, and Titusville), and Volusia County (New Smyrna Beach, Daytona Beach, and Ormond Beach). The southern part of this region is nicknamed "The Treasure Coast" for the many Spanish galleons bearing tons of gold and silver from Mexico and South America that were wrecked off the coast here. Destroyed by hurricanes in the seventeenth and early eighteenth centuries, several of these ships have been found and their treasures recovered. The middle part of the area is called "The Space Coast." Many times since America's space program began in the 1950s the nation's attention has focused on Brevard County and its John F. Kennedy Space Center. The northern part proclaims it has the "world's safest beaches."

As on the lower east coast of Florida, most of the cities and towns (and therefore most of the population) in this region are on a strip of land along the coast less than 20 miles wide. The land west of this narrow coastal strip is low-lying marshes, ranch land, or—in the northern part—pine forests and small towns. The St. Johns River begins here as a tiny stream, almost invisible as it flows through swampy prairies, wide shallow ponds covered with water hyacinths, and a series of increasingly larger lakes. It becomes a powerful river, more than 4 miles wide in places, as it twists and turns for 300 miles on its way to Jacksonville and the Atlantic Ocean.

Along the eastern border of this region are long lagoons known in the southern part as the Indian River and in the northern part as the Halifax River. Across the lagoon from the mainland is a narrow barrier island that stretches from Stuart to Jacksonville, broken only by a few inlets. In this region some communities, Daytona Beach for example, are on both sides of the Intracoastal Waterway, while others are on either the mainland side or the beach side. Every city and town seems to have been oriented to take advantage of beautiful river views. Protected by the barrier island, the Indian River and the Halifax River are part of the Intracoastal Waterway.

The communities along the coast are linked by several north-south roads and highways, making transportation between the cities and towns in the region easy. U.S. Highway 1, the old major thoroughfare for the entire east coast of the United States, goes through the center of almost every city. It also runs along the Indian River for several stretches. U.S. A1A runs the length of the barrier island except where it is blocked by the Kennedy Space Center or by inlets without bridges. While these two roads are by far the most interesting, they are also the slowest, with heavy traffic at times and a great many traffic lights. I–95 runs the entire length of Florida's east coast, usually from 3 to 5 miles inland. There are exits to all major points along the coast. From south of Miami to Fort Pierce, where it turns inland, the Florida Turnpike parallels the coast 5 to 8 miles inland. The turnpike, a toll road, is the fastest of Florida's highways.

The major appeal of this region to retirees is a combination of delightful weather, wonderful beaches, stunning water views, and truly affordable housing. Its pleasant small and midsize towns offer many of the same amenities as towns farther south on the "Gold Coast" without the crowds or expense. The services provided at Patrick Air Force Base in Brevard County and at MacDill Air Force Base in Tampa make this entire area popular with military retirees.

As you go north in this region the scenery changes from tropical to subtropical. Coconut palms and other very tender trees and shrubs disappear. Once again we see more pines, oaks, and cold-hardy palms such as cabbage and Sabal palms, the latter Florida's state tree. While the weather may be a few degrees cooler in winter than farther south, the sun is just as bright and winter is very brief. The always-cool Atlantic Ocean moderates summer heat, and its Gulf Stream warms up the winter months.

When Grandkids Visit. For campers, hikers, and nature lovers in general it is hard to beat *Jonathan Dickinson State Park* at the southern tip of this region. The park comprises 10,328 acres of natural wood and swampland with diverse plant and animal life as well as 135 campsites, biking and hiking trails, and nature walks. Admission to the park is $3.25 per vehicle with up to eight passengers and $1.00 for each additional person.

Florida Power and Light's Energy Encounter on South Hutchinson Island is an interesting and educational museum showing how energy powers the world, complete with hands-on displays and exhibits. There is no admission charge.

This part of Florida is known as the Treasure Coast, and two museums are dedicated to shipwrecks and sunken treasure. *The McLarty Treasure Museum* presents, through dioramas and exhibits of actual treasure, a fascinating record of the eleven Spanish galleons that sank in a hurricane just off the coast here in 1715. From the museum you can see the actual site of the sinking. Admission to the state-funded museum is $1.00 and children under 6 are free. There is no treasure hunter more famous or more successful than Mel Fisher, and the *Mel Fisher Treasure Museum* in Sebastian has displays of treasure he retrieved from wrecked Spanish galleons. Admission is $5.00 for adults, $4.00 for seniors, and $1.50 for kids ages 6 to 12. Admission is free for those age 5 and under.

The *U.S. Astronaut Hall of Fame* in Titusville is an excellent introduction to the Space Coast. The museum showcases the training and experiences of America's first astronauts. Hands-on interactive exhibits simulate a training mission for a jet fighter pilot, a shuttle landing, and floating weightless in outer space. Admission is $13.95 for adults and $9.95 for children ages 6 to 12.

For the real thing take the grandkids to the *Kennedy Space Center Visitor Complex*. This exciting visit includes an IMAX theater, simulated blast-offs and landings on the moon, an observation gantry overlooking the space shuttle launch pads, and a look at the International Space Station being readied for launch. Admission to the tour, which includes access to all the attractions and takes about four hours, is $19.00 for adults and $15.00 for children.

If your grandkids like speed and all the noise and excitement of auto racing, take them to the *Daytona International Speedway*, home to several of the most famous auto races in the world. Admission prices vary according to the event. Walt Disney World, SeaWorld, and Universal Studios are only an hour away from most locations in this region.

MARTIN COUNTY: Stuart

Martin County (population 114,464) is bordered on the east by the Atlantic Ocean. Its western border, some 30 miles away, is Lake Okeechobee, the second largest inland lake in the United States. In between, you find ranch land, farms, and citrus groves. Stuart (population 13,773) is the county seat and by far the largest municipality. The rest of the population lives in unincorporated areas of Martin County, most in communities near the coast. Martin County's beach and coastal communities have become very popular with retirees. In recent years Martin County ranked fortieth among all U.S. counties in attracting retirees from other states. I suspect that a recent boom in retiree population in this area will change that ranking in future studies. Martin county has one of the highest ratios of people over age sixty-five to total population in the state.

Cost of Living. Martin County ranks ninth in the state with a cost of living exactly at the state average. The sales tax is 6 percent. The cost of housing is 2.2 percent above the state average. The average purchase price of a home is $105,578. Martin County ranks twenty-second in the state with an average monthly apartment rent of $560.

Climate. The wide St. Lucie River, the Indian River, and the Atlantic Ocean keep Martin County's winters mild and its summers breezy and pleasant.

Vero Beach–Martin County Weather

	In degrees Fahrenheit				
	Jan.	Apr.	July	Oct.	Annual Rainfall
DAILY HIGHS	72.5	81.5	90.1	84.0	51.16"
DAILY LOWS	50.7	61.0	72.1	66.9	

Medical Care. One hospital with 336 beds serves the people of Martin County.

Transportation. The nearest major airport is Palm Beach International 40 miles away. There is no local bus transportation.

Opportunities for Continuing Education. Martin County schools and Indian River Community College's Chastain Center in Stuart offer continuing-education courses geared to the needs of the county's retirement population.

Stuart

The St. Lucie River, nearly a mile wide at this point, makes a sweeping horseshoe turn around the city of Stuart (population 13,773) before it flows into the Indian River and, via the St. Lucie Inlet, into the Atlantic Ocean. With the St. Lucie River on three sides and views across a narrow spit of land to the Indian River, Stuart has one of the loveliest water orientations of any city on Florida's east coast. And Stuart has one of the most appealing downtowns you will find anywhere. It is the result of a $500,000 grant in 1987 that generated $12.5 million in private capital to renovate downtown Stuart. Historic old buildings were given a cleaning and a face-lift. (It helps the district's ambience that a city ordinance limits buildings to four stories.) Now, old-fashioned street lights sparkle and new pink sidewalks encourage strolling through the historic district. A river walk stretches for more than a mile and a half along the St. Lucie River, and an outdoor bandstand attracts people to concerts and festivals throughout the year. All of this effort has had the desired effect. There are people in the downtown area now, new shops and restaurants have opened, and there is a vitality to Stuart that will make you want to visit again and perhaps make it your new home.

The St. Lucie River is the eastern terminus of the waterway that runs from the Gulf of Mexico through Lake Okeechobee to the Atlantic Ocean. With access to the St. Lucie River, the Indian River, Lake Okeechobee, the Gulf of Mexico and the Atlantic Ocean, it is easy to see why Stuart is a major center for fishing and pleasure boating on Florida's east coast. It is also known as the "Sailfish Capital of the World," and fishing in the Atlantic for these game fish is a huge business for charter boat owners in the area.

Housing. From Sewall's Point's luxurious riverfront estates to very inexpensive inland housing, Stuart offers something for everyone at relatively low prices. (It should be noted that throughout this area the term "inland" refers to land not directly on either the Indian River or the Atlantic Ocean, but rarely more than a few minutes from either.) Deepwater and country club condominiums may be found for around $80,000. A recent listing for a two-bedroom two-bath condo with a dock on a deepwater canal was priced at $82,900. For even less, a one-bedroom unit in a very handsome newer condominium building with one and a half baths and a glass-enclosed patio was on the market for

$43,500. A three-bedroom three-bath pool home in a parklike setting located in an established neighborhood was for sale for $119,900. Ranches, a little farther inland with several acres of land, often list for well under $200,000. I saw a three-bedroom log "ranchette" situated on a five-acre lot with a 2,000-square-foot barn priced at $175,000. For those needing loads of space to entertain, a 3,800-square-foot five-bedroom mansion with three baths, plus a three-car garage with an office was for sale for $279,000. On the high end, luxury homes with acres of riverfront property on Sewall Island—like living on the water in Boca Raton or Palm Beach at half the price—can be found starting at around $500,000. The property tax rate in Stuart is $20.15 per $1,000 nonexempt valuation. In unincorporated Palm City the rate is $18.15.

Culture and Entertainment. The Martin County Council for the Arts coordinates the activities of a number of cultural organizations in Martin County. Part of the downtown redevelopment project, the old Martin County Courthouse has been restored to its original 1937 design and now houses art galleries and historical exhibits. A December outdoor art festival is held in Memorial Park in the historic area. The Lyric Theater is another successful restoration project in downtown Stuart. This 1925 Mediterranean Revival theater now houses concerts, plays, and lectures. Barn Theater is a local group of players presenting a season of live theater.

Sports and Recreation. Stuart's access to water encourages boating, fishing, swimming, and all water sports. Access to Lake Okeechobee, with some of the best freshwater fishing in the state, and easy access to the Atlantic Ocean for outstanding saltwater fishing give Stuart's anglers the best of both worlds. Miles of nearby beaches bring out swimmers and sun worshippers. Thirty golf courses within a 15-mile radius of Stuart are a major draw for those whose retirement dream is to golf year-round. Baseball fans have a real treat during spring training season with five major league teams practicing within an hour's drive of Stuart.

Law Enforcement and Safety. In 1996 there were eighty-six criminal offenses reported per 1,000 year-round residents in Stuart. In unincorporated Martin County the rate was forty-six.

Senior Centers. The Martin County Council on Aging is a private, nonprofit agency that operates a Meals on Wheels program, provides in-home assistance for the homebound elderly, provides transportation to shopping centers, doctors' offices, and recreational destinations, and coordinates loans of medical equipment such as wheelchairs and walkers. The Log Cabin Senior Center in nearby Jensen Beach serves congregate meals and provides space for continuing-education classes and activities.

Nearby Communities. **Sewall's Point** (pop. 1,736) is a posh and expensive community located on a narrow peninsula of land with the Indian River on one side and the St. Lucie River on the other. **Jensen Beach** (pop. about 12,000) is an unincorporated community north of Sewall's Point. A movement is afoot to restore Jensen Beach to its quaint "old-Florida beach community" look. Housing here is less expensive than in Sewall's Point, but still fairly pricey. **Port Salerno** (pop. about 26,000) is another rapidly growing unincorporated neighbor of Stuart. Located at the end of a long cove called the Manatee Pocket at the junction of the Indian River and the St. Lucie River, Port Salerno is the deep-sea fishing capital of Martin County. With almost unlimited room to expand on its western side, Port Salerno is a growing community attractive to retirees and to young families. There is a wide range of housing prices here. **Palm City** (pop. about 17,000) is an unincorporated community on the banks of the St. Lucie River just west of Stuart. It is self-contained with shopping centers, movie theaters, and schools. In addition to its water orientation, Palm City is a city of golf courses—eight in all. With a great deal of available land, Palm City's housing prices are lower than in the cities and towns nearer to the coast. **Hobe Sound** (pop. about 14,000) and **Jupiter Island** (pop. 581) are two communities about 10 miles south of Stuart. Jupiter Island is undoubtedly the wealthiest and most exclusive community in Florida and probably the only place where the residents can look down their noses at Palm Beach society to the south. Most of its huge estates front on the Atlantic Ocean with acres of jungle between them and the public road. **Hobe Sound** is only a couple of notches down in cost and prestige. **Indiantown** is an unincorporated community of about 6,000. Located 30 miles west of Stuart, it is the only significant Martin County town away from the coast. The town is named for the Seminole Indian settlement that existed in the area until the early 1880s. Indiantown is a haven for retirees who want land and open spaces yet want to be only a few minutes from larger cities. Golf course communities are beginning to spring up in the area. With the low cost of land and easy access to retirement communities on the coast, you may expect this area to grow rapidly in the coming years.

Addresses and Connections

Chambers of Commerce: Hobe Sound Chamber of Commerce, 8779 Bridge Road, Hobe Sound, FL 33475; (561) 546–4724

Indiantown Chamber of Commerce, P.O. Box 602, Indiantown, FL 34956; (561) 597–2184

Jensen Beach Chamber of Commerce, 1910 North East Jensen Beach Boulevard, Jensen Beach, FL 34957; (561) 334–3444

Palm City Chamber of Commerce, 901 Martin Downs Boulevard, Palm City, FL 34990; (561) 286–8121

Stuart/Martin County Chamber of Commerce, 1650 South Kanner Highway, Stuart, FL 34994; (561) 278–1088; Fax, (561) 220–3437; http://www.stuartmartinchamber.org

Newspapers: The Stuart News (daily), P.O. Box 9009, Stuart, FL 34995; (561) 287–1550

Palm Beach Post (daily), 8290 Business Park Drive, Port St. Lucie, FL 34952; (561) 871–0472

Internet: http://www.tcgo.com

ST. LUCIE COUNTY: Fort Pierce and Port St. Lucie

St. Lucie County (pop. 175,458) is another coastal Florida county with miles of beautiful beaches, a few towns near the coast, and thousands of acres of sparsely populated interior land. Books such as this are not in the business of predicting the future, but if I may be allowed one speculation, it is that fifty years from now these interior lands will be as developed and populated as the areas along the coast. Already you can see the population spreading westward, where there is ample land for golf courses and planned communities. Throughout the length of St. Lucie County, the Indian River separates the mainland from the barrier island—called Hutchinson Island here—and its 22 miles of beaches. The North Fork of the St. Lucie River reaches far up into St. Lucie County, providing additional waterfront property. St. Lucie County ranks thirty-second among all U.S. counties in attracting retirees from other states. More than one in five residents are sixty-five or older in St. Lucie County. In Port St. Lucie the ratio is closer to one in three.

Cost of Living. St. Lucie County ranks twenty-eighth in the state with a cost of living 95.51 percent of the state average. The sales tax in St. Lucie County is 6.5 percent. The cost of housing is 9.37 percent below the state average. The average purchase price of a home is $87,000. St. Lucie County ranks twenty-fourth in the state with an average monthly apartment rent of $549.

Climate. Proceeding northward on Florida's Atlantic Coast, expect temperatures to be a little cooler than farther south. Summer temperatures are still moderated by the ocean and almost daily afternoon showers.

Vero Beach–St. Lucie County Weather

| | In degrees Fahrenheit | | | | |
	Jan.	Apr.	July	Oct.	Annual Rainfall
DAILY HIGHS	72.5	81.5	90.1	84.0	51.16"
DAILY LOWS	50.7	61.0	72.1	66.9	

Medical Care. Two hospitals with 513 beds serve the residents of St. Lucie County.

Transportation. Palm Beach International Airport, 70 miles away, is the nearest commercial airport. There is no local bus service.

Opportunities for Continuing Education. St. Lucie County schools, Indian River Community College, and the Treasure Coast campus of Florida Atlantic University all provide continuing-education courses and programs of interest to retirees

Fort Pierce and Port St. Lucie

Fort Pierce (pop. 37,273) is another city in this region with a spruced-up and restored downtown. It seems that more and more Florida towns are rediscovering their roots and making the most of their historic buildings. Fort Pierce has the advantage of a downtown that looks out on the Indian River, almost 2 miles wide at this point, and it is developing its plans to make the most of these views.

Founded in 1961 as a planned community, Port St. Lucie (pop. 74,894) is a new community compared to an old Florida town like Fort Pierce. Its mushrooming growth, however, has already made it one of the larger towns in the state, and community leaders predict a population of

250,000 residents before it has reached its planned maximum size. Port St. Lucie is one of the communities with enough vision to see the wisdom of locating away from the crowded coast. In terms of land mass, Port St. Lucie's 85 square miles makes it the third largest city in Florida. It also seems to be one of the best managed. The original design—that of individual residential communities with their own schools, parks, and shopping centers—is still being followed today.

Housing. You can let your imagination run wild in selecting a home in Fort Pierce or Port St. Lucie. Huge historic homes fronting on the Indian River list in the high $200,000s. Large executives homes range from $120,000 to $175,000. Modest three-bedroom family homes abound in the $90,000 price range, but little two-bedroom gems for less than $40,000 can be found in nice neighborhoods nestled among more expensive homes. I found a handsome three-bedroom two-bath home on a double lot with a fireplace, a fenced yard, and mature landscaping in town for $52,750. Nearby, I saw a three-bedroom two-bath main home with a pool and a detached garage with two rental apartments—all in move-in condition—for $89,500. And a lakefront villa on a golf course offered two bedrooms, two baths and a two-car garage for $92,000. You can buy a lot for your money if you want to spend more. A custom-built five-bedroom home on a beautiful treed lot featured a great room with 17-foot ceilings and guest quarters with a separate entrance for $115,000. For island and beach living, two-bedroom high-rise condominiums are often found for less than $90,000—prices almost impossible to find in most other Florida beach communities. Property taxes in St. Lucie County range from $21.54 to $28.59 per $1,000 nonexempt valuation. The average for the county is $25.06.

Culture and Entertainment. The St. Lucie County Cultural Affairs Council is charged with developing, coordinating, and promoting cultural arts in the county. The Council publishes a quarterly newsletter, *ArtsView.* Recent activities of the council include art and architecture tours, public forums on cultural issues, inventories of local public art, and publication of tour guides to local art and architecture. The performing arts are alive and well in Fort Pierce. In one recent announcement the following were scheduled in Fort Pierce: *The Glass Menagerie* at the St. Lucie Community Theater, the Treasure Coast Opera Society's production of *Madama Butterfly* and performances by the Treasure Coast Symphony, and Indian River Community College's Fall Fine Arts Festival that included two plays, three concerts, a Broadway musical, a lecture, and a concert by the St. Lucie Chorale.

Sports and Recreation. There are 22 miles of beaches with twenty beach parks for swimming and sunning. On South Hutchinson Island the beach has a boardwalk, picnic tables, lifeguards, and dressing areas with showers. The coasts of St. Lucie County and her neighboring counties have spectacular reefs and wrecked ships for scuba diving. There are thirteen championship golf courses in the area. Three of them are PGA courses rated in the top twenty by *Golf Digest*. The Fort Pierce Fronton offers a season of jai alai with pari-mutuel wagering, and seniors are admitted free to all matinee games. The New York Mets hold spring training in Port St. Lucie.

Law Enforcement and Safety. In 1996 there were 150 criminal offenses reported per 1,000 year-round residents in the city of Fort Pierce. In unincorporated St. Lucie County the rate was forty. In 1996 there were thirty-seven criminal offenses reported per 1,000 year-round residents in Port St. Lucie. In 1994 the Florida Attorney General designated the Port St. Lucie Police Department as having Florida's best crime prevention unit in a city with a population less than 100,000.

Senior Centers. The St. Lucie Council on Aging coordinates activities for seniors including two day-care centers.

Nearby Communities. **St. Lucie West** (population about 7,000) is actually in the city of Port St. Lucie, but it is so typical of developments one now finds in Florida it deserves special mention. St. Lucie West is a billion-dollar 4,600-acre development on the western edge of Port St. Lucie. It is being developed as a self-contained community with banks, office buildings, health care providers, a huge shopping center, an industrial park, restaurants, movie theaters, churches and temples, and golf courses. St. Lucie West is being developed at the rate of one and one-half residences built and sold every day. It is expected that when the community is completed it will have 30,000 residents, 12,500 homes, and five million square feet of industrial and commercial space. While it is not specifically a retirement community, you can bet a large percentage of its residents will be retirees.

Addresses and Connections

Chamber of Commerce: St. Lucie County Chamber of Commerce, P.O. Box 8209, Port St. Lucie, FL 34985; (561) 595–9999;

http://www.co.st-lucie.fl.us; E-mail: slccom@gate.net

Newspapers: The Fort Pierce Tribune (daily), P.O. Box 69, Fort Pierce, FL 34985; (561) 461–2050

Port St. Lucie News (daily), 1591 Port St. Lucie Boulevard, Suite K, Port St. Lucie, FL 34952; (561) 337–5800

Palm Beach Post (daily), 8290 Business Park Drive, Port St. Lucie, FL 34952; (561) 871–0472

INDIAN RIVER COUNTY: Vero Beach

Indian River County (pop. 102,211) is in the very center of Florida's east coast and at the heart of the famous Indian River citrus belt. The barrier island along the coast here is about 80 percent developed with rather luxurious, small, mostly unincorporated beach communities. Indian River County (combined with Okeechobee County) ranks thirty-ninth among all U.S. counties in attracting retirees from other states.

Cost of Living. Indian River County ranks twelfth in the state with a cost of living 98.55 percent of the state average. The sales tax is 7 percent. The cost of housing is 3.12 percent below the state average. The average sale price of a home is $94,000. The county ranks forty-first in the state with an average monthly apartment rent of $440.

Climate. Situated in the middle of Florida's Atlantic Coast, Indian River County enjoys mild winters and pleasant summers.

Indian River County Weather

	In degrees Fahrenheit				
	Jan.	Apr.	July	Oct.	Annual Rainfall
DAILY HIGHS	72.5	81.5	90.1	84.0	51.16"
DAILY LOWS	50.7	61.0	72.1	66.9	

Medical Care. Two hospitals with 480 beds serve Indian River County.

Transportation. Melbourne International Airport, 35 miles north of Vero Beach, offers commercial jet service. Palm Beach International Airport, 68 miles away, and Orlando International Airport, 100 miles away, offer extensive jet service. The Community Coach Transportation System provides local weekday bus service. The Indian River Council on Aging provides door-to-door service for the elderly and the handicapped.

Opportunities for Continuing Education. Indian River County schools and Indian River Community College provide continuing-education courses and activities.

Vero Beach

Vero Beach is a beautiful little coastal community with much to offer its 17,697 residents. Its downtown is small and open to wonderful vistas of the Indian River, seemingly at every turn. Most buildings are no taller than three stories, so there is a light and open feel to even the busiest part of the city.

Housing. Housing in Vero Beach offers a wide range of options, from the interesting and historic downtown area to newer country club communities. Although it has its share of million-dollar waterfront estates, retirees easily find affordable, immaculate homes in parklike settings in the downtown area. In town on a cul-de-sac, a four-bedroom two-bath lakeside ranch with a split floor plan was priced at $78,500. For buyers who appreciate owning a bit of local history, a completely renovated downtown manor, one of Vero's oldest mansions, offered three bedrooms, three baths, a new kitchen, and a detached two-car carriage house on a gorgeous lot, all for an asking price of $249,000. For the more modest budget, there was a small three-bedroom home with a tropical pool area for $90,000. The wonderful challenge in Vero Beach is finding the perfect house in the perfect neighborhood, for here you should settle for nothing but the best in your price range. Property taxes in Vero Beach are about $21 per $1,000 nonexempt valuation.

Culture and Entertainment. Vero Beach's Center for the Arts is the focal point for the visual arts in the local area. Already the largest cultural facility of its kind on the Treasure Coast, it is currently under expansion to double its size to 43,000 square feet. The center offers art shows with local and international artists represented, lectures, classes, concerts, a library, and films. In his 1994 book *The 100 Best Small Art Towns in America,* author John Villani praised the Center for the Arts. A number of commercial galleries offer a wide variety of contemporary art by national and regional artists. The 633-seat Riverside Theater presents professional theater, touring Broadway shows, and classical music concerts. Its Riverside 2 series, referred to as "off-off-Broadway," offers innovative and avant-garde theater productions. The Vero Beach Theater Guild is a local amateur theater group that presents a full season of live theater.

Sports and Recreation. Swimming, sunning, sailing, fishing, and all the possibilities of the Atlantic Ocean and its beaches lure retirees to Vero Beach. Along with sunny beaches, golf seems to be a major attraction bringing retirees to Florida, and the Vero Beach area offers twenty-three courses for year-round play. Fishing in the Atlantic, in the Indian River, and in nearby lakes where the bass fishing is considered outstanding, brings fishermen to Indian River County. Public tennis courts are available at eight parks throughout the county. For spectator-sports fans Vero Beach runs the gamut from the Los Angeles Dodgers in the spring to a December to April season of polo.

Law Enforcement and Safety. In 1996 there were eighty-three criminal offenses reported per 1,000 year-round residents in Vero Beach. In unincorporated Indian River County the rate was forty-seven.

Senior Centers. The Indian River County Council on Aging, Inc., coordinates programs for seniors and operates a professional day-care center for the elderly. There are senior centers in Sebastian and Vero Beach.

Nearby Communities. **Fellsmere** (pop. 2,412) is a rural community about 30 miles northwest of Vero Beach. **Indian River Shores** (pop. 2,640) is an exclusive community of very wealthy retirees. **Orchid** (pop. 44) is the newest enclave for the super-rich on the barrier island. **Sebastian** (pop. 13,967), on the Indian River north of Vero Beach, is one of the fastest-growing communities in Indian River County.

Addresses and Connections

Chamber of Commerce: Indian River County Chamber of Commerce, P.O. Box 2947, Vero Beach, FL 32961; (561) 567–3491; Fax, (561) 778–3181; http://www.vero-beach.fl.us/chamber; E-mail: chamber@verobeach.fl.us

Newspaper: The Press Journal (daily), P.O. Box 1268, Vero Beach, FL 32961; (561) 562–2315

BREVARD COUNTY: Melbourne and Palm Bay, Cocoa and Cocoa Beach, and Titusville

With 72 miles of beaches on the Atlantic Coast, Brevard County (population 450,164) has the distinction of being the longest county in the state. Less than 10 miles wide in places, it is also the narrowest. Brevard County has profited and suffered from being the host county for NASA and the Kennedy Space Center. In the 1950s Brevard's population exploded from 23,653 to 111,435, and the county scrambled to provide housing, schools, and other services. Years later, when NASA went through a series of cutbacks, population dwindled in some areas and housing became very inexpensive. Now 10,000 new citizens arrive each year. Recently Brevard County ranked fifteenth out of all U.S. counties in attracting retirees from other states. In *Retirement Places Rated* Melbourne ranked tenth among the 183 most popular retirement locations in the United States.

A string of small and midsize communities parade up U.S. 1 on the mainland. The lower two-thirds of the barrier island is home to several little towns and the larger communities of Cocoa Beach and Merritt Island. North of the town of Cape Canaveral, all of the barrier island becomes the Space Center.

Cost of Living. Brevard County ranks twenty-second in the state with a cost of living 96.67 percent of the state average. The sales tax is 6 percent. The cost of housing is 3.06 percent below the state average. The local chamber of commerce states that Brevard County is the tenth most affordable housing area in the nation. The average sale price of a home is about $91,000. The county ranks twenty-fifth in the state with an average monthly apartment rent of $548.

Climate. North Brevard County cities such as Titusville are closer to the NOAA station at Daytona Beach, while those in the southern part of the county, Melbourne for example, are closer to the station at Vero Beach.

Northern Brevard County Weather

| | In degrees Fahrenheit | | | | |
	Jan.	Apr.	July	Oct.	Annual Rainfall
DAILY HIGHS	68.0	80.0	89.8	81.5	47.89"
DAILY LOWS	46.9	58.6	72.5	65.2	

Southern Brevard County Weather

| | In degrees Fahrenheit | | | | |
	Jan.	Apr.	July	Oct.	Annual Rainfall
DAILY HIGHS	72.5	81.5	90.1	84.0	51.16"
DAILY LOWS	50.7	61.0	72.1	66.9	

Medical Care. Four hospitals with 1,191 beds serve Brevard County.

Transportation. Space Coast Area Transit provides bus service throughout the county with seventeen routes year-round and nineteen during the summer. The company also provides transportation for the disabled and "vanpool" programs. Melbourne International Airport provides limited jet service. Orlando International Airport, 67 miles west, provides more extensive domestic and international service.

Opportunities for Continuing Education. Brevard County schools, Brevard Community College, the Brevard campus of the University of Central Florida, Florida Institute of Technology, and the Brevard campus of Rollins College provide degree programs and continuing education to the area.

Melbourne and Palm Bay

Melbourne (pop. 66,970) and Palm Bay (pop. 74,395) are adjacent communities in the southern part of Brevard County. Melbourne is the older city (named in 1880), now growing more slowly and beginning to take pride in its history. Palm Bay is the sprawling new town with almost unlimited land (66 square miles) to grow on. Palm Bay extends several miles west from the Indian River.

Housing. If you want a beautiful home in a beautiful small city, the Melbourne–Palm Bay area is the place for you. Where else can you find a new, three-bedroom Victorian-style home with three baths, Italian tile, mahogany cabinetry, a fireplace with an antique mantel, a master bath with claw-foot tub, and more than one acre of land for $135,000? A two-bedroom two-bath villa with ocean access had a loft, porch, garage, community pool, and a community pier for $105,000? Or you might want to live within walking distance of Melbourne's cozy historic downtown area in a restored, older three-bedroom home for just $80,000. For the same price I spotted a newer three-bedroom two-bath home with a two-car garage and a screened in-ground pool surrounded by a privacy fence, all on a lot with mature trees that backed onto a greenbelt. Palm Bay has expansive country club communities of $150,000 homes, but it also offers neighborhoods of small, pastel-colored storybook homes for about $60,000. I saw an attractive three-bedroom two-bath home with an oversize two-car garage and a custom-built in-ground pool listed for $86,000. A new three-bedroom two-bath split plan home on a lake was listed for $122,900. Also inland, a huge lakefront home with four bedrooms and three baths on a half-acre lot was priced at $179,900. Even the beach communities offer relatively affordable homes. Small contemporary homes near the water can start at less than $130,000. I noticed a four-bedroom home with a solar-heated pool just a block from the beach listed for $199,000. You won't find homes like these for even double the price in many other Florida towns. Property taxes in the Melbourne–Palm Bay area range from $19.66 to $20.60 per $1,000 nonexempt valuation, depending on municipality and neighborhood.

Culture and Entertainment. The Brevard Museum of Art and Science in Eau Gallie (a neighboring town that is now part of Melbourne) exhibits the work of international contemporary artists. Several art galleries are clustered in the historic districts of Eau Gallie and Melbourne. The 500-seat theater in the Henegar Center for the Arts is used by the Melbourne Civic Theater, the Central Florida Lyric Opera, Fantasy Theater Factory, and by touring shows. The King Center for the Performing Arts brings major events to the community throughout the year.

Sports and Recreation. All the water sports and activities associated with the Atlantic Ocean and the Indian River are available in Melbourne and Palm Bay. Of the twenty golf courses in Brevard County, nine are in Melbourne or Palm Bay. The Miami-based Florida Marlins baseball team holds spring training in Melbourne.

Law Enforcement and Safety. In 1996 there were ninety-two criminal offenses reported per 1,000 year-round residents in Melbourne. In Palm Bay the rate was fifty-five. In unincorporated Brevard County the rate was forty-three.

Senior Centers. The South Brevard Seniors Association, Inc. provides many services to retirees in the Melbourne area. When I visited the center, dance, art, bridge, and exercise classes were underway and the

SHINE (Serving Health Insurance Needs of Elders) program was in full swing. The flyer I picked up listed several outings and excursions. I was told by a friendly volunteer that annual dues were $1.00, but that they would be waived if I couldn't pay.

Nearby Communities. Several small communities are primarily bedroom communities for Melbourne and Palm Bay: **Malabar** (pop. 2,364), **Palm Shores** (pop. 578), and **West Melbourne** (pop. 9,171). The following are beach communities across the Indian River from Melbourne: **Melbourne Beach** (pop. 3,198), **Indialantic** (pop. 2,938), **Indian Harbour Beach** (pop. 7,579), and **Satellite Beach** (pop. 10,106).

Cocoa and Cocoa Beach

Cocoa (population 17,874) and Cocoa Beach (population 12,794), along with Titusville, profiled below, are the nearest towns to the Kennedy Space Center. As such they bear the greatest tourist crunch and have benefited and suffered the most as NASA has flourished and declined. Cocoa is on the mainland; Cocoa Beach, on the outer barrier island, is a typical Florida beach community with houses and apartments for residents and many motel accommodations for tourists.

Housing. Cocoa and Cocoa Beach are very diverse in terms of homes. Busy condo areas share the coast with quiet stretches of undeveloped beach property. Small cottages and mid-rise condominium complexes coexist in quiet harmony. Immaculate three-bedroom one-story homes in Cocoa are often available for less than $80,000. And waterfront pool homes sell for a fraction of the prices demanded in other areas. Inland, the bargains are even more stunning. A recent listing for a three-bedroom home included a detached two-car garage with a one-bedroom apartment above it and a barn, all on one acre of land, for an asking price of $119,000. A five-bedroom five-bath home with a heated pool and an acre of land was listed for $169,000. To spend much more, you have to be looking for loads of acreage or several thousand square feet of living space. For example, a three-bedroom three-bath home with nearly 4,000 square feet of living space, an in-ground pool, an oversize two-car garage with a utility bathroom, and a professionally landscaped, fenced yard was priced at $210,000. Property taxes in the Cocoa–Cocoa Beach area are about $20 per $1,000 nonexempt valuation.

Culture and Entertainment. As in the rest of Brevard County, the Brevard Cultural Alliance coordinates and promotes art and cultural agencies and activities in Cocoa and Cocoa Beach. A monthly newsletter, *ART-A-FACTS*, publicizes activities throughout the county. The Cocoa Village Playhouse, Brevard Community College's Experimental Theater, and the Surfside Playhouse provide live theater. The Brevard Museum of History and Natural Science in Cocoa presents local exhibits and touring shows.

Sports and Recreation. Four golf courses in the Cocoa area (as well as all the others in nearby Brevard County communities) provide year-round golf opportunities. Miles of beaches and several marinas provide access to every type of water sport.

Law Enforcement and Safety. In 1996 there were seventy-four criminal offenses reported per 1,000 year-round residents in Cocoa. In Cocoa Beach the rate was seventy-nine.

Senior Centers. Brevard Elderlearning, an affiliate of the Elderhostel Institute, is housed on the Brevard Community College campus in Cocoa. The Martin Anderson Senior Center in Rockledge schedules activities and programs for seniors.

Nearby Communities. **Rockledge** (pop. 18,434) is a very old Florida town just a few miles south of Cocoa on U.S. 1. **Merritt Island** (pop. about 38,603) is a burgeoning unincorporated community on a middle island with the Indian River on one side and another lagoon, the Banana River, on the other. **Cape Canaveral** (pop. 8,375) is north of Cocoa Beach on the outer barrier island and at the edge of the Kennedy Space Center. **Port St. John** (pop. about 16,649) is an unincorporated community north of Cocoa.

Titusville

Titusville (population 41,321) is the county seat of Brevard County. Located directly across the Indian River from the Kennedy Space Center, Titusville proudly calls itself "Space City, USA." Another city polishing up its downtown, Titusville is designated a Florida Main Street City. Downtown Titusville has a national historic district with twenty-seven buildings from the late 1800s and early 1900s listed on the National Register of Historic Places. An ongoing community study and development program, Transformation Titusville, is involving the community in planning for the future.

Housing. Titusville is a town that faces the challenge of the scaled-down space program, and for retirees that is one of the attractions of this area. The cutbacks resulted in the loss of jobs from the Titusville–Cape Canaveral area, and as population declined housing became very inexpensive. If you'd prefer a quieter town, just a bit removed from the beach life to the south, Titusville has a lot to offer. Three-bedroom pool homes can be found for less than $75,000. In a lovely golf community a Spanish-style two-bedroom two-bath home overlooking a fairway was recently on the market for $67,900. A nice in-town home with a one-bedroom guest house and in perfect condition was listed for $130,000. A new contemporary home might start at $100,000. For those who need living space and elbow room, a 3,000-square-foot country home on two acres of land with a barn, a pool, and a detached garage was listed for $129,000. Affordable real estate and the proximity to metropolitan Orlando are certainly factors that cause some retirees to choose Titusville. Property taxes in Titusville are about $20.80 per $1,000 nonexempt valuation.

Culture and Entertainment. Titusville shares in all of the art and cultural activities of its sister communities in Brevard County. The Brevard Symphony Orchestra and the Space Coast Philharmonic Orchestra perform in Titusville. All of the cultural and entertainment activities of Orlando are only an hour away.

Sports and Recreation. Titusville boasts four championship eighteen-hole golf courses and is home to the Canadian PGA. Fishing in the Atlantic, the Indian River, and the St. Johns River is popular here. The Canaveral National Seashore/Merritt Island National Wildlife Refuge is a 57,000-acre wilderness that protects more endangered species than any other refuge in the United States. One of the nation's most natural beaches, Playalinda Beach, is located here.

Law Enforcement and Safety. In 1996 there were sixty-seven criminal offenses reported per 1,000 year-round residents in Titusville.

Senior Centers. The North Brevard Senior Center provides social, recreational, and educational services to area seniors.

Nearby Communities. **Mims** (pop. about 9,400) is an unincorporated community 4 miles north of Titusville. **Scottsmoor** (pop. about 2,500) is another unincorporated community 7 miles north of Mims.

Addresses and Connections

Chambers of Commerce: Cocoa Beach Area Chamber of Commerce, 400 Fortenberry Road, Merritt Island, FL 32952; (407) 459–2200

Melbourne–Palm Bay Area Chamber of Commerce, 1005 East Strawbridge Avenue, Melbourne, FL 32901-4782; (407) 724–5400; Fax, (407) 725–2093; http://www.melpb-chamber.org; E-mail: mail@ melpb-chamber.org

Titusville Area Chamber of Commerce, 2000 South Washington Avenue, Titusville, FL 32780; (407) 267–3036

Newspapers: Brevard Senior Life (monthly), P.O. Box 541208; Merritt Island, FL 32953

The Orlando Sentinel (daily), 633 North Orange Avenue, Orlando, FL 32801; (800) 359–5353

VOLUSIA COUNTY: New Smyrna Beach, Daytona Beach, and Ormond Beach

While Volusia County (population 407,199) has an attractive inland side with cities such as De Land and Deltona, it is famous for its beaches and beach communities. New Smyrna Beach, Daytona Beach, and Ormond Beach are the best known. Volusia County's beaches are on a long, narrow barrier island separated from the mainland by the Halifax River. Very popular with retirees, 23 percent of Volusia County's population is age sixty-five or older.

Cost of Living. Volusia County ranks sixteenth in the state with a cost of living 97.30 percent of the state average. The sales tax is 6 percent. The cost of housing is 4.49 percent below the state average. The average purchase price of a home is $89,600. Volusia County ranks thirty-first in the state with an average monthly apartment rent of $517.

Climate. Volusia County's climate is moderated by its proximity to the Atlantic Ocean. The following figures are from the NOAA station in Daytona Beach.

Volusia County Weather

| | In degrees Fahrenheit | | | | |
	Jan.	Apr.	July	Oct.	Annual Rainfall
DAILY HIGHS	68.0	80.0	89.8	81.5	47.89"
DAILY LOWS	46.9	58.6	72.5	65.2	

Medical Care. Seven hospitals with 1,452 beds serve Volusia County.

Transportation. Volusia County Transit (VOTRAN) provides local bus service throughout East Volusia County. Daytona Beach International Airport provides limited service, and Orlando International Airport, about an hour away, provides excellent domestic and international jet service.

Opportunities for Continuing Education. Volusia County schools, the University of Central Florida, and Daytona Beach Community College with campuses in Daytona Beach, Palm Coast, New Smyrna Beach, and De Land provide adult and continuing-education programs.

New Smyrna Beach

New Smyrna Beach (population 18,239) is a small community with an interesting historic downtown on the mainland and a pleasant, residential beach side. While there are condominiums, rental apartments, private homes, and some motels on New Smyrna's beach, it seems to have been spared the blatant commercialism and tourist attractions of other beach communities. All in all, New Smyrna Beach will strike you as a very livable town with a wonderful beach and very pleasant weather.

Housing. Because it is still exceedingly affordable, you may not notice that housing in New Smyrna Beach is slightly more expensive than in other nearby towns. However, for the small additional amount you will spend on real estate, you get a lot in return. Appealing condominiums and single-family homes are everywhere in this friendly community with a small-town atmosphere. Just five minutes from the beach, a pleasant downtown bungalow with three bedrooms was recently listed for $47,000. A small, older two-bedroom one-bath home surrounded by a white picket fence included a garage with a separate one-bedroom apartment for $93,000. In the downtown historic district, a stately, restored 1890 Victorian home with six bedrooms, heart of pine floors, 11-foot ceilings and a two-bedroom cottage in the rear was for sale at $179,900. A unique four-bedroom three-bath executive home with a three-car garage was on the market for $139,900. Near downtown, condominium living provides a lot of carefree space for a reasonable price. For example, a two-bedroom condo with two and a half baths, wood floors, a new kitchen, and an attractive community pool area was for sale for $72,500.

At the beach, a two-bedroom two-bath condo with tiled floors and a new kitchen in a mid-rise building listed for $74,000. Even single-family homes at the beach are within reach of many retirees. For example, a beach duplex, each unit with two bedrooms, two baths, a separate garage, and a sprawling ocean-view deck was listed for $174,500. Property taxes in New Smyrna Beach are about $25.60 per $1,000 nonexempt valuation.

Culture and Entertainment. Primarily because of the Atlantic Center for the Arts, New Smyrna Beach has become known as an art community. An artist-in-residence facility, the center brings nationally and internationally known master artists from the visual arts, literature, music, and the performing arts to work with talented midcareer artists. Harris House, the Center's community education and outreach space, offers classes, seminars, gallery talks, and changing gallery shows. Programs, lectures, and concerts are scheduled at the center throughout the year. There are several commercial art galleries here. New Smyrna Beach was featured in John Villani's book *The 100 Best Small Art Towns in America.* The Little Theatre is a local community playhouse with a year-round schedule of performances. Residents of New Smyrna Beach take part in the cultural and entertainment offerings of nearby Daytona Beach and Orlando.

Sports and Recreation. There are more than thirty golf courses within a half hour of New Smyrna Beach. Tennis is available throughout the area. Fishing in the Indian River and the Atlantic Ocean is a major activity here, and fans of all water sports enjoy New Smyrna's miles of coastline and beaches.

Law Enforcement and Safety. In 1996 there were fifty-two criminal offenses reported per 1,000 year-round population in New Smyrna Beach.

Senior Centers. The Council on Aging in New Smyrna Beach provides information about senior centers and various services available in the area.

Nearby Communities. **Edgewater** (pop. 17,761) is immediately south of New Smyrna Beach on the Indian River and is very popular with retirees. **Oak Hill** (pop. 1,083) is about 12 miles south of New Smyrna Beach.

Daytona Beach

If all you know about Daytona Beach (population 63,796) is that it is home to an internationally acclaimed automobile speedway, an annual gathering of motorcyclists, a week of adolescent high jinks known as Spring Break, and a very touristy beach, you will be surprised to learn that there is also a very livable community here. The center part of the beach is mainly for tourists, with the requisite motels, fast-food shops, and T-shirt emporiums, but just a few blocks south or north you find quiet beach communities. The world-famous beach, wide and safe, is as attractive to residents as it is to tourists.

Housing. In this area, sprawling high-rise condominium buildings, large modern beach homes, and wonderful old homes coexist in surprising harmony. Properties for sale are plentiful, and vary dramatically in price. A bayshore condo with two bedrooms, two baths, and a wrap-around balcony with sunset views was available for $95,000. A large two-bedroom two-bath condo in a modern high-rise building listed for $115,000. And a two-bedroom two-bath condo in a luxurious, round high-rise with wonderful pie-shaped units, spectacular ocean and Halifax River views, and semiprivate elevator foyers was recently listed for $130,000. For much less money, simple but attractive two-bedroom condos in small buildings are plentiful for around $43,000. For absolute luxury in Daytona Beach, two-bedroom condos in new oceanfront buildings with every conceivable recreational amenity were priced at around $168,000. Property taxes in Daytona Beach are about $27.70 per $1,000 nonexempt valuation.

Culture and Entertainment. The Museum of Arts and Sciences is the primary museum and the major center for the visual arts in Daytona Beach. There is a fine permanent collection and changing exhibitions. The sciences are represented with a planetarium and a ninety-acre nature preserve with interpreted trails. The Harvey W. Lee Jr. Memorial Gallery, a component of the $22 million Mary McLeod Bethune Fine Arts Center on the campus of Bethune-Cookman College, exhibits works of local and nationally known artists. There is also a fine permanent collection of African art on display. The Art League of Daytona Beach, Inc., which features classes, monthly exhibitions, and several commercial art galleries, bring the visual arts to the community.

The performing arts are well represented in the Daytona Beach area.

The 2,560-seat Peabody Auditorium is host to touring dance companies, symphony orchestras, Broadway musicals, the Daytona Beach Symphony Society, the Civic Ballet of Volusia County, and the pride of Daytona Beach's cultural community, the Florida International Festival, which brings the London Symphony Orchestra to town every other summer for a brief season of performances. A variety of free concerts is scheduled at the Dayton Beach Bandshell, a unique oceanfront amphitheater built entirely of coquina, a rock made up of shells and coral. Daytona Beach Community College's 500-seat Theater Center presents student plays and events and is host to the Seaside Music Theater. This company of professional actors, directors, musicians, and technicians produces five musicals each summer. The Daytona Beach Playhouse is an all-volunteer community theater bringing live theater to the community year-round.

Sports and Recreation. Of course all of the water sports of any Atlantic Ocean community are popular in Daytona Beach. Walking, running, lying in the sun, and swimming make the beach the major outdoor scene here. More than thirty golf courses with great year-round play attract golfing retirees to the area. The Daytona International Speedway is truly a spectacular racing venue and the events hosted here are popular with visitors and residents alike.

Law Enforcement and Safety. In 1996 there were 120 criminal offenses reported per 1,000 year-round residents in Daytona Beach. This figure is particularly misleading in a community such as Daytona Beach, where tourists and sports events greatly inflate the population numbers.

Senior Centers. Two very active centers with activities and programs for seniors are operated by the City of Daytona Beach Leisure Services Department. Both the Schnebly Recreation Center and the City Island Recreation Hall and Senior Center offer complete schedules of courses and activities such as physical fitness, ballroom and country-western dancing, arts and crafts, choral singing, and tax assistance.

Nearby Communities. **Port Orange** (pop. 40,543) is one of the fastest-growing municipalities in the county. Located on the Halifax River immediately south of Daytona Beach, Port Orange boasts the lowest crime rate of any Florida city with a population between 25,000 and 50,000. **Daytona Beach Shores** (pop. 2,870) is a newer municipality, incorporated in 1967. Much of the housing here consists of high-rise condominiums, and many of the residents are winter-only.

Ormond Beach

Created in the 1870s by John D. Rockefeller, Henry Flagler, and a group of millionaire cronies who decided it was the best place in the world to spend winter, Ormond Beach (population 32,426) is still trying to live down the reputation of being only for the very rich. Today it is a beautiful, quiet (compared to bustling Daytona Beach a few miles south), and self-contained residential community that is very popular with retirees. Most of the city is on the mainland, but several miles of beautiful, natural beaches are also part of Ormond Beach.

Housing. Ormond Beach is another area where you will benefit from the sheer number of condos and homes on the market. In a small complex with a private beach and a community pool, a two-bedroom condo with a balcony and oversize garage was for sale at $84,900. A very private four-bedroom (two master suites) three-bath home with hardwood floors, situated on an oversize lot with views of the Intracoastal Waterway, was listed for $148,000. A newer two-bedroom villa in a golf community was for sale for $79,900. I also saw, for the same price, a furnished penthouse beach condo with an eat-in kitchen. In newer family neighborhoods you can find larger executive homes in the mid-$100,000 range. A three-bedroom three-bath home in a pastoral setting on a full acre of land was priced at $169,900. Property taxes in Ormond Beach are about $23.90 per $1,000 nonexempt valuation.

Culture and Entertainment. The Casements, Rockefeller's winter home, is now a cultural center and museum that hosts many community cultural events and the city's summer musical festival, Jazz Matazz. The Ormond Beach Performing Arts Center sponsors children's theater, community theater, and concerts. The Ormond Memorial Art Museum and Gardens features monthly exhibits of Florida artists, a permanent art collection, and a tropical garden.

Sports and Recreation. There are six golf courses in Ormond Beach and many more within an easy drive. Twenty-two tennis courts keep those athletes busy and happy. Fishing in the Halifax River and the Atlantic is popular with residents and visitors.

Law Enforcement and Safety. In 1996 there were forty-two criminal offenses reported per 1,000 year-round residents.

Senior Centers. The Ormond Beach Senior Center, operated by the Department of Leisure Services of the City of Ormond Beach, sponsors a variety of programs and activities for the area's seniors including day, weekend, and extended trips; visits to dinner theaters; physical fitness classes; bridge and poker games; self-defense; current-events lectures and discussions; several kinds of dance; and arts and crafts.

Addresses and Connections

Chambers of Commerce: Southeast Volusia Chamber of Commerce, 115 Canal Street, New Smyrna Beach, FL 32168; (800) 541–9621

Daytona Beach/Halifax Area Chamber of Commerce, P.O. Box 2475, Daytona Beach, FL 32115; (904) 255–0981

Ormond Beach Chamber of Commerce, 165 West Granada Boulevard, Ormond Beach, FL 32174; (904) 677–3454

Newspapers: The Observer (daily, Tuesday through Saturday), 823 South Dixie Highway, New Smyrna Beach, FL 32168; (904) 428–2441

Daytona Beach News-Journal (daily), 901 Sixth Street, Holly Hill, FL 32117; (904) 252–1511

Internet: http://www.daytonabeach-tourism.com

E-mail: DaytonaBea@aol.com

NORTHEAST FLORIDA

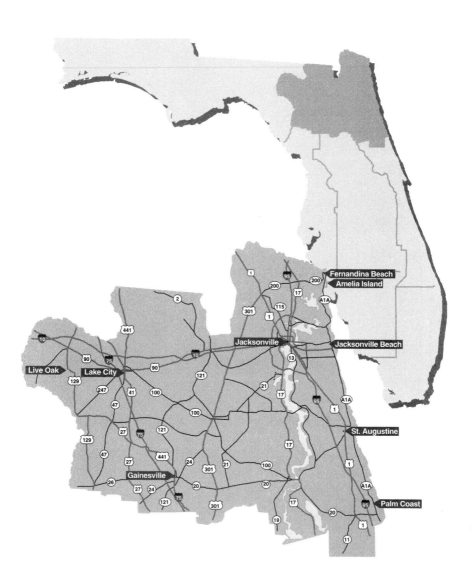

NORTHEAST FLORIDA

The Northeast Florida region stretches for more than 100 miles along the Atlantic coast, from Flagler County to the Georgia state line, and about 100 miles west to the Suwannee River. For many visitors coming from the northeast, it is the gateway to Florida and, indeed, Duval County calls its beach area the "First Coast," a play on words because in addition to being a major point of entry to Florida, Duval County claims the first European settlement in the United States, dating back to 1562. It is an area that tourists and snowbirds seeking winter warmth and tropical surroundings most often fly over or drive through on their way farther south. However, retirees looking for mild winters with a touch of four seasons and economical living have discovered the exciting gems along Florida's northeast Atlantic coast, the quiet charm of small rural communities near the Suwannee River, and the cultural joys of Gainesville.

No region in Florida is more diverse or more interesting. In a short drive you may go from the oldest city in the United States to a modern planned community with expansion and construction proposed well into the next century. You may go from busy, urban Jacksonville to sleepy Live Oak or historic Fernandina Beach. Go in any direction from Gainesville, where educators, scientists, and doctors work in laboratories discovering wonders of tomorrow, and you find yourself in author Marjorie Kinnan Rawlings' Cross Creek or Micanopy, where yesterday seems to linger patiently. The one thread common to all of this diversity is Florida's natural beauty—the Atlantic Ocean seen from a dune high above the beach on Amelia Island, the wide St. Johns River as it flows quietly through countryside or bustling city, the sparkling black waters of the Suwannee River reflecting festoons of Spanish moss, the vastness of Paynes Prairie with its mysterious sinkholes and lakes that, like Brigadoon, appear only to disappear again, and much, much more. And here, no matter where you choose to live, it is all within your reach!

From south to north along the Atlantic coast those counties and their cities most popular with retirees are Flagler County (Palm Coast), St. Johns County (St. Augustine), Duval County (Jacksonville and Jacksonville Beach), and Nassau County (Fernandina Beach and Amelia

Island). Inland counties and cities are Suwannee County (Live Oak), Columbia County (Lake City), and Alachua County (Gainesville).

When Grandkids Visit. Wherever you choose to retire in Florida, take the grandkids to historic St. Augustine. Founded in 1565 and recognized as the oldest city in the United States, all the old part of the city is like a museum. To mention just a few of the interesting attractions, there is *The Oldest House* (adults $5.00, seniors $4.50, students 6 to 18 $3.00), the *Oldest Wooden Schoolhouse* (adults $2.00, seniors $1.50, kids 6 to 12 $1.00), the *Old Jail* (adults $4.25, kids ages 6 to 12 $3.25), and *Castillo de San Marcos*, an intact Spanish fort built in 1672 ($2.00 per person). A good way to begin your visit is to view the free orientation film and pick up maps and brochures at the Visitor Information Center.

Jacksonville Beach has loads of fun things for kids of all ages, from miniature golf to water parks. You and the grandkids will also enjoy the *Mayport Ferry* that takes you and your automobile from the northern tip of Jacksonville Beach across the St. Johns River to Fort George Island. The fare is $2.50 each way for automobiles. Check at the Pass and Decal office to arrange a tour of the *Mayport Naval Station*, one of the largest naval facilities in the United States.

The western part of this region around Lake City, Live Oak, and Gainesville has very different activities for your visiting grandkids. The Suwannee River offers many opportunities to canoe or kayak, and the many springs that flow into the Suwannee provide swimming in cold, pure water as it bubbles up from deep underground caverns. One of the best-known in this area is *Itchetucknee Springs State Park* where numerous springs create a crystal clear river that runs for 3.5 miles before it flows into the Suwannee River. The park is popular for hiking, picnicking, swimming, snorkeling, canoeing, and tubing. At the northern entrance to the park the fee for tubing is $4.25 per person and the float time is about 3 hours.

Florida is known for its sink holes, places where an underground river or cave causes the land to cave in. Many round lakes throughout the central part of the state began as sink holes. One of the best places to show the grandkids a real sink hole is *Devil's Millhopper* in Gainesville. Here you can take 232 steps to the bottom of a 120-foot deep, 500-foot wide ancient sink hole. Small waterfalls and springs flow into the sink hole and out through underground streams. Admission is $2.00 per vehicle. The *Florida Museum of Natural History* on the campus of the

University of Florida in Gainesville provides an excellent free opportunity to view ancient fossils and other historical exhibits. Walt Disney World, SeaWorld, Universal Studios, and the Kennedy Space Center are between 2 and 3 hours from most locations in this region.

FLAGLER COUNTY: Palm Coast

While Flagler County (pop. 39,052) grew more than 200 percent between 1980 and 1992, making it the fastest-growing county in the country, it remains the least-populated of the counties on Florida's Atlantic coast. It is an area of small towns (no municipality is larger than 5,000 population) and large, heavily populated unincorporated areas. Its population density of sixty-nine people per square mile ranks it fortieth in the state. Why Flagler County has lagged behind the rest of Florida's east coast is a mystery, with the answer perhaps hidden somewhere in its history. It has all of the assets of its neighboring counties, including beautiful beaches, excellent high ground for building, and verdant wooded areas.

The county is increasingly attractive to retirees, and its percentage of residents over age sixty-five is ninth highest in the state. Flagler County (along with neighboring Putnam and St. Johns Counties) ranks thirty-first among all U.S. counties in the number of retirees moving in from other states.

Cost of Living. Flagler County ranks thirty-fifth in the state with a cost of living 94.53 percent of the state average. The sales tax is 7 percent. The cost of housing is 8.55 percent below the state average. The average purchase price of a house is about $86,900. Flagler County ranks fifty-sixth in the state with an average monthly apartment rent of $339.

Climate. The climate in Flagler County is similar to that of Volusia County, its neighbor to the south.

Daytona Beach–Flagler County Weather

	Jan.	In degrees Fahrenheit Apr.	July	Oct.	Annual Rainfall
DAILY HIGHS	68.0	80.0	89.8	81.5	47.89"
DAILY LOWS	46.9	58.6	72.5	65.2	

Medical Care. One hospital with eighty-one beds serves Flagler County. The county's residents have access to hospitals in St. Augustine, 23 miles north, or in Daytona Beach, 23 miles south.

Transportation. The nearest airports are Daytona Beach International and Orlando International, about an hour and a half away. There is no public bus service.

Opportunities for Continuing Education. Flagler County schools and Daytona Beach Community College's Palm Coast Campus provide adult and continuing education.

Palm Coast

Palm Coast, the largest community in Flagler County, is not a municipality but a planned development that has now reached the status of an unincorporated town. Begun in 1970 by the ITT Development Corporation on a 42,000-acre site between I–95 and the Intracoastal Waterway, Palm Coast now has about 35,000 residents. Since only about 10,000 of the 46,000 possible home sites have been used, there is potential for immense growth. While Palm Coast is extremely popular with retirees, it should be noted that it is not a retirement community. It is a community with mixed ages, and many of the residents are young families. The Palm Coast representative I recently spoke with reported that the average age in the development at this time is forty-seven. Neither is Palm Coast just a housing development. From the very beginning it was planned that there would business parks and sites for light industry. Except for the fact that it is better planned, Palm Coast today has most of the attributes of a typical Florida community.

Palm Coast is one of the most beautiful developments you will ever see. From the time you leave I–95 on Palm Coast's parkway, you feel you are in a very special place. Landscaping is near perfect with tasteful use of native plant materials. As much of the natural growth as possible has been maintained to give the feel of a Florida woodland, and 5,000 acres have been set aside as a natural area.

Housing. Palm Coast is still building, with home sites advertised for "as low as $20,000." New homes range in price from less than $100,000 to more than $1,000,000. The newest project is Hammock Dunes, a very upscale oceanfront development billed as "the last great oceanfront resort in Florida." Palm Coast is a development of condominiums, town homes, and many single-family homes. Single-family homes are available here for about the cost of a two-bedroom condo elsewhere. An attractive ten-year-old home with three bedrooms, three baths and a two-car garage was recently listed for $72,000. In the low $100,000 range there is a great supply of appealing newer homes. A four-bedroom golf course home with a two-car garage was priced at $129,900. And a three-bedroom two-bath home with a two-car garage and 2,149 square feet of living space was listed for $127,500. A large home with nearly 3,000 square feet of space including four bedrooms, three baths, a two-car garage, a living room, family room, den, and vaulted ceilings was listed for $154,900. An immense contemporary home with nearly 5,000 square feet of living space including four bedrooms, four and a half baths, and a heated in-ground swimming pool was for sale for $219,000. Property taxes in unincorporated Flagler County are about $15.40 per $1,000 nonexempt valuation.

Culture and Entertainment. The Flagler Auditorium brings some performing arts to the community, and the Palm Coast Little Theatre presents several plays each year. For other cultural activities residents go to nearby Ormond Beach, Daytona Beach, and St. Augustine.

Sports and Recreation. Palm Coast is built around five golf courses designed by such well-known golf figures as Jack Nicklaus, Gary Player, and Arnold Palmer. Palm Coast also boasts a sixteen-court tennis complex where the head pro is captain of the U.S. Davis Cup team. Palm Coast has its own private ocean beach club an easy walk over the Intracoastal Waterway. Other activities here relate to the county's 26 miles of beach with easy public access. Fishing is great from the 884-foot Flagler Beach Pier where the water is 25 feet deep.

Law Enforcement and Safety. In 1996 there were thirty-five criminal offenses reported per 1,000 year-round residents in unincorporated Flagler County. In Bunnell, the county seat, the rate was ninety-five.

Senior Centers. The Flagler County Council on Aging operates a senior center in Bunnell and a satellite center in Flagler Beach.

Nearby Communities. **Bunnell** (pop. 2,048) is about 5 miles inland on U.S. Highway 1. The largest municipality in Flagler County is **Flagler Beach** with a population of 4,225.

Addresses and Connections

Chamber of Commerce: Flagler County Chamber of Commerce, Star

Route 18N, Bunnell, FL 32110; (800) 881–1022

Newspapers: The St. Augustine Record (daily), P.O. Box 1630, St. Augustine, FL 32805; (904) 829–6586; Fax, (904) 829–6664

Daytona Beach News-Journal (daily), 901 Sixth Street, Holly Hill, FL 32117; (904) 252–1511

Other Resources: Palm Coast Information, (800) 458–2305

ST. JOHNS COUNTY: St. Augustine

St. Johns County (pop. 101,729) is the center of Florida's "History Coast." St. Augustine (pop. 12,149) is the largest city in the county, but there are 84,816 people scattered among small towns and unincorporated communities throughout the county. The county's eastern border is the Atlantic Ocean and the western border is the St. Johns River, 2 to 3 miles wide here. South of the St. Augustine Inlet the Matanzas River separates the barrier island from the mainland and serves as the Intracoastal Waterway. North of the Inlet it is the Tolomato River. With water on two sides plus the Intracoastal Waterway and several interior rivers and creeks, much of the county is on or near water. The three-county area of Flagler, Putnam, and St. Johns Counties recently ranked thirty-first among all U.S. counties in the number of retirees attracted from other states.

Cost of Living. St. Johns County ranks nineteenth in the state with a cost of living 97 percent of the state average. The sales tax is 6 percent. The cost of housing is 3.43 percent below the state average. The average purchase price of a home is about $91,600. St. Johns County ranks fifth in the state with an average monthly apartment rent of $720.

Climate. The January average low temperatures shown below indicate that St. Johns County is more of a four-season area than its neighbors farther south, but frost and freezing temperatures are still a rarity.

Daytona Beach–St. Johns County Weather

| | In degrees Fahrenheit | | | | |
	Jan.	Apr.	July	Oct.	Annual Rainfall
DAILY HIGHS	68.0	80.0	89.8	81.5	47.89"
DAILY LOWS	46.9	58.6	72.5	65.2	

Medical Care. One hospital with 230 beds serves the residents of St. Johns County.

Transportation. The nearest major airport is Jacksonville International Airport about 50 miles away. There is no public bus service.

Opportunities for Continuing Education. St. Johns County schools and the St. Augustine campus of St. Johns River Community College provide adult and continuing-education courses and activities.

St. Augustine

No matter where in Florida you choose to live, you should visit St. Augustine! In addition to having an interesting and exciting time, you will come to understand that U.S. history did not begin at Jamestown or Plymouth Rock, and you will appreciate your new state's heritage. Called a "time capsule of 500 years of American history," no city in the United States is more historic than St. Augustine. Whether it is the oldest house, occupied since the early 1600s; Castillo San Marcos, the fort begun in 1672; or the gorgeous, grand hotels built by Henry Flagler in the late nineteenth century, the city displays its history very well indeed! Behind the history, however, you will find a charming and very livable small city, one that deserves your consideration as a retirement destination.

Housing. Wait until you see what your real estate dollars can buy in extraordinary St. Augustine. Not only do you have to choose what kind of home you want, you have to decide in which century you want it to have been built. Unique, centuries-old homes are scattered throughout this amazing town. Affordable new condos and homes are abundant in every price range, and many nice three-bedroom homes in family neighborhoods are sold for less than $120,000, but it may well be the astounding supply of unique historic homes that will capture your imagination and your heart! Within walking distance of ancient St. George Street, a vintage five-bedroom home with hardwood floors and renovated kitchen and baths was priced at $139,900. A lovely, historic four-bedroom home with a private courtyard patio, a huge front porch, and a two-car garage with workshop was listed for $155,000. A four-bedroom three-bath Victorian with hardwood floors in a prime downtown location was listed for $199,000. If you're after recent history for the same price, a three-bedroom three-bath home on one acre of land in a gated community featured an in-ground pool with a separate bath house and oversize two-car garage. Just steps from the Fountain of Youth in downtown St. Augustine, I found a brand-new three-bedroom home designed with a 1930s look but with 1990s amenities for $93,450. Prices at St. Augustine Beach also seem reasonable. A three-bedroom two-bath condo with vaulted ceilings, ocean views, indoor parking, and access to a marina, health club, pool, and tennis courts was priced at $128,000. Property taxes in the city of St. Augustine are about $24.60 per $1,000 nonexempt valuation. They are far lower in unincorporated areas of the county.

Culture and Entertainment. The St. Augustine Art Center organizes art shows and displays its permanent collection. The Little Theater produces several plays annually. The official state play, *The Cross and the Sword*, is presented in an outdoor amphitheater for a couple of months each summer. For other cultural and entertainment activities, residents go to either Jacksonville or Daytona Beach, both about an hour away.

Sports and Recreation. With 43 miles of oceanfront, the two broad rivers that make up the Intracoastal Waterway, and the St. Augustine Inlet all at hand, St. Augustine is equipped for every imaginable kind of water sport. There are several golf courses in or near St. Augustine and the PGA tour headquarters is in nearby Ponte Vedra Beach, but the biggest news in golf in the United States this year is the opening of World Golf Village. It is part of the mammoth Saint Johns development, a $1.5 billion project underway on 6,300 acres about 5 miles north of St. Augustine. World Golf Village will ultimately include the World Golf Hall of Fame, a 300-seat IMAX theater, the International Golf Library and Resource Center, the super-posh 300-room World Golf Village Resort Hotel and Convention Center, a Mayo Clinic facility, an eighteen-hole championship golf course, and 5,630 residences. World Golf Village has its own web site (http://www.wgv.com), and is expected to draw one million visitors annually.

Law Enforcement and Safety. In 1996 there were 120 criminal offenses reported per 1,000 year-round residents in St. Augustine, where summer tourists greatly inflate the population. In unincorporated St. Johns County the rate was thirty-four.

Senior Centers. The Elder Helpline refers seniors to services and activities including home-delivered meals, congregate meals, transportation, and homemaker assistance.

Addresses and Connections

Chamber of Commerce: St. Augustine and St. Johns County Chamber of Commerce, 1 Riberia Street, St. Augustine, FL 32084; (904) 829–5681; Fax, (904) 829–6477; http://www.staug.com/biz/chamber/index.htm; E-mail: chamber@staug.com

Newspaper: The St. Augustine Record (daily), P.O. Box 1630, St. Augustine, FL 32805; (904) 829–6586; Fax, (904) 829–6664; E-mail: record@staugustine.com

DUVAL COUNTY: Jacksonville and Jacksonville Beach

Duval County (pop. 728,437) has a unique form of government. In 1967 the county and city consolidated, making Jacksonville's 774 square miles the largest city in the United States in terms of land mass. The city of Jacksonville (Duval County) now stretches more than 20 miles inland from the Atlantic Ocean. Since Jacksonville and Duval County are coterminous, further description and discussion are continued below.

Cost of Living. Duval County ranks twenty-sixth in the state with a cost of living 95.91 percent of the state average. The sales tax is 6 percent. The cost of housing is 6.67 percent below the state average. The average price of a home is $88,000. Duval County ranks sixteenth in the state with an average monthly apartment rent of $594.

Climate. Duval County is one of Florida's northernmost counties, and except for areas directly on the coast, frost and occasional freezes do occur in the coldest months.

Duval County Weather

| | In degrees Fahrenheit | | | | |
	Jan.	Apr.	July	Oct.	Annual Rainfall
DAILY HIGHS	64.2	79.1	91.4	80.2	51.32"
DAILY LOWS	40.5	54.9	71.9	59.3	

Medical Care. Eight hospitals with a total of 2,833 beds serve the residents of Duval County.

Transportation. The city bus system has fifty routes covering most neighborhoods. The Automated Skyway Express is a state-of-the-art people mover covering much of the downtown area. Jacksonville International Airport provides excellent international and domestic jet service.

Opportunities for Continuing Education. The four campuses of Florida Community College at Jacksonville offer the Golden Opportunities for Lifelong Development (GOLD) program designed to provide for the learning and development needs of those over age fifty-five. Duval County schools and the University of North Florida also serve the adult and continuing-education needs of Duval County's senior population.

Jacksonville and Jacksonville Beach

Although city and county governments have been consolidated, local municipalities still exist with a limited form of local government. Jacksonville (pop. 686,172) and Jacksonville Beach (pop. 20,086) are separate municipalities under the strong mayoral form of county/city government. For our purposes we will consider Jacksonville one big city with many neighborhoods and smaller municipalities.

Jacksonville claims to have been the site of the first European settlement in the United States, Fort Caroline, established by the French in 1562 on a bluff overlooking the St. Johns River 12 miles east of today's downtown Jacksonville. Fort Caroline was destroyed three years later by Pedro Menéndez de Avilés, the Spanish founder of St. Augustine. Some historians dispute this claim, citing a very short-lived Spanish colony established in Georgia in 1526. Jacksonville, however, is proud of its history and maintains several monuments to its interesting past.

Jacksonville seems surrounded by water. The wide St. Johns River makes big horseshoe turns as it goes through the city on its way to the ocean at Mayport. Several rivers and many bayous pour into the St. Johns along the way. More than 20 miles of the Intracoastal Waterway separate the mainland from Jacksonville's miles of oceanfront.

With huge Mayport Naval Station on the east and Jacksonville Naval Air Station to the south, there is a big military presence in Jacksonville. Approximately 4,000 Navy and other military personnel retire or exit the service each year in Jacksonville, and many choose to stay in the area. All of the city, particularly Jacksonville Beach and the Mayport area, is popular with military retirees; it is estimated that more than 50,000 live here. In recent years Duval County ranked fifty-second out of all U.S. counties in the number of retirees moving there from other states. There are more than fifty retirement communities in Duval County.

Jacksonville is a very well-organized and maintained city. Even the beach area, where you might expect a degree of tackiness, is neat, clean, and orderly. Highways and bridges are in good repair and you may go from one side of the huge city to the other in a few minutes. In *Money* magazine's 1995 "Top Places to Live" list Jacksonville ranked first in the midsize city category and third overall.

Housing. Housing in Jacksonville reflects the needs and purchasing power of a large, working middle class, but Jacksonville also has a broad range of home prices with many on the high end. It would be realistic to spend around $90,000 for a nice small home and more than a half million dollars for a unique, luxurious property in a prime location. An attractive three-bedroom home near downtown was priced at $149,900. In a nice, quiet neighborhood, a large two-story brick colonial-style home with five bedrooms, three and a half baths, two master suites, an island kitchen, and an in-ground spa was on the market at $244,900. Because the city's highways make suburban living a breeze, you may want to look into newer neighborhoods just a few minutes' drive from the downtown culture and business districts. In a convenient suburb a two-bedroom townhome with two and a half baths and a stone fireplace was for sale at $58,900. An upgraded, newer home with three bedrooms, two baths, 12-foot ceilings, skylights, a fireplace, and a two-car garage was listed for $128,900. A large executive home with three bedrooms, a double garage, and a custom-built in-ground pool, hot tub, and gazebo was priced at $154,900.

In Jacksonville Beach an oceanfront two-bedroom penthouse condo with 10-foot ceilings was listed at $199,900. Three blocks from the beach, a large three-bedroom three-bath home with decks and balconies taking advantage of Intracoastal Waterway views, was priced at $234,900. A more modestly priced Bermuda-style waterfront home for $165,000 had three bedrooms, two baths, a great room overlooking the Waterway, a two-car garage, and a dock with boat lift. Property taxes in Jacksonville range from $21.48 to $25.12 per $1,000 nonexempt valuation, depending on location.

Culture and Entertainment. I was surprised on my last visit to

Jacksonville to find what an art city it has become. The Crummer Museum of Art, the Jacksonville Museum of Contemporary Art, and the Alexander Brest Museum and Gallery at Jacksonville University have excellent permanent collections and regularly sponsor special shows and touring exhibits. A host of commercial galleries showcase works of local and nationally recognized artists. Florida Community College at Jacksonville has just completed a 135,000-square-foot arts complex and its Artist Series is a major contribution to the community's cultural calendar. The University of North Florida brings many cultural activities to the community. The Florida Theatre Performing Arts Center hosts more than 200 cultural events each year in a magnificently restored 1920s movie palace. The Jacksonville Symphony Orchestra performs each season at the city's new Robert E. Jacoby Symphony Hall in the Florida Times Union Center for the Performing Arts. In operation since 1919, Theater Jacksonville is the oldest continuously operating community theater in the United States. All in all, Jacksonville competes favorably with any city in Florida when it comes to the arts.

Sports and Recreation. Like most of Florida's coastal cities, much of the sports and recreational activities in Jacksonville relate to water. Freshwater fishing in the many lakes and streams and saltwater fishing from the beach, from piers like the 983-foot fishing pier in Jacksonville Beach, and from charter boats far out in the Atlantic are major sports activities here. Every type of boating, from canoes and kayaks to sailboats and power boats of all sizes, is popular. There are more than two dozen public boat ramps and docking facilities in Duval County and more than 25 miles of beaches. One of the favorite outings for locals is to the Kathryn Abby Hanna Park on the beach near the naval station. The 450-acre park has a 1½-mile beach, nature trails, freshwater lakes for fishing, a picnic area, and campsites. There are twenty-two golf courses in Duval County and too many tennis courts to count. Sports spectators can now watch professional football, hockey, and soccer as well as many golf and tennis tournaments in Jacksonville.

Law Enforcement and Safety. In 1996 there were eighty-six criminal offenses reported per 1,000 year-round residents in Jacksonville/Duval County. In the municipality of Jacksonville Beach the rate was eighty-seven.

Senior Centers. The Jacksonville Senior Services Program (JSSP) provides services to seniors over the age of sixty. JSSP operates twenty-six senior centers in the Jacksonville area providing social, recreational, and educational activities and programs.

Nearby Communities. **Atlantic Beach** (pop. 13,116) and **Neptune Beach** (pop. 7,503) are popular beach towns immediately north of Jacksonville Beach.

Addresses and Connections

Chambers of Commerce: Jacksonville Chamber of Commerce, 3 Independent Drive, Jacksonville, FL 32202; (904) 366–6600

Jacksonville Chamber of Commerce, Beach Office, 1101 Beach Boulevard, Jacksonville Beach, FL 32250; (904) 249–3868; Fax, (904) 241–7556

Newspapers and Magazines: The Florida Times Union (daily), P.O. Box 1949F, Jacksonville, FL 32231; (800) 553–0541; http://www.jacksonville.com

Jacksonville (monthly), 1032 Hendricks Avenue, Jacksonville, FL 32207; (800) 962–0214; Fax, (904) 396–0926; http://www.jacksonvillemag.com; E-mail: mail@jacksonvillemag.com

NASSAU COUNTY: Fernandina Beach and Amelia Island

Nassau County (pop. 51,097) is at the very northeast corner of Florida. When the first cross-Florida railway was built in the 1850s, Amelia Island was its eastern terminus and Cedar Key its western. Both towns flourished until after the Civil War when the railroad closed. Henry Flagler's railroad, which brought prosperity to most of Florida's east coast, bypassed eastern Nassau County, and both Fernandina Beach and Amelia Island languished. Years of little growth put Nassau County far behind other coastal counties in development, but far ahead in terms of historic and ecological preservation. The Victorian beauty of the area's civic, commercial, and residential buildings survived, and now fifty blocks of downtown Fernandina Beach are listed on the National Register of Historic Places. Even the local chamber of commerce is in the old train station. Because rapacious building booms passed the county by, miles of natural beaches, huge sand dunes, coastal hammocks, and saltwater marshes remain. Today, Nassau County is one of the most beautiful and unspoiled coastal spots in Florida.

Cost of Living. Nassau County ranks forty-fifth in the state with a cost of living 93.23 percent of the state average. The sales tax is 6 percent. The cost of housing is 8.93 percent below the state average. The average purchase price of a home is $87,000. Nassau County ranks eleventh in the state with an average monthly apartment rent of $632.

Climate. Nassau County is far enough north to have four seasons, but winters are almost always sunny and pleasant.

Jacksonville–Nassau County Weather

| | In degrees Fahrenheit | | | | |
	Jan.	Apr.	July	Oct.	Annual Rainfall
DAILY HIGHS	64.2	79.1	91.4	80.2	51.32"
DAILY LOWS	40.5	54.9	71.9	59.3	

Medical Care. One hospital with fifty-four beds serves Nassau County. All the medical services of Jacksonville are nearby.

Transportation. The nearest airport is Jacksonville International, 25 miles away. There is no public transportation system in the area.

Opportunities for Continuing Education. Nassau County schools and the Fernandina Beach Center of Florida Community College at Jacksonville provide adult and continuing-education programs and services.

Fernandina Beach and Amelia Island

Fernandina Beach (population 9,988) is on the north end of Amelia Island. The rest of the island is unincorporated. All of Amelia Island is of interest to tourists and more recently to retirees. This corner of Florida is quiet, and those who seek a serene and beautiful natural environment are ecstatic here. If nightlife and big city amenities are your thing, then you will find this part of Florida far too quiet. For history buffs, Amelia Island has a unique standing. It is the only place in the United States to have been under eight flags: French, Spanish, English, Patriots, Green Cross of Florida, Mexican, Confederate, and United States.

Housing. Single-family home prices in Fernandina Beach are very reasonable. I found a modest but attractive home from the 1950s that included four bedrooms, two baths, and a one-car garage for $79,900.

In a more upscale neighborhood, a four-bedroom two-bath home with a great room and an in-ground pool listed for $122,500. A new three-bedroom frame-and-stucco home on an ample lot with mature trees featured tile flooring, a two-car garage, a lawn sprinkler system, and a separate laundry room for $148,900. Prices of executive and luxury homes can go well above $300,000; however, I saw a 2,224-square-foot brick home with four bedrooms, two baths, a two-car garage, a laundry room, a separate workshop, and all appliances included located on a huge lot overlooking a golf course for $219,000. There are some impressive options at the beach too. Although its rooms were somewhat small, a beautiful new condominium offered a three-bedroom three-bath unit with a fireplace for $156,900.

Although island living in Florida usually translates into real estate prices out of the reach of most retirees, Amelia Island has some attractive properties at affordable prices. An appealing, small three-bedroom home with an in-ground pool was recently listed for $110,900. A handsome two-bedroom two-bath condominium in a lovely development with pools and tennis courts, overlooking the community golf course, was listed for $118,600. More typically priced was a circa 1880 restored Victorian home with pine floors and original stained-glass windows for $249,500. Another historic home featured four bedrooms, two baths, and five fireplaces with a beautiful fenced yard for $227,500. For period charm with up-to-date conveniences, a new Victorian-style home with a one-car garage, three covered porches, and hardwood floors, located just two blocks from the beach, was listed for $175,500. Property taxes in Fernandina Beach are $23.66 per $1,000 nonexempt valuation. In unincorporated Amelia Island the rate is about $17.

Culture and Entertainment. A couple of commercial art galleries and the Island Art Association Gallery bring the visual arts to the community. The performing arts are represented by the Amelia Community Theatre, the Fernandina Little Theatre, and the Amelia Fine Arts Series. All of the cultural and entertainment activities of Jacksonville are only forty minutes away.

Sports and Recreation. There are several golf courses and many tennis courts here. The twenty-seven-hole public golf course in Fernandina Beach is challenging. The Amelia Island Plantation's twenty-five excellent tennis courts are considered to be in the top fifty in the United States.

For most visitors and residents, however, fishing, boating, and all the other water sports are the most important activities. The 13 miles of scenic beaches provide ample space for walking, sunning, and swimming.

Law Enforcement and Safety. In 1996 there were sixty-eight criminal offenses reported per 1,000 year-round residents in Fernandina Beach. In unincorporated Nassau County, including Amelia Island, the rate was thirty-three.

Senior Centers. The Northeast Florida Area Agency on Aging provides information and referrals for seniors needing assistance. Senior centers are located in Fernandina Beach and on Amelia Island.

Addresses and Connections

Chamber of Commerce: Amelia Island–Fernandina Beach–Yulee Chamber of Commerce, 102 Centre Street, Fernandina Beach, FL 32034; (904) 261–3248

Newspapers: Newsleader (weekly), 511 Ash St., Fernandina Beach, FL 32034; (904) 261–3696

The Florida Times Union (daily), P.O. Box 1949F, Jacksonville, FL 32231; (800) 553–0541; http://www.jacksonville.com

SUWANNEE COUNTY: Live Oak

Nestled in an area where the Suwannee River makes great, looping horseshoe turns, Suwannee County (population 31,424) is bordered on three sides by one of the South's most beautiful and famous rivers. Although Stephen Foster never saw the Suwannee (or "Swanee," as he called it in his song "Old Folks At Home"), Florida has adopted the song as its state song and its composer as a native son. With its mysterious black water reflecting the sky and the ancient oaks and cypresses that hang over it, the Suwannee is one of the most magical rivers in this country. It twists and turns in huge loops, at times between high sandy bluffs and at other times through swampy prairies, across this section of Florida. *Suwannee River: Strange Green Land*, a wonderful book by Cecile Matschat, traces the river from the Okefenokee Swamp in Georgia to its delta in the Gulf of Mexico. Suwannee County is a rural area, heavily wooded where the land has not been cleared for farming, and the towns you find here are southern country towns.

Cost of Living. As you might expect in such a rural area, the cost of living in Suwannee County is low. The county ranks sixty-sixth in the state with a cost of living 90.57 percent of the state average. The sales tax is 7 percent. The cost of housing is 16.58 percent below the state average. The average purchase price of a house is about $70,700. Suwannee County ranks fifty-second in the state with an average monthly apartment rent of $370.

Climate. You will definitely find four seasons (or at least Florida's version of them) in this part of the state. Winter temperatures may be slightly lower than those below, provided by the NOAA station in Gainesville.

Gainesville–Suwannee County Weather

	In degrees Fahrenheit Jan.	Apr.	July	Oct.	Annual Rainfall
DAILY HIGHS	65.6	80.7	90.7	81.0	51.81"
DAILY LOWS	42.5	55.8	70.9	59.7	

Medical Care. There is one hospital with 30 beds in Suwannee County. Three nursing homes have a total of 281 beds. The nearest major hospital is the University of Florida's Shands Teaching Hospital in Gainesville some 50 miles away. Suwannee County is served by four helicopter ambulance services.

Transportation. The nearest airport is in Gainesville, about 65 miles away. The Suwannee Valley Transit Authority offers local and regional transportation, but this is an area where you really must have your own automobile to get around.

Opportunities for Continuing Education. Suwannee County public schools and nearby Lake City Community College provide adult and continuing education programs.

Live Oak

Live Oak, the county seat, is located squarely in the middle of Suwannee County. The town has a charming, old-fashioned feel about it, as though by living here you could turn the clock back to a simpler time. With a population of 6,465 and a total county population of 31,424 people spread across 688 square miles, you will never feel crowded in Live Oak. If you need bright lights and urban amenities, do not even stop here. However, if living a quiet life near or on the usually lazy, meandering Suwannee River is your cup of tea, you will think you've died and gone to heaven in Live Oak or almost anywhere in Suwannee County.

Housing. If you enjoy the outdoors, like to have some land separating you from neighbors, are happiest living in a quiet, small-town neighborhood, and enjoy a nice taste of all four seasons each year, then Live Oak may be just the place for you. Chances are with Suwannee County's housing costs at 83.4 percent of the state average, you'll live in a more comfortable and more affordable home here than in just about any other location in Florida. Housing here is truly inexpensive. The average house purchase price in Suwannee County is $70,652. In-town homes on large lots with mature trees and well-established landscaping (azaleas and camellias are huge and gorgeous here) may be found for around $120,000. Country homes with lots of acreage are easy to find and affordable. Even homes on the Suwannee River are within easy reach of almost all retirement budgets. Recently I noticed a listing for a newer 2,800-square-foot three-bedroom two-bath home with a two-car garage situated on a ten-acre lot for $139,600. It is fortunate that most of these are on high bluffs overlooking the river, because the Suwannee drains the vast Okefenokee Swamp and is prone to flooding. When I was there recently, the river had risen almost 30 feet, and large areas of its floodplain were underwater. In this part of old north Florida a nineteenth-century home with acres of land, several bedrooms and baths, marble foyers, and custom-built spiral staircases can be found for around $200,000. For those of us with more modest needs and lifestyles the options are extraordinary. This area offers comfortable to luxurious small-town living at sometimes ridiculously low costs. Property taxes in Live Oak are $23.66 per $1,000 of nonexempt valuation.

Culture and Entertainment. Suwannee and its surrounding counties are big on festivals and celebrations. The Suwannee River Jubilee is an annual celebration of gospel music. Several events are held each year at the Stephen Foster State Folk Culture Center in nearby White Springs. Included are the Florida Folk Festival, the annual Rural Folklife Days, a number of Elderhostel programs, and the annual Jeanie Auditions and Ball, where an outstanding Florida female vocalist is selected to receive a scholarship and reign as "Jeanie" (as in Foster's "Jeanie with the Light Brown Hair") for the coming year. The new Spirit of the Suwannee Music Park, just a few miles north of Live Oak, is host to country, western, bluegrass, and gospel music festivals. For more sophisticated cultural activities you must drive to Gainesville, 65 miles south on I–75, or to Jacksonville, 84 miles east on I–10. It has been taken for granted that there are movie theaters in other cities and towns profiled thus far and they have not been mentioned, but it should be noted there are none in Live Oak at this time.

Sports and Recreation. Hunting, fishing, camping, canoeing, swimming, and just about every other activity you can think of to do in the woods or on a river are popular in Live Oak. When you look at a map of the Suwannee River as it curves around Suwannee County, you realize how many springs surface to feed this great river. There are twelve on my map, in almost every direction from Live Oak. Every one of the springs has swimming and some have camping, canoeing, and other park activities.

Law Enforcement and Safety. In 1996 there were thirty-five crimes per 1,000 year-round residents reported in Live Oak. In the unincorporated area of the county the ratio was fifteen per 1,000 residents.

Senior Centers. The Suwannee County Senior Center provides a range of services for retirees in the area.

Nearby Communities. **Branford** (population 659) is 25 miles south of Live Oak near the confluence of the Santa Fe and Suwannee Rivers.

Addresses and Connections

Chamber of Commerce: Suwannee County Chamber of Commerce, P.O. Drawer C, Live Oak, FL 32060; (904) 362–3071; Fax, (904) 362–4758; E-mail: schamber@hankins.com

Newspapers: The Gainesville Sun (daily), 2700 Southwest Thirteenth Street, Gainesville, FL 32614–7147; (352) 374–5000

The Suwannee Democrat (semiweekly), P.O. Box 370, Live Oak, FL 32064; (904) 362–1734

COLUMBIA COUNTY: Lake City

Columbia County (population 52,565) is much like Suwannee County. The Suwannee River forms most of its western border and a great deal of the county's acreage is in the huge Osceola National Forest. Columbia County and its county seat, Lake City, have benefited from being at the junction of two major interstate highways: I–75, the major north-south interstate that runs from south Florida to the upper

Midwest, and I–10, the major east-west interstate that runs from Jacksonville to the west coast of the United States. The county's recreation areas are popular with visitors from all over the state. Both O'Leno State Park and Ichetucknee Springs State Park have swimming, camping, picnicking, fishing, and canoeing. The latter, with its mammoth springs, is one of the best-known locations in the state for snorkeling and for tubing down the crystal-clear, spring-fed Ichetucknee River.

Cost of Living. Columbia County ranks sixty-third in the state with a cost of living 90.86 percent of the state average. The sales tax is 6 percent in Columbia County. The cost of housing is 18.36 percent below the state average. The average purchase price of a house is $74,777. Columbia County ranks forty-fourth in the state with an average monthly apartment rent of $432.

Climate. Another four-season area away from the coast, Columbia County's climate is virtually the same as for neighboring Suwannee County.

Gainesville–Columbia County Weather

	Jan.	In degrees Fahrenheit Apr.	July	Oct.	Annual Rainfall
DAILY HIGHS	65.6	80.7	90.7	81.0	51.81"
DAILY LOWS	42.5	55.8	70.9	59.7	

Medical Care. Lake City is served by two hospitals with a total of 203 beds. A Veterans Administration medical center has 152 beds and a VA nursing home has 210 beds. The Shands Teaching Hospital of the University of Florida is in Gainesville 45 miles away.

Transportation. The nearest airports are in Gainesville and Jacksonville. There is no local bus service.

Opportunities for Continuing Education. Lake City Community College and Columbia County schools offer adult and continuing-education programs.

Lake City

Much of what has been said above about Live Oak and Suwannee County can be said of neighboring Columbia County and its county seat, Lake City. The major difference—and it is an obvious one—is that Lake City is nearly twice the size of Live Oak, and Columbia County has nearly

twice the population of Suwannee County. You feel this difference immediately. With 10,049 citizens, Lake City is obviously more of a town. Yet
just beyond the city limits, Columbia County has all of the rural charm of
its neighboring counties. Retirees who would like their country living a little closer to a bigger town may prefer Lake City to Live Oak.

Housing. With a similar cost of housing, Lake City shares many of the
economic advantages of Live Oak but in a slightly larger town. Single-
family homes for sale are plentiful and affordable. A ten-year-old three-
bedroom two-bath contemporary home offered 1,190 square feet of living space on a large lot in a family neighborhood for $59,900. In the
downtown area a very handsome 1937 frame home with three bedrooms, two baths, hardwood and terrazzo floors, and a fireplace was
priced at $93,000. A four-bedroom home with two and a half baths, tile
floors, and a two-car garage on nearly an acre of land was for sale for
$107,000. A beautiful four-bedroom three-bath home on a one-half-acre
lot, with a fenced yard, a two-car garage, and a separate workshop was
listed for $117,000. For a little more than $200,000 you can have one
of the largest homes in town. A four-bedroom home on four acres of land
with three and a half baths, a screened, in-ground pool, an oversize two-
car garage, tile and terrazzo floors, and a laundry room provided nearly
4,000 square feet of living space for $240,000. In Lake City condomini-
ums are a bit rare, but I did find a large town house with four bedrooms,
three full baths, an indoor laundry room, a utility room, all appliances
included, and a large community pool for $84,900. Property taxes in
Lake City are $23.73 per $1,000 nonexempt valuation.

Culture and Entertainment. Residents of Lake City participate in
the music and folk festivals listed above for Live Oak. Lake City also
has the Columbia Art Guild, the Community Concert and Lyceum
Series, the Performing Arts Center, an art gallery, and a movie theater
with six screens.

Sports and Recreation. In addition to all of the outdoor sports and
activities listed above for Live Oak, there are two semiprivate golf courses,
a skating rink, seven tennis courts, and a bowling alley in Lake City.

Law Enforcement and Safety. In 1996 the crime rate in Lake City was
151 per 1,000 residents. In unincorporated Columbia County the rate
was fifty-one per 1,000 residents.

Senior Centers. Columbia County Senior Services, Inc., funded by
the state of Florida, United Way of Suwannee Valley, Columbia County

Commissioners, the City of Lake City, and the town of Fort White, provides a variety of services to the senior population of the area including congregate meals, transportation, home delivered meals, education, recreation, health screening, telephone reassurance to the elderly who live alone, homemaker assistance, assistance with personal care, legal assistance, and support for caregivers of Alzheimer's patients.

Addresses and Connections

Chamber of Commerce: Lake City–Columbia County Chamber of Commerce, 106 South Marion Street, Lake City, FL 32025-4343; (904) 752–3690

Newspaper: Lake City Reporter (daily), P.O. Box 1709, Lake City, FL 32056; (904) 752–1293

ALACHUA COUNTY: Gainesville

Alachua County (population 202,140) is at the northern edge of central Florida's hill and lake country. It is a largely rural farming and timber area with one large city and many small towns and unincorporated communities. If it were not for the University of Florida and all the related services required by a major university, even Gainesville would be a small country town. The countryside is beautiful with many lakes and streams, extensive stands of tall pines, stately magnolia trees with their glossy green leaves and fragrant white flowers, and many huge old oak trees draped with gray Spanish moss. The best book written about this part of Florida is Marjorie Kinnan Rawlings' *Cross Creek.* It is the story of her life in the rural community between two lakes southeast of Gainesville. *The Yearling* or any of her other books will give you an excellent historical perspective.

Cost of Living. Alachua County ranks seventeenth in the state with a cost of living 97.04 percent of the state average. The sales tax is 6 percent. The cost of housing is 7.95 percent below the state average. The average sale price of a home is $85,360. Alachua County ranks fourteenth in the state with an average monthly apartment rent of $607.

Climate. Alachua County has a four-season climate. Winter evenings can be chilly and there will almost certainly be a few times each winter when the temperature drops below freezing. Days, however, are almost always sunny.

Alachua County Weather

| | In degrees Fahrenheit | | | | |
	Jan.	Apr.	July	Oct.	Annual Rainfall
DAILY HIGHS	65.6	80.7	90.7	81.0	51.81"
DAILY LOWS	42.5	55.8	70.9	59.7	

Medical Care. Three hospitals with 1,349 beds serve the residents of Alachua County. The Shands Hospital of the University of Florida is recognized as one of the finest teaching hospitals in the country.

Transportation. The Gainesville Regional Airport provides domestic jet service. The Regional Transit System provides bus service throughout the Gainesville area, but it is not countywide.

Opportunities for Continuing Education. Alachua County schools, the University of Florida, and particularly Santa Fe Community College with its strong commitment to community lifelong learning provide many programs and services for adults.

Gainesville

Gainesville (population 97,693) is first and foremost a college town. In this case it is the huge, sprawling, 40,000-student, 11,000-employee University of Florida. The university is the city's major industry, source of culture, and preoccupation. Gainesville is the pleasant city it is because of the university's cultural activities, academic focus, athletic events, and educated work force. You could say that Gainesville is a "one-factory town" and you would be right. Here, however, it is a factory that isn't going to close and move its production line elsewhere, and it is a factory whose main product is education and whose by-product for its community is culture. For some retirees, the downside of living in Gainesville will be the large number of young people, and indeed those who are bothered by youth should consider a community where retirees predominate. For many others, however, Gainesville will be more of a "fountain of youth." For the past several years Gainesville has ranked high on *Money* magazine's "Best Places to Live in the U.S." list, and in 1995 it was at the head of the list.

Housing. Housing in Gainesville reflects the diverse tastes and incomes of those who work for or attend the University of Florida. For less than $100,000 you can expect to find a three- or four-bedroom two-bath home without difficulty. There is not an abundance of condominium offerings, but Gainesville compensates with almost forty nearby subdivisions with town homes and single-family houses in every price range. And there are many small rural communities just a few minutes from Gainesville that offer peaceful, small-town living at even more affordable prices. When I was there last a custom-built four-bedroom four-bath home on seven acres featured a tin roof, oak floors, and a wraparound porch for $184,500. In town, a two-bedroom two-bath condo in a small building was priced at $40,000. A new three-bedroom two-bath home with double garage on a landscaped corner lot in a convenient subdivision was listed for $118,500. A four-bedroom three-bath contemporary Victorian home with 17-foot ceilings, hardwood floors, a huge front porch, and more than two acres of land was priced at $172,900. In a wooded hilly setting, a contemporary three-bedroom two-bath home was priced at $89,900. In a nearby community, a custom-designed craftsman-style lakefront home with two bedrooms, two baths, a two-car garage, and a wraparound porch was listed for $68,000. Property taxes in Gainesville are about $28.70 per $1,000 nonexempt valuation.

Culture and Entertainment. There is more culture and entertainment per capita in Gainesville than in any other city its size in Florida. The University of Florida, Santa Fe Community College, and the city of Gainesville have together assembled an outstanding array of venues and programs for an intelligent and discriminating community. For the performing arts the shining star is the university's 1,800-seat Performing Arts Center, which presents theater, dance, and orchestral concerts. Adjacent to the Performing Arts Center is the Samuel P. Harn Museum of Art, with galleries for a fine permanent collection, shows of faculty and student work, and touring exhibitions. The Harn also presents a film series, lectures, and seminars. The Hippodrome State Theater, housed in an elegant neoclassical former post office building in downtown Gainesville, is one of four state-supported theaters in Florida. It brings a continuous series of plays, many with nationally known artists, to the community. The Hippodrome has a second theater for films and an art gallery featuring the work of local artists. Other performing arts groups in Gainesville include the Gainesville

Civic Chorus, Gainesville Ballet, Danscompany, the Gainesville Symphony, and the Gainesville Friends of Jazz. Live theater is represented by the Gainesville Community Playhouse, Santa Fe Players, Across-town Repertory Theatre, and the University's excellent Florida Players. In addition to the Harn Museum of Art, the visual arts are presented at the University Gallery, the Santa Fe Gallery at Santa Fe Community College, and the Center for Modern Art.

Sports and Recreation. Mention sports in Gainesville and you will immediately be told about the Florida "Gators," the University's nationally ranked football team. Throughout much of the year the team's progress is a major topic of conversation here. But for exercise and sports participation Gainesville isn't lacking. There are seven golf courses and numerous tennis courts. Freshwater fishing in the many lakes and streams is excellent and, of course, both the Gulf of Mexico and the Atlantic Ocean are only an hour away. For diving, snorkeling, swimming, canoeing, and tubing there are five springs nearby. The Hawthorne Trail, another part of Florida's Rails-to-Trails program, encourages biking, walking, skating, or horseback riding. Its 17-mile length passes through two fascinating natural sites: the 19,000-acre Paynes Prairie State Preserve and the Lochloosa Wildlife Management Area. Because of its 60 miles of roadways with on-street bicycle lanes or paved shoulders, Gainesville has been ranked among the top ten bicycling communities in the United States by *Bicycling* magazine.

Law Enforcement and Safety. In 1996 there were 102 criminal offenses reported per 1,000 year-round residents in Gainesville. In unincorporated Alachua County the rate was seventy-seven.

Senior Centers. The Mid-Florida Area Agency on Aging is headquartered in Gainesville. The Elder Helpline for Alachua County provides information and referral to services available in the county including congregate meals, home delivered meals, homemaker assistance, transportation, and educational programs.

Nearby Communities. Gainesville is ringed with smaller towns that have been very popular with all of Gainesville's residents, including retirees. Most offer small-town living close to a major cultural center. **Micanopy** (pop. 645) is a charming, historic town about 10 miles south of Gainesville. Micanopy gives you the feeling it hasn't changed in a hundred years. **Alachua** (pop. 5,882), about 10 miles northwest of

Gainesville, is the second largest municipality in Alachua County. **Newberry** (pop. 2,289) is about 15 miles west of Gainesville. **Hawthorne** (pop. 1,381) is about 15 miles east of Gainesville and is near Rawlings's beloved Cross Creek.

Addresses and Connections

Chamber of Commerce: The Gainesville Area Chamber of Commerce, 300 East University Avenue, Gainesville, FL 32602-1187; (352) 334–7100; Fax, (352) 334–7141

Newspaper: The Gainesville Sun (daily), 2700 Southwest Thirteenth Street, Gainesville, FL 32614-7147; (352) 374–5000

Internet: http://www.afn.org

CENTRAL FLORIDA

Central Florida is very different from the Florida most people know. There are no lagoons, no barrier islands with inviting beaches, and no vast ocean or gulf. Instead, there are broad vistas of hills, forests, rivers, and lakes. Except for stretches of level ranch land in the southernmost part, central Florida is made up of gentle hills. Much of it is heavily wooded, and thousands of acres of these woodlands are protected in national and state forests containing recreation areas for swimming, hiking, camping, fishing, and hunting. There are springs, rivers, and thousands of lakes of all sizes. Many of these lakes are connected by creeks or canals to become chains of lakes, and some connect with rivers leading ultimately to the Atlantic Ocean or the Gulf of Mexico. Several of the towns we will visit have developed around clusters of lakes.

Other than Orlando, the towns of central Florida are not well known by the hundreds of thousands of tourists who visit the state every year. They have, however, been discovered by retirees who are settling by droves into small and midsize towns and into the many new retirement communities. In addition to lovely terrain and a near-perfect climate, this area's major asset is land so plentiful that even a new community of modestly priced manufactured homes may include an eighteen-hole golf course among its amenities. All of the counties we will visit in this region rank high among U.S. counties in attracting retirees from other states.

Even though no part of this region is more than an hour or so from the coast, retirees I interviewed here seem happy to have traded the open waters of the Gulf and the Atlantic for lovely lakes and springs, and the faster lifestyle of the coastal areas for a slower pace in smaller towns. Over and over, when I asked retirees why they had chosen a town like Mount Dora or Winter Haven as their retirement destination, I was told that it was more peaceful and less crowded than other parts of Florida. Some said that the hills and woodlands reminded them more of their former homes than Florida's coasts and beaches did. Talking with these retirees after meeting so many who love the coasts and couldn't imagine living inland always reminds me how varied the tastes of America's

CENTRAL FLORIDA

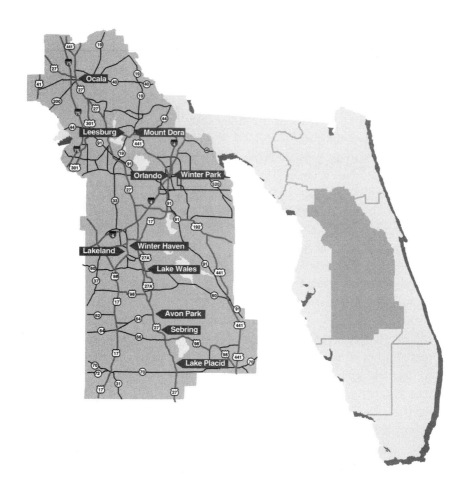

retirees are and how fortunate Florida is to offer an environment and a lifestyle for just about everyone.

The Central Florida Region includes from north to south the following counties and their cities and towns most popular with retirees: Marion County (Ocala), Lake County (Leesburg and Mount Dora), Orange County (Orlando and Winter Park), Polk County (Lakeland, Winter Haven, and Lake Wales), and Highlands County (Avon Park, Sebring, and Lake Placid).

When Grandkids Visit. *Silver Springs* in Ocala is an attraction well worth a visit. The main attraction is Florida's largest spring itself gushing 550 million gallons of water daily. There are glass bottom boat rides, an alligator habitat, a jeep safari, a petting zoo, a reptile institute, a jungle cruise, and, of course, swimming in the spring. Admission to the park and all the attractions is $29.95 for adults and $20.95 for kids ages 3 to 10. *The Ocala National Forest* is a 383,220-acre forest preserve with numerous springs and campgrounds. One of the best is Juniper Springs with facilities for camping, swimming, and canoeing down the 12-mile long river flowing from the spring.

It's stating the obvious to say that a book could be written about the theme parks in the Orlando area alone, since several have been. Chances are your grandkids will arrive knowing exactly what they want to see and do in these parks. *Walt Disney World* seems to grow daily with new attractions. As of now you can visit the Magic Kingdom, Epcot, MGM Studios, and Disney's newest park, Animal Kingdom. Single-day admission prices for each of the Disney parks are $42 for adults and $34 for kids ages 3 to 9. Several packages combine entry to multiple parks for two or more days. *SeaWorld* also continues to add new attractions beyond its famous performing killer whales. It is a beautiful and refreshing park with many entertaining and educational features. Single-day admissions to the entire park, including all shows and attractions, are $42 for adults and $34 for kids ages 3 to 9. *Universal Studios* offers one admission price for the entire park with a variety of rides and shows. The price for adults is $42, and for kids ages 3 to 9, $34. Different combinations allow entrance to more than one of the parks. A convenient web site with information about all of them is www.insidecentralflorida.com

If, after Orlando's theme parks, you are ready for something free and fun, take the grandkids to *Spook Hill* in Lake Wales to experience the eeriest optical illusion you may ever encounter. Once you've located

Spook Hill, follow the instructions on a sign and your car will appear to roll back up hill. It is on most maps of Lake Wales, but anyone there can tell you how to get to Spook Hill. The *Kennedy Space Center* is 1 to 2 hours from most locations in this region.

MARION COUNTY: Ocala

Low hills, abundant land, and a good climate have made Marion County (population 229,260) the thoroughbred-horse capital of Florida. Several horse farms in the area have become famous as the homes of Kentucky Derby winners, and raising and training thoroughbreds is a billion-dollar business here. The well-cared-for green fields of the more than 1,200 horse farms (with an estimated 20,000 horses) are visible from almost every road and highway in the county. Another attraction popular with tourists is Silver Springs. One of the largest natural springs in the world, more than 550 million gallons of pure cold water gushes from it daily. The park is now a 350-acre commercial attraction. Marion County boasts 430,000 acres of national forests and more than 200 spring-fed lakes and rivers.

Juniper Springs, Rainbow Springs, and several other springs have been developed into popular recreation sites. Their crystal-clear depths and underwater caves lure divers and snorkelers. People come from all over the state to canoe or float on large inner tubes down the rivers that flow from these springs through natural woodlands. The 450,000-acre Ocala National Forest with its springs, rivers, and woodlands attracts more than two million visitors each year to its campgrounds, hiking and riding trails, swimming areas, and hunting and fishing preserves.

Recently Marion County ranked twenty-third among all U.S. counties in attracting retirees from other states. Almost 25 percent of Marion County's population is sixty-five or older, and it is expected that the percentage will continue to increase in the coming decade. The developer of The Villages, a huge retirement community near Leesburg in Lake County, has announced plans to begin a similar development with 5,000 homes in Marion County. The Del Webb Corporation has purchased two retirement communities near Ocala and has announced plans for expanding them.

Cost of Living. Marion County ranks forty-ninth in the state with a cost of living 92.56 percent of the state average. The sales tax is 6 percent. The cost of housing is 14.05 percent below the state average. The average purchase price of a house is about $76,700. Marion County ranks twenty-sixth in the state with an average monthly apartment rent of $544.

Climate. You will find the climate a little cooler in winter and warmer in summer in this region than along the coasts. The following figures are from the NOAA station in Gainesville.

Marion County Weather

	In degrees Fahrenheit				
	Jan.	Apr.	July	Oct.	Annual Rainfall
DAILY HIGHS	65.6	80.7	90.7	81.0	51.81"
DAILY LOWS	42.5	55.8	70.9	59.7	

Medical Care. Two hospitals with 553 beds serve the residents of Marion County.

Transportation. The newest airports with jet service are Gainesville Regional, about 40 miles away, and Tampa International, about 90 miles away. There is no public transportation in Marion County.

Opportunities for Continuing Education. Marion County schools and Central Florida Community College offer adult and continuing-education programs and activities.

Ocala

Ocala (population 43,332) is the center of a largely agricultural area, and it retains all the charm of a small town right down to its town square and domed Victorian bandshell. It benefits culturally from its proximity to Gainesville and from the wealth of its "farmers." While there are many traditional, small farms in the area, the major farms here are horse farms whose products bring in a considerable amount of money and where one Kentucky Derby winner is worth many millions. The surrounding countryside with its many hills and lakes has become one of the most popular areas in the state for the development of retirement communities.

Housing. Real estate in Ocala is a good value, and there are many choices in low, middle, and higher priced homes. Single-family homes in nice neighborhoods are listed frequently for less than $50,000. A newer, three-bedroom one-bath ranch house with an attached one-car garage in a beautiful setting recently listed for $49,900. For the same price a charming lakeside condominium in a golf community offered two bedrooms, two baths, and all furnishings. Among the growing number of restored homes in Ocala's historic district, a recent listing offered a living room with stone fireplace, three bedrooms, two baths, and original hardwood floors for $74,900. Many homes are available in the low $100,000 range. A three-bedroom home with a stone chimney, cathedral ceilings, an in-ground pool, a pole barn, and five acres of land was listed for $109,000. A beautifully landscaped, three-bedroom pool home with new carpet, a great room with fireplace, an oversize double garage, and a split bedroom plan was for sale at $120,000. Even larger homes are still very affordable in Ocala. For example, a four-bedroom three-bath newer home on one acre with a 40-foot pool, two waterfalls, and a two-car garage with an apartment was priced at just $147,900. To spend more in the Ocala area, you're probably looking at homes with considerable acreage or prime riverfront locations. A four-bedroom home on a one-acre lot overlooking a park in Ocala's historic district offered hardwood floors throughout, a brick-enclosed pool and hot tub area, screened porches, balconies, a two-car garage, and a workshop for $239,000. Property taxes in Ocala are about $23.30 per $1,000 nonexempt valuation.

Culture and Entertainment. The Appleton Museum of Art houses a permanent collection of European, pre-Columbian, African, and Asian art in a beautiful, contemporary $8.5 million building set amid thirty-four wooded acres just outside Ocala. Special shows and touring exhibitions are scheduled throughout the year. The Museum was a gift to Central Florida Community College and Florida State University from the Appleton family, owners of a 900-acre horse farm nearby. Next door to the Appleton is the Ocala Civic Theatre. All of the cultural and entertainment activities in Gainesville are about forty minutes away.

Sports and Recreation. Ocala has its share of golf courses. Sixteen are currently listed in Ocala or nearby communities. The major focus of recreation in this area, however, relates to all of the possibilities offered by the mammoth Ocala National Forest, Rainbow Springs State Park, and the many lakes, springs, and rivers that run through the nearby forests. There are forests for hunting, lakes and rivers for fishing, springs for swimming, diving, and snorkeling, and clear spring-fed rivers for tubing and canoeing. Many of the parks have campgrounds. For sports spectators, Ocala Jai Alai is open from May 30 through August 30. The athletic teams of the University of Florida in nearby Gainesville have an enthusiastic following in Ocala.

Law Enforcement and Safety. In 1996 there were 139 criminal offenses per 1,000 year-round residents in Ocala. The rate was thirty-five per 1,000 in unincorporated Marion County.

Senior Centers. Marion County Senior Services, a private nonprofit corporation funded through several state, county, and local sources, coordinates activities and services for seniors in the area. The group publishes the *Senior Times*, which features activities of seniors, promotes volunteerism, and informs seniors of programs and activities. Classes and social activities are held at the multipurpose senior center.

Nearby Communities. **Dunellon** (pop. 1,785) is on the southwestern corner of Marion County. It is the nearest town to Rainbow Springs State Park and the beautiful Rainbow River. The area between Dunellon and Ocala is home to several age fifty-five and over communities.

Addresses and Connections

Chamber of Commerce: Ocala-Marion County Chamber of Commerce, 110 East Silver Springs Boulevard, Ocala, FL 34470; (352) 629–8051

Newspaper: Star Banner (daily), P.O. Box 490, Ocala, FL 34478; (352) 867–4010; Fax, (352) 867–4018

LAKE COUNTY: Leesburg and Mount Dora

Lake County (population 182,309) is aptly named. The county boasts more than 1,400 named lakes with 350 miles of shoreline. Lake County also claims the most diverse terrain in the state, with altitudes ranging from 53 feet to 192 feet above sea level. It is a county that prides itself on its attractive small towns. In addition to appealing communities, a wonderful climate, and lovely views of lakes and hills, the two most important reasons retirees come to Lake County are fishing and golf. Because of its many lakes, rivers, creeks, and marshes, this area is one of the nation's premier freshwater fishing spots, and the county's nineteen golf courses with all levels of difficulty offer great year-round play. In recent years Lake County ranked twenty-second among all U.S. counties in attracting retirees from other states. With so many new and rapidly growing retirement communities, Lake County is moving higher on the list.

Several factors have fueled the growth of Lake County's retiree population. Every year more retirees are considering Florida as a destination, and more of these retirees are forgoing the coastal areas for the more peaceful life of central Florida. Many retirees choose to retire in an area they have visited as tourists, and for many years that meant primarily Florida's beach cities and towns. The growth of Orlando as a premier tourist destination has introduced many potential retirees to the beauty of the "other" Florida.

The shift away from citrus production to housing development has been an important factor, and Lake County is an excellent example. Located on the northern edge of Florida's inland citrus belt, it has been the area most affected by a few disastrous freezes in the late 1980s. It isn't that this part of Florida has unpleasant winters, it is just that it takes only a few hours of just-below-freezing temperatures in the middle of the night to destroy an orange grove. Those weather conditions, coupled with a demand for land for housing, caused a great many grove owners to sell or develop their land for housing and move their grove businesses farther south. Since citrus trees grow best on high, well-drained land, and areas around lakes and on hillsides are always the least prone to freezes, orange and grapefruit groves have long occupied some of the most attractive acreage in Florida. When frozen groves were not replanted, acres of prime real estate were freed for development. The area around Clermont in south Lake County, where groves were once so abundant that a tourist attraction there is named the Citrus Tower, is now one of the fastest growing retirement areas in the state.

Cost of Living. Lake County ranks twenty-ninth in the state with a cost of living 95.45 percent of the state average. The sales tax is 7 percent. The cost of housing is 5.58 percent below the state average. The average purchase price of a house is $90,250. Lake County ranks forty-second in the state with an average monthly apartment rent of $438.

Climate. Without the moderating effects of the Gulf of Mexico or the Atlantic Ocean, Lake county has four seasons. Winters are sunny, however, and the lakes help keep summer pleasant.

Orlando–Lake County Weather

	In degrees Fahrenheit				
	Jan.	Apr.	July	Oct.	Annual Rainfall
DAILY HIGHS	70.8	83.0	91.5	84.6	48.11"
DAILY LOWS	48.6	59.4.	73.1	65.8	

Medical Care. Three hospitals with a total of 544 beds meet the needs of Lake County residents.

Transportation. Orlando International Airport, less than an hour away from most points in Lake County, is the nearest major airport with domestic and international jet service. There is no local bus transportation.

Opportunities for Continuing Education. Lake-Sumter Community College near Leesburg and Lake County schools provide adult and continuing-education programs.

Leesburg

Leesburg is an appealing small town located on high ground between two of the area's largest and prettiest lakes. With a population of 15,352, it is the largest municipality in Lake County, but with many unincorporated communities nearby, the population it serves has been estimated at closer to 50,000. Leesburg was first settled in 1857 and has taken excellent care of its historic heritage. Picturesque buildings from Leesburg's main building booms (the 1870s, 1920s, and 1950s) have been maintained and are still in use. With an ongoing rehabilitation of its historic downtown area, it was designated a Florida Main Street City in 1994. Retirees who have moved here comment on the friendliness of the people.

Housing. You can be very particular about the kind of home and amenities you'd like to look for in Leesburg. Here you may be tempted to go all out for a large, custom-built home. For example, I recently looked at a very unique home. The open floor plan had three bedrooms, three baths, an eat-in kitchen with a separate pantry, a master bath with an adjoining spa and gym, numerous skylights, a central vacuum system, an attached two-car garage with an air-conditioned workshop, and a second detached two-car garage. It was designed with state-of-the-art energy efficiency on a four-acre, professionally landscaped lot. This gem listed for $209,500. At the other end of the scale was a two-bedroom two-bath condo with 1,134 square feet of living space and a nice community pool for $35,000. A two-bedroom townhouse with two and a half baths in a gated community listed for $60,950. This area seems to have a number of unusual properties. I noted several listings with multiple dwellings, such as two small houses on six acres of land with a small pond and a separate workshop priced at $94,900. Property taxes in Leesburg are about $20.25 per $1,000 nonexempt valuation.

Culture and Entertainment. The Melon Patch Players in Leesburg and the Bay Street Players in Eustis bring live theater to the area. The Great American Music Hall, located 7 miles away in Weirsdale, produces shows throughout the year and is host to touring shows. Lake-Sumter Community College presents plays, lectures, and art shows, and there are festivals year-round in one or another of the small towns in Lake County. For other cultural and entertainment activities residents of Leesburg go to Mount Dora, 20 miles away, and to Orlando, less than 50 miles away.

Sports and Recreation. Fishing in the many lakes and streams, canoeing through the chain of lakes, and swimming and diving in the springs are major sports activities here. Golfing year-round at any one of the more than twenty courses in the area keeps many retirees active and happy. There are miles of hiking and biking trails. Venetian Gardens, on the shore of Lake Harris, is a hundred-acre public park with boat ramps, a beach, baseball fields, tennis and shuffleboard courts, a cultural center, and a swimming pool open in summer.

Law Enforcement and Safety. In 1996 there were eighty-eight criminal offenses reported per 1,000 year-round residents of Leesburg. In unincorporated Lake County the rate was thirty-six per 1,000.

Senior Centers. The Leesburg Senior Center is an independent center with support from the local United Way and from donations. The work is carried on by a largely volunteer staff. The center offers educational, social, and recreational activities.

Nearby Communities. **Lady Lake**, 7 miles north of Leesburg, is one of the fastest-growing communities in the state. With a population of only 1,200 a decade ago, it has now reached 12,287. Most of the growth is attributable to the success of a huge development known as The Villages, a 10,000-acre retirement community of site-built homes that spreads out into Lake, Marion, and Sumter Counties. Typical of the new, self-contained "golf-cart communities" being developed for retirees in Florida, The Villages' selling point is "hometown living in Florida's friendliest hometown." The Villages entices prospective retirees with its nine golf courses, nine pools, eighteen tennis courts, two bowling alleys, fourteen shuffleboard courts, twenty-two bocci ball courts, 6 miles of nature trails, and two polo fields. Recreational activities advertised in The Villages' flyer include tennis, softball, horseshoes, water volleyball, shuffleboard, dance clubs and classes, table tennis, bingo, bridge, canasta, Scrabble, mah-jongg, pinochle, a photography club, chess, whist, a singles club, water aerobics, cribbage, and a computer club. More than 200 activities per week are scheduled through the community's recreation department. With 1,000 homes being sold annually, the population of The Villages is expected to top 70,000 in a few years.

Mount Dora

Mount Dora (population 8,483) is the Sara Lee of Florida towns—nobody doesn't like Mount Dora. It seems to be everyone's favorite small town. Wherever I go in Florida, people know Mount Dora, and even those who have no desire to live in central Florida or in a small town love to visit Mount Dora. The reason is that it is in every respect one of the prettiest little towns you will ever see. It sits on a high bluff overlooking Lake Dora, and there are wonderful views from almost every part of the town. Huge old oak trees shade narrow streets lined with turn-of-the-century shops and some of the most beautifully restored Victorian homes in the country. Mount Dora will remind you more of a little New England town than a community only thirty minutes from bustling, modern Orlando. Even the chamber of commerce is in a renovated 1913 railroad depot. However, it isn't just the charm of the town that brings people to Mount Dora. The downtown area is a thriving community center with antique shops, art galleries, craft shops, cafes, and restaurants.

Housing. Like Ocala, Mount Dora offers an array of interesting new and historic homes at affordable prices, but here there is an arty twist to much of the real estate. I fell in love with a three-bedroom home on a hilltop corner lot overlooking the lake, with an in-ground pool, a two-car garage with a workshop, a two-car carport, and mature professional landscaping, on the market at $129,990. A similarly appealing but smaller nearby home without the lake view was priced at $96,900. A modest but comfortable three-bedroom pool home in a neighborhood of new construction was for sale for $103,500. Mount Dora also has many charming old bungalows in the downtown area. One, in a great location but needing a bit of renovation, was listed for $35,900. Nearby, a two-bedroom bungalow in perfect condition was listed for $39,000. For the ardent golfer, a three-bedroom three-bath executive pool home on a corner lot in a golf community listed for $150,000. Renovated bungalows, some with commercial zoning suitable for mixed use as a home/gallery, are scattered throughout the town. On the higher end, you can expect a unique home for a fair price in Mount Dora. For $201,000 you could buy a large home with a private interior courtyard garden, all-wood flooring, three bedrooms, including a master suite with a bath and a private garden spa, and a living room with vaulted ceilings and a fireplace. Property taxes in Mount Dora are about $22.60 per $1,000 of nonexempt valuation.

Culture and Entertainment. Mount Dora prides itself on its reputation as an art community, and its annual art festival attracts more than 200,000 attendees. Other popular festivals during the year have earned Mount Dora the title "Florida's Festival City." The Mount Dora Center for the Arts and several private galleries bring art exhibitions to the town. The Community Concert Association performs in an annual series of concerts. The IceHouse Players present a season of live theater in a 300-seat theater. Orlando, with all its cultural and entertainment activities, is only thirty minutes away.

Sports and Recreation. The Mount Dora Yacht Club is the state's oldest lakeside club, and an annual sailing regatta is a major event in central Florida. Lake Dora, on the chain of lakes with eventual access to the Atlantic Ocean, is so popular with boaters that it is one of the few lakes with its own lighthouse. Palm Island Park, 3 blocks from downtown Mount Dora, is twelve acres of forested wetland. Raised boardwalks allow visitors to explore the park without harming its delicate ecology, and ten picnic areas with mulched nature trails encourage community use. There are eight golf courses and many tennis courts in and around Mount Dora.

Law Enforcement and Safety. In 1996 there were eighty-seven criminal offenses reported per 1,000 year-round residents in Mount Dora.

Senior Centers. The nearest senior center is in Eustis 7 miles away.

Nearby Communities: **Tavares** (pop. 8,233) is the county seat of Lake County. It is 11 miles east of Leesburg and 4 miles west of Mount

Dora, on the Dora Canal between Lake Dora and Lake Eustis. The Dora Canal, a quiet, black stream that meanders among ancient cypress trees, has been called "the most beautiful half mile of water in the world." **Eustis** (pop. 14,286) is in the center of what Lake County calls its "Golden Triangle": Mount Dora, Umatilla, and Tavares. Downtown Eustis is a step back in time with brick streets, village shops, and Florida's oldest department store. **Clermont** (pop. 7,291), once known for its miles of hillside orange groves, is now fast becoming one of Florida's most popular retirement destinations, as groves are being replaced by planned retirement communities.

Addresses and Connections

Chambers of Commerce: Eustis Chamber of Commerce, 1 Orange Avenue, Eustis, FL 32727-1210; (352) 357–3434

Lady Lake Chamber of Commerce, P.O. Box 1430, Lady Lake, FL 32159; (352) 753–6029

Leesburg Area Chamber of Commerce, P.O. Box 490309, Leesburg, FL 34749-0309; (352) 787–2131; Fax, (352) 787–3985; http://www.lake-county.org; E-mail: chamber@lake-county.org

Mount Dora Chamber of Commerce, 341 North Alexander Street, Mount Dora, FL 32757; (352) 383–2165

South Lake Chamber of Commerce, 691 West Monotrose Street, Clermont, FL 34712-0417; (352) 394–4191

Tavares Chamber of Commerce, 912 Sinclair Avenue, Tavares, FL 32778; (352) 343–2531

Umatilla Chamber of Commerce, 23 South Central Avenue, Umatilla, FL 32784; (352) 669–3511

Newspaper: The Daily Commercial (daily), P.O. Box 490007, Leesburg, FL 34749-0007; (352) 787–0600

Internet: http://www.lakecountyfl.com

ORANGE COUNTY: Orlando and Winter Park

Until the late 1960s, Orange County (population 777,556) was primarily an agricultural center with many citrus groves in the hilly western part and farms and nurseries in the rich soil of the Lake Apopka area. Winter residents had discovered Winter Park in the late 1800s, and the huge Martin Marietta plant that manufactures sophisticated guidance systems for missiles had brought in new residents in the 1950s, but Orlando and its neighbors were still somewhat sleepy Florida cities and towns when Walt Disney announced plans to build the world's largest tourist attraction on the outskirts of Orlando. In the thirty years since the opening of Walt Disney World, other theme parks, including SeaWorld and Universal Studios, have been built near Orlando, and the city has become the number one tourist destination in the nation. As the hospitality industry has grown, bringing jobs and economic prosperity, the population of Orlando and its neighboring towns has mushroomed. There are still farms and nurseries around Lake Apopka, and the nearby Kennedy Space Center still keeps an electronics industry thriving in Orange County, but there is no doubt that tourism is now the driving force of the area's economy. At the same time tourism was growing, so was the number of retirees discovering all of central Florida. Orange County ranks twenty-ninth out of all U.S. counties in attracting retirees from other states.

Cost of Living. Orange County ranks tenth in the state with a cost of living 99.42 percent of the state average. The sales tax is 6 percent. The cost of housing is just 0.97 percent below the state average. The average purchase price of a house is $94,150. Orange County ranks tenth in the state with an average monthly apartment rent of $637.

Climate. While you may have an occasional frost in Orange County, the climate is generally temperate year round. The sun shines all winter and almost daily afternoon showers keep summers pleasant.

Orange County Weather

	In degrees Fahrenheit				
	Jan.	Apr.	July	Oct.	Annual Rainfall
DAILY HIGHS	70.8	83.0	91.5	84.6	48.11"
DAILY LOWS	48.6	59.4	73.1	65.8	

Medical Care. Six hospitals with 3,402 beds serve Orange County residents.

Transportation. The Orlando International Airport has expanded to meet the needs of Orange County's tourist boom and is now one of the nation's busiest airports. The Orange, Seminole, and Osceola Transportation Authority operates a tricounty bus service called LYNX. The colorful buses cover all three counties.

Opportunities for Continuing Education. Orange County schools, Valencia Community College with three campuses and several centers, the University of Central Florida, and Rollins College in Winter Park provide for every conceivable continuing-education need of the area's retiree population.

Orlando and Winter Park

Orlando (population 173,122) is the county seat of Orange County and the largest municipality in the county. Winter Park (population 24,750) is Orlando's northern neighbor and the second largest city in the county. These cities have distinct personalities, but they are so close and share so many cultural and recreational amenities that for our purposes here they may be considered one large community.

Orlando is a city with a wide variety of neighborhoods and environments. Its downtown will strike you as very up-to-date. Tall, modern banks and public buildings with stunning architecture dominate the skyline, and much seems fresh and new. Yet if you go a few blocks in any direction from the town center, you find yourself in neighborhoods of brick streets, spreading oak trees, and restored older homes from the early 1900s. Craftsman bungalows and stucco Mediterranean homes predominate. Several of these neighborhoods have sought and received "historic district" status. Old oaks spread out so that many neighborhood streets are completely covered, making Orlando one of the greenest cities you will find. It began in 1889 when the mayor of Orlando persuaded the city council to purchase 400 oak trees for $500. Other citizens became involved when an offer was made to plant oak trees and guarantee them to live for fifty cents apiece. Lake Eola Park, in the busiest part of downtown Orlando, is a refreshing oasis of water and greenery where large oaks, beds of azaleas, and flower gardens encircle a lake. Sidewalks for walking and running and benches for relaxing and observing the natural beauty bring people to the park throughout the day, and an open-air amphitheater brings them back for performances in the evenings. Visitors in swan boats paddle among the real black and white resident swans. Hundreds of lakes are scattered throughout Orlando. Some cover hundreds of acres, and some are less than 100 feet across.

Winter Park is an elegant college town laid out around a chain of seventeen lakes connected by canals. The town is proud of its image as the cultural and fashion hub of central Florida. Rollins College, a small, highly regarded liberal arts college, occupies a prominent position in the town—geographically, socially, and culturally. The Mediterranean architecture of its campus seems to have created the prevailing style of the community, and its many cultural activities set the pace for the rest of the town. Park Avenue—Winter Park's street with bougainvillea-draped arcades of upscale shops, boutiques, cafes, and gourmet restaurants—draws strollers and shoppers from throughout the area. A recent inventory revealed that the city has seventy-five parks and 27,000 trees within its eight square miles.

In the first chapter, Orlando was given as an example of a city that is very livable in spite of great numbers of tourists. The theme parks that draw so many tourists are several miles outside the city, and it is true you may live almost anywhere in Orlando and its neighboring towns and be oblivious to the crowds of tourists at the parks, even in the busiest seasons. These theme parks have done a great service to their surrounding cities and towns and indeed to the entire state. The standards they have set in terms of safety, beautification, and cleanliness have mandated that surrounding communities and other tourist attractions keep pace. No longer can a seedy roadside "tourist trap" expect to survive, and Florida's cities and towns, particularly those nearby, must also measure up or look very sad by comparison.

Housing. If you decide to live in the suburbs around Orlando, you will find everything from new homes in the $70,000 range to high-end gated communities where new homes start well over $300,000. And some unusual properties a short drive from Orlando offer interesting alternatives. For $265,000 a four-bedroom home on two and one-half acres near Orlando included a four-stall horse barn and a separate guest home. One thing that makes Orlando so appealing is the abundance of interesting, quiet neighborhoods in the city proper where every type of home imaginable may be found. On the border between Orlando and Winter Park is Orwin, a small, diverse community of older homes that has become very popular in recent years. In spite of its great location and popularity you can still find bargains here. A recent listing for a three-bedroom two-bath ranch was priced at $119,000. In a nice neighborhood northwest of Orlando a historic, recently renovated two-story home with four bedrooms and three baths was put on the market for $219,000. An irresistible, updated three-bedroom two-story bungalow on a brick street was priced at $109,500. And a small, classic bungalow in the Lake Cherokee Historic District with high ceilings and wood floors throughout was placed for sale at $79,900. A four-bedroom three-bath bungalow in the same neighborhood offered two master suites and a fireplace for $129,900.

In spite of its reputation for luxury living, Winter Park also has neighborhoods of more modest homes, although you must always pay a bit of a premium for that Winter Park address. An older lakefront home with four small bedrooms and three baths was listed for $144,900. A two-bedroom two-bath condo in an attractive modern complex overlooking Winter Park's Park Avenue was for sale for $104,000. In "Old Winter Park," an updated two-bedroom home with one and a half baths was priced at $124,900. Property taxes in Orlando are about $21.65 per $1,000 nonexempt valuation. Winter Park's rate is $18.41.

Culture and Entertainment. Winter Park is a town of museums! The Cornell Fine Arts Museum on the Rollins College campus, with a permanent collection of more than 6,000 works of European and American artists, hosts changing exhibitions and concerts throughout the year. The Morse Museum of American Art houses the world's largest collection of the stained-glass art of Louis Comfort Tiffany and an impressive collection of American Art Pottery. The Albin Polasek Museum and Sculpture Gardens features 200 works of the noted Czech-American sculptor in the setting where he worked. The Crealdé School of Art houses exhibitions in its galleries. Winter Park's annual Sidewalk Art Festival is one of the largest and best-known in the nation. For three days it fills the town's Central Park and nearby streets as 300,000 visitors look and buy from the carefully selected 250 participating artists.

The Maitland Art Center is one of the most unusual places you will find anywhere. Built in 1937 and now on the National Register of Historic Places, it was the studio, art school, art research center, and gallery of the late American artist and architect Jules André Smith. Resembling a Mayan temple with fantastic designs sculpted by hand into the cement and stucco facades, the entire compound is itself a work of art. It now houses a permanent collection, galleries for special shows, and studios for artists. The Orlando Museum of Art has a fine permanent collection, but its greatest contribution is bringing to town excellent touring exhibitions. Galleries at Valencia Community College's East Campus present changing exhibitions of prominent local, state, and national artists.

The Orlando–Winter Park area also excels in the performing arts. Rollins College's Annie Russell Theater is home to plays and musicals of outstanding quality put on by students of the college's superb drama department. The college sponsors concerts throughout the year, and the sixty-three-year-old October-to-April Bach Festival brings its noted Bach Festival Chorus and internationally acclaimed musicians to the community. Orlando's lakeside Lockhaven Park is that city's cultural heart. In addition to the Orlando Museum of Art, the park is home to the dazzling new $48 million Orlando Science Center and the Civic Theaters of Central Florida, an excellent regional theater with three performance spaces. A real gem is the highly regarded Orlando-University of Central Florida Shakespeare Festival, a nine-month season of theater with many of the plays performed outdoors in the Walt Disney Amphitheater at Lake Eola Park. The Bob Carr Performing Arts Centre provides a venue for the Orlando Opera Company, the Southern Ballet Theater, and the fledgling Orlando Philharmonic for their performances as well as for the MasterCard Broadway Series.

Sports and Recreation. The Orlando area is an outdoor paradise for almost any degree of physical activity you may prefer. There are eighty-two lakes in the city of Orlando and more than 2,000 in the metropolitan area. Some are mere beauty spots in the urban and residential landscapes while others are big enough to invite sailing, waterskiing, fishing, and boating. There are about 4,000 acres of parks, many with tennis courts and other sports facilities. Several hiking and biking trails wind through parks and natural areas. Another Rails-to-Trails project, the current 5-mile West Orange Trail, will eventually reach most of central Florida, with 20 miles of paved pathway for biking, running, and in-line skating. Golf is perhaps king among participatory sports in central Florida, and the Orlando area is hard to beat. There are more than seventy golf courses in Orlando's metropolitan area. One of the best-known is Arnold Palmer's Bay Hill Club, home of the annual Bay Hill Invitational. Disney World's acclaimed golf courses include ninety-nine holes with every level of difficulty.

Spectator sports hold their own, too, in Orlando. A professional basketball team, the Orlando Magic, makes its home at the 17,000-seat

"Orena," which is also home to the arena football team, the Orlando Predators. The Atlanta Braves hold spring practice at Disney's Wide World of Sports complex. The Kansas City Royals come to Polk County's Baseball City, and the Houston Astros come to the Osceola County Stadium each spring.

Law Enforcement and Safety. In 1996 there were 139 criminal offenses reported per 1,000 year-round residents in Orlando. In Winter Park the rate was seventy-six. It should be kept in mind that numbers of tourists inflate these figures. In unincorporated Orange County the rate was eighty-four per 1,000 year-round residents.

Senior Centers. The following agencies based in Orlando provide a variety of services to seniors: the Senior Resource Alliance, a multicounty agency providing information on all issues affecting seniors in Brevard, Orange, Osceola, and Seminole Counties; Community Care for the Elderly, a provider of services and information to help seniors function in their homes; ADNET, a consortium of nonprofit adult day-care providers; and Orange County Seniors First, a congregate meal service for seniors. The Beardall Senior Center, the L. Claudia Allen Senior Center, and the Marks Street Senior Center in Orlando; the Maitland Senior Center; and the Apopka Senior Recreation Center all provide full calendars of social, recreational, and educational programs and activities.

Nearby Communities. **Apopka** (pop. 19,255) is still primarily agri-cultural, with the booming foliage and houseplant business dominating. With thirty million square feet of greenhouse space, nurseries here produce 60 percent of the world's foliage plants. Instead of a local hero, downtown Apopka proudly displays a sculpture of a Boston fern! **Eatonville** (pop. 2,506) is proud of its distinction as this nation's oldest incorporated African- American community. **Maitland** (pop. 9,871) is a mainly residential community built around several of the prettiest lakes in Orange County. It is located just north of Winter Park and the two towns' borders have merged. *Ocoee* (pop. 19,261) was known as citrus country until recently. Now subdivisions of luxury homes mix with older rural neighborhoods. **Windermere** (pop. 1,776) is very proud of its small-town atmosphere. Homes here are expensive and the atmosphere is deliberately rural—one of the few places you may find million-dollar lakefront mansions on unpaved roads that wind through palmetto thick-ets. Windermere is on the Butler Chain of Lakes. **Winter Garden** (pop. 12,413), on the western edge of Orange County, is still more rural than urban. **Kissimmee** (pop. 38,175) is in Osceola County, just south of Orange County. Perhaps because it is closer to Disney World and perhaps because it was a much smaller town to begin with, Kissimmee seems more impacted by the motel and tourist attraction boom than Orlando. Once the center of Florida's cattle industry, Kissimmee still hosts a major annual rodeo. **Altamonte Springs** (pop. 38,200) is in Seminole County, Orange County's neighbor to the north. The fastest-growing municipality in Seminole County, Altamonte Springs's many new subdivisions and apartment complexes serve as a bedroom community for Orlando. In fact, 70 percent of the residents of Seminole County work outside the county.

Addresses and Connections

Chambers of Commerce: Greater Orlando Chamber of Commerce, P.O. Box 1234, Orlando, FL 32802-1234; (407) 418–4462; Fax, (407) 418–4463; http://www.orlando.org

Maitland South Seminole Chamber of Commerce, 110 North Maitland Avenue, Maitland, FL 32751; (407) 644–0741

Winter Park Chamber of Commerce, P.O. Box 280, Winter Park, FL 32790; (407) 644–8281; Fax, (407) 644–7826

Newspaper: The Orlando Sentinel (daily), 633 North Orange Avenue, Orlando, FL 32801; (800) 359–5353; http:www.orlandosentinel.com

Internet: http://www.ci.orlando.fl.us
http://www.osceola.org

POLK COUNTY: Lakeland, Winter Haven, and Lake Wales

Polk County (population 452,707) is a very large county south of Lake County and west of Orange and Osceola Counties. When you look at a map of Polk County, the most obvious features are the many lakes—more than 600 large enough to be named and counted. Polk County, far enough south to be spared some of the freezing temperatures that destroyed groves in Lake and Orange Counties, is the leading citrus-producing county in the state. Citrus is a billion-dollar industry here. The county is also a leader, along with Pasco county, in the number of mobile homes—more than 51,000 according to one recent count. In 1996 *Money* magazine ranked Polk County number ten on its list of the best places to live in the United States. Polk County recently ranked fourteenth out of all U.S. counties in the number of retirees moving in from out of state.

Cost of Living. Polk County ranks twenty-first in the state with a cost of living 96.68 percent of the state average. The sales tax is 6 percent. The cost of housing is 6.01 percent below the state average. The average purchase price of a house is $89,190. Polk County ranks twenty-seventh in the state with an average monthly apartment rent of $542.

Climate. As you would expect of the area that produces most of Florida's huge citrus crop, winters are mild and sunny.

Orlando–Polk County Weather

| | In degrees Fahrenheit | | | | |
	Jan.	Apr.	July	Oct.	Annual Rainfall
DAILY HIGHS	70.8	83.0	91.5	84.6	48.11"
DAILY LOWS	48.6	59.4	73.1	65.8	

Medical Care. Six hospitals with 1,917 beds serve all of Polk County.

Transportation. Residents of Polk County have a choice of airports. Both Tampa International and Orlando International are about an hour from most points in the county. At present, Lakeland is the only city in Polk County with scheduled local bus service, the Citrus Connection.

Opportunities for Continuing Education. Polk County schools and Polk Community College with campuses in Lakeland and Winter Haven provide adult and continuing education to retirees throughout Polk County.

Lakeland

Lakeland (population 75,422) is the largest city in Polk County. Located almost midway between Orlando and Tampa, Lakeland's residents may take advantage of all the offerings and amenities of both nearby cities. Lakeland is a city of green parks and, wherever you look, sparkling lakes. There are at least thirty named lakes in the city and another thirty or so too small to be named on my city map. There is a restored antiques district surrounding Munn Park, Lakeland's town square, that contains shops, galleries, and restaurants. In 1997 *Money* magazine ranked Lakeland the fourteenth "Best Place to Live in America." A beautiful colonnaded walkway overlooking Lake Mirror in downtown Lakeland is on the National Register of Historic Places.

Housing. If you choose to retire in Lakeland, not only will you have chosen a wonderful town, you will be able to choose a wonderfully priced home. For example, a three-bedroom two-bath home with a tile foyer, a fireplace, and a deck surrounding the in-ground pool was recently listed for $107,900. And a fully furnished two-bedroom condo in a newer complex with a community pool and clubhouse went on the market at $28,500. In Lakeland's historic district a handsome three-bedroom home with one and a half baths and original hardwood floors was placed on the market for $79,500. A three-bedroom three-bath pool home with hardwood floors, a detached apartment, and a screened pool on a one-half-acre lot was listed for $94,900. And a three-bedroom three-bath town house with a balcony overlooking a golf course was offered for $106,000, including all furnishings. A sprawling four-bedroom three-bath executive home that featured a master suite with double fireplace, whirlpool tub, and custom-built octagonal shower was listed for $168,000. Property taxes in Lakeland range from $19.80 to $22.35 per $1,000 nonexempt valuation.

Culture and Entertainment. Although near enough to take in all the cultural and entertainment activities in Orlando and Tampa, the residents of Lakeland have access to a very full range of offerings right at home. The performing arts are well represented. The Imperial Symphony Orchestra, made up of 120 professional and amateur musicians, presents a season of classical music from October to May. The Lakeland Center, the county's largest performing arts venue, also functions as a convention and conference complex. Its 2,186-seat Youkey Theatre is home to a series of Broadway shows, touring dance companies, and the Imperial Symphony. The Polk Theater, built in 1927, has been restored and now provides a home for films, live performances, and special events. The Pied Piper Players, Lakeland's community theater company, presents a season of plays in the 386-seat Lake Mirror Theater.

Lakeland's publicly supported Arts on the Park is the city's center for the creative arts. The center sponsors competitions, shows, and coordinates arts activities for the city. The Polk Museum of Art, housed in a very contemporary redbrick building in downtown Lakeland, has a fine collection of pre-Columbian artifacts. The museum has a student gallery, a sculpture garden, 37,000 square feet of exhibit space for local and touring art shows, studio classrooms, and a 152-seat theater. The museum sponsors the Mayfair-by-the-Lake Art Festival on the shores of Lake Morton every May. In September the Fall Festival brings arts and crafts exhibitors to Munn Park. Without question the best-known cultural attraction in Lakeland is the campus Frank Lloyd Wright designed for Florida Southern College. The breathtaking twelve-structure complex, called "Child of the Sun," is the largest single-site collection of Wright architecture in the world.

Sports and Recreation. In a city with so many lakes within its limits and others nearby, it stands to reason that fishing, boating, and water sports will be high on the recreation agenda of Lakeland's residents. The largemouth bass fishing in Polk County's lakes is legendary. The Lakeland Shuffleboard Club has more than one hundred members and is recruiting more. The club gives free lessons and holds tournaments on its forty-one courts throughout the year. There are nine public and four private golf courses in Lakeland. The Detroit Tigers hold spring training in Lakeland, and the annual Orange Cup Regatta brings hydroplane boat racers and fans from all over the country to Lakeland's Lake Hollingsworth every March.

Law Enforcement and Safety. In 1996 there were 126 criminal offenses reported per 1,000 year-round residents in Lakeland. In unincorporated Polk County the rate was fifty-nine per 1,000.

Senior Centers. Lake Morton Senior Center provides congregate meals, educational programs, and recreational activities to seniors. Volunteers in Service to the Elderly provides a range of services including telephone reassurance, housekeeping assistance, senior ride programs, and volunteer recruitment and placement.

Nearby Communities. **Bartow** (pop. 15,025) is 14 miles southeast of Lakeland. It is the county seat of Polk County and a very pretty historic city with many blocks of elegant old homes.

Winter Haven

Winter Haven (population 25,485) is so proud of its unusual chain of fourteen lakes that it has a Chain of Lakes Convention Center and a Chain of Lakes Stadium Complex where the Cleveland Indians hold spring training. One of the city's most enduring claims to fame is Cypress Gardens. A magnificent 223-acre botanical garden built around several connected lakes, it is Florida's oldest tourist attraction (it recently celebrated its sixtieth anniversary). The background for several movies, the park has popularized Florida's lake country and its beautiful flowering trees and shrubs. Winter Haven is known as the waterskiing capital of the world. Cypress Gardens' founder, Dick Pope, almost single-handedly made waterskiing a major sport in the United States, and the water-ski shows at Cypress Gardens are still a major tourist draw. Winter Haven's city limits touch or surround more than twenty lakes.

Housing. Your housing dollars go a long way in Winter Haven. A beautifully landscaped home with more than 2,000 square feet of living space was recently priced at $78,500. And a two-bedroom lakeside condo with sunset views went on the market for $54,900. An older three-bedroom home with one and a half baths, large rooms, high ceilings, wood floors, and a detached garage was priced at $49,500. For more upscale living at a great price, a 1930s home with 3,000 square feet of living space including four bedrooms, three and a half baths, hardwood floors, and an in-ground pool on a large city lot was completely renovated before being put for sale at $159,900. Property taxes in Winter Haven range from $22.23 to $23.74 per $1,000 nonexempt valuation.

Culture and Entertainment. The Winter Haven Arts Festival showcases the works of 140 artists from throughout the United States. More than $7,200 in prizes and purchase awards are presented each year. Theater Winter Haven presents six productions each year in the city's 350-seat theater in the Chain of Lakes Convention Center. Polk Community College presents many musical and theatrical productions in its 500-seat auditorium.

Sports and Recreation. The twenty-one-court Winter Haven Shuffleboard Club has one hundred members and is open for new members. A low membership fee also includes entry fees to tournaments. There are four public and three private golf courses in Winter Haven. There are twelve lighted tennis courts open to the public. Fishing, boating, and waterskiing on the area's many lakes are Winter Haven's most popular sports. Public boat ramps can be found on most of the city's lakes. Lake Shipp Park is an eighteen-acre county park with boat ramps, a swimming beach, and picnic areas.

Law Enforcement and Safety. In 1996 there were 104 criminal offenses reported per 1,000 year-round residents in Winter Haven.

Senior Centers. The Neighborhood Service Center and the Winter Haven Senior Adult Center provide a range of services to Winter Haven's senior population.

Nearby Communities. Winter Haven is surrounded by communities that are popular with retirees. **Lake Alfred** (pop. 3,771) is about 2 miles north. **Haines City** (pop. 12,911) is 10 miles northeast. **Eagle Lake** (pop. 1,903) is 2 miles southwest. **Auburndale** (pop. 9,323) is about 5 miles northwest.

Lake Wales

Lake Wales (population 9,928) is located atop Florida's central ridge and boasts the highest elevation in the peninsular part of the state: Iron Mountain at 295 feet. Much of the historic downtown, an area of low stucco buildings from the city's early years, has been placed on the National Register of Historic Places. All of the downtown area has been tastefully landscaped with trees and planting boxes. Old-fashioned lighting and wide sidewalks add to the charm. The big lake in the middle of the city is Lake Wailes. According to one story, that was the name of the city too, until someone observed that it sounded too mournful.

Housing. Housing costs in Lake Wales are even lower than in popular Winter Haven. This will give you plenty of options, particularly among single-family homes. Homes here can dip below $50,000 and occasionally soar above the million dollar mark, particularly in the older, exclusive neighborhoods like Mountain Lake. A modest, in-town bungalow with three bedrooms, two baths, a fireplace, living room, family room, and screened front porch was recently on the market for $42,500. When I was in Lake Wales last, very affordable listings included a newer three-bedroom two-bath home with a one-car garage and a separate one-bedroom apartment for $89,900. A small home on a lake offered three bedrooms, two baths, and two porches overlooking a quiet lake for $88,500. A handsome three-bedroom two-bath log home with parquet floors, a fireplace, and a large yard shaded by mature oaks was for sale for $95,000. A three-bedroom home with professional landscaping featured two fireplaces, separate dining and breakfast rooms, an oversize two-car garage, a workshop, and all appliances for $120,000. In a very upscale neighborhood, a country club villa with a split bedroom plan with vaulted ceilings, skylights, an interior atrium, and a two-car garage was listed for $240,000. Beautiful newer condos are available. For example, a two-bedroom two-bath unit overlooking a large community pool and tennis courts had an asking price of $44,500. Property taxes in Lake Wales are $24.82 per $1,000 nonexempt valuation.

Culture and Entertainment. In the annual Lake Wales Art Festival 120 artists compete for $17,000 in prize money. Scheduled along with the festival is a student art show held at the Lake Wales Art Center. The show's sponsor, the Lake Wales Art Council, is located in a former church built in 1927. The council has adapted the church into its Arts Center with rotating exhibitions, concerts, and films. The Lake Wales Museum and Cultural Center, located in a former railway depot built in 1928, contains exhibits of historical and cultural interest. The Lake Wales Amphitheater is the winter home of the Black Hills Passion Play, a religious drama of Christ's last days.

Sports and Recreation. There are three public and two private golf courses in Lake Wales. The city maintains 110 acres of parks and recreational sites. Lake Kissimmee State Park, east of Lake Wales, contains 5,000 acres around three lakes with 13 miles of hiking trails, picnic areas, boat ramps, fishing, and camping facilities. The Audubon Center and Nature Trail 6 miles south of Lake Wales and the Tiger Creek Nature Preserve are two huge natural areas with trails and facilities for bird-watching and nature observation. The new Lake Wailes Trail is a path for running, biking, or skating around most of the big downtown lake for which the city was named.

Senior Centers. The Lake Wales Community Center provides services for the area's senior residents. The Lake Wales Tourist Club sponsors many activities for those over fifty. You do not have to be a tourist to participate.

Nearby Communities. **Frostproof** (pop. 2,904) is a small community in southeast Polk County. As its name implies, the town is proud of its moderate climate.

Addresses and Connections

Chambers of Commerce: The Greater Bartow Chamber of Commerce, P.O. Box 956, Bartow, FL 33831-0956; (941) 533–7125; Fax, (941) 533–3793; http://www.bartowchamber.com; E-mail: info@bartowchamber.com

Lakeland Area Chamber of Commerce, P.O. Box 3607, Lakeland, FL 33802-3607; (941) 688–8551; Fax, (941) 683–7454; http://www.lakeland.net/chamber; E-Mail: chamber@lakeland.net

Lake Wales Area Chamber of Commerce, P.O. Box 191, Lake Wales, FL 33859-0191; (941) 676–3445; Fax, (941) 676–3446; http://www.cityoflakewales.com

Winter Haven Chamber of Commerce, P.O. Box 1420, Winter Haven, FL 33882-1420; (800) 871–7027; E-mail: chamber1 @winterhavenfl.com

Newspapers: The Ledger (daily), P.O. Box 408, Lakeland, FL 33802; (800) 282–3200; http://www.theledger.com

The News Chief (daily), P.O. Box 1440, Winter Haven, FL 33882-9986; (941) 294–7731

The Lake Wales News (weekly), 138-140 East Stuart Avenue, Lake Wales, FL 33853-4198; (941) 676–3467

HIGHLANDS COUNTY: Avon Park, Sebring, and Lake Placid

Highlands County (population 77,996) is the southernmost county we will visit in the Central Florida region. The state's central ridge with its gentle hills and lakes comes to an end with Highlands County, but it ends with a flourish! No county in central Florida is more scenic. Country roads here go over hills, around lakes, through miles of orange and grapefruit groves, and by fields of brightly colored caladiums. Highlands County calls itself "The Heart of Florida" and it is no idle claim, for it sits squarely in the middle of peninsular Florida. Avon Park is about 70 miles from the Atlantic coast and about 65 miles from the Gulf of Mexico. It is about 170 miles to the southern tip of the state and the same distance to Gainesville, where the peninsula begins. Retirees are attracted to Highlands County by its mild weather, lovely terrain, appealing small towns, and low cost of living, particularly for housing. Lumped together with neighboring DeSoto, Glades, Hardee, and Hendry Counties, Highlands County ranks thirty-third among all U.S. counties in the number of retirees attracted from out of state.

Immediately south of Highlands County the land becomes flat and is used mainly for grazing cattle. A little farther south, around Lake

Okeechobee, you begin to see the rich black dirt of the farmlands wrested years ago from the northern stretches of the Everglades. Folks here refer to that whole area as the "Glades." While there is no county in Florida without some retirees, Highland's neighboring counties are sparsely populated, and—without lakes, hills, or a coast—they are less attractive to retirees.

Like Polk County to its north, Highlands County depends upon citrus as its major industry. The county's 74,000 acres of citrus groves with 8.8 million trees produce 22,226,000 boxes of fruit annually. Ranching and the raising of caladium bulbs are also important to the local economy. More than 90 percent of the world's caladium bulbs are produced here each year.

Cost of Living. Highlands County ranks forty-sixth in the state with a cost of living 93.12 percent of the state average. The sales tax is 6 percent. The cost of housing is 14.42 percent below the state average. The average purchase price of a house is about $75,300. Highlands County ranks fifty-fourth in the state with an average monthly apartment rent of $357.

Climate. Located inland and away from the Atlantic's moderating affect, the climate in Highlands County will be a little cooler in winter and warmer in summer than the temperatures listed below, obtained from the NOAA station in Vero Beach.

Highlands County Weather

| | In degrees Fahrenheit | | | | |
	Jan.	Apr.	July	Oct.	Annual Rainfall
DAILY HIGHS	72.5	81.5	90.1	84.0	51.16"
DAILY LOWS	50.7	61.0	72.1	66.9	

Medical Care. Two hospitals with 277 beds serve Highlands County.

Transportation. The nearest major airport is Orlando International, about 75 miles away. There is no public transportation within Highlands County.

Opportunities for Continuing Education. South Florida Community College presents many educational programs and activities through its Adult and Continuing Education Department including a "Lifetime Learning" program oriented to senior citizens and a ten-week "Senior Enrichment Series." The main campus is between Avon Park and Sebring. The college maintains a center in Lake Placid.

Avon Park, Sebring, and Lake Placid

Three small incorporated towns—Avon Park, population 8,110; Sebring, population 8,955; and Lake Placid, population 1,427—are the major municipalities in Highlands County. These towns are about 15 miles apart along U.S. Highway 27, the major north-south highway that runs the length of central Florida. They are also connected by State Road 17, a two-lane country road that takes you through miles and miles of beautiful, glossy green citrus groves. In early spring these trees are almost white with blossoms and the fragrance is intoxicatingly delicious. By late summer and into the fall, the trees are filled with oranges and grapefruit. The rest of the county's 59,500 residents are scattered throughout the county, many in small developments of manufactured homes or in mobile-home parks. Some of these developments are on lakes, some are in orange groves, many have clubhouses and pools for recreation, and a few have their own golf courses.

Avon Park is a small town tucked away in the midst of orange groves and thirty lakes. The most striking thing about this little country town is its Main Street, a mile-long mall with more than 1,000 different plants and trees planted in its wide parkway. The street is lined with historic buildings and many antique shops. One of the most interesting buildings is the elegant 1926 Hotel Jacaranda. Now owned by the South Florida Community College Foundation, it has been renovated and is used as a laboratory for training students for the restaurant and hospitality industries. It is now open as a restaurant, and a buffet lunch in the quaint, old-fashioned hotel dining room is a step back in time. Like its sister cities in Highlands County, Avon Park's population grows by about 50 percent in the winter.

Sebring, the county seat of Highlands County, has one of the most impressive downtown historic districts in the state. Sebring is known as "The City on the Circle." When the city was founded in 1911, it was envisioned that all roads would lead into the park at the town's center, like spokes in a wheel. Today that centerpiece of the city is Circle Park, a lovely round park filled with huge old oaks, flowering shrubs, and beds of annuals. The drive around the park has many historic buildings, including the neoclassical County Court House. Most of the city's streets still radiate from this hub. The city's western border is 3,000-acre Lake Jackson.

One of Lake Placid's earliest promoters was Dr. Melvil Dewey, creator of the Dewey Decimal System, a name familiar to all librarians and scholars. The town and one of the nearby lakes now bear the name of Dr. Dewey's hometown, Lake Placid, New York. Lake Placid is a little gem, surrounded by lakes and hills and sitting in the middle of orange groves. It is a charming, small town with an obvious community spirit. Everyone I met was not only friendly and helpful, they all were Lake Placid boosters. On my impromptu visit, the executive director of the chamber of commerce was so enthusiastic and informative I was ready to relocate! Lake Placid was named "Rural Community of the Year 1995" and the "Outstanding Rural Community of the Year 1996" by Enterprise Florida and the Department of Transportation. With twenty-seven lakes ranging in size from ten acres to 27,000-acre Lake Istokpoga, Lake Placid is known as "Lake Country."

One unique and eye-catching thing about Lake Placid is its murals. In 1993 a large mural was painted on the side of the local arts-and-crafts cooperative building, and the Lake Placid Mural Society was formed. By mid-1997 there were twenty-six beautifully executed original murals throughout the town depicting the history, the ecology, the industry, and the culture of Lake Placid and its surrounding countryside. Most of the murals are large enough to cover the entire side of a building. Several are more than 100 feet wide and the largest, an overwhelming depiction of a cattle drive from the area's ranching past, is 175 feet wide by 30 feet high.

Housing. Life in this area of rural Florida has many benefits, not the least of which is very inexpensive housing. In Avon Park small condos occasionally sell for around $15,000 and single-family homes for about $65,000 are the norm. Even the most desirable lakefront homes are within reach of many, like a recent home for sale that offered a spacious two-bedroom ranch on the lake for $139,000. In an established neighborhood a three-bedroom two-bath brick home with living room, great room, and a screened pool on an acre of land listed for $121,500. Interesting homes at very affordable prices are in great supply, like a lakefront A-frame chalet with two bedrooms and a sleeping loft for $75,000. Property taxes in Avon Park are $26.85 per $1,000 nonexempt valuation.

It hardly seems fair that housing costs in one of the prettiest towns in Florida should be so low! In Sebring a great little bungalow in a nice in-town location but in need of a bit of a "face-lift" offered two bedrooms, two baths, and hardwood floors throughout for $28,900. A similar bungalow in perfect condition was listed for $39,900. It included a small office and was even zoned for mixed residential/commercial use. I saw a two-bedroom two-bath villa with new Berber carpet for $34,900, and a handsome two-bedroom end-unit condo with new interior decor, a split bedroom plan, and all furnishings and appliances for sale for $46,900. An attractive duplex building with a pool comprised a three-bedroom two-bath unit and a two-bedroom two-bath unit for just $89,900. A large four-bedroom newer ranch home with an oversize garage, in-ground heated pool, situated on a private double lot listed for $97,000. For more luxurious living, a four-bedroom three-bath golf course home with cathedral ceilings and an in-ground pool was for sale for $157,500. Property taxes in Sebring are $25.85 per $1,000 nonexempt valuation.

Lake Placid is one of the few places in Florida where most of us can even afford waterfront real estate. Although condominiums are in very short supply here, single-family homes for every budget are easy to find. Where else could you find a small but immaculate two-bedroom home with a new kitchen for $43,900? And a two-bedroom wood frame "Cracker home" featured two bedrooms, two baths, two porches, and a peaceful lake view for $68,500. A brand-new custom-built canal home with three bedrooms, two baths, and a large two-car garage was priced at $125,000. A newer three-bedroom three-bath two-story home on nearly five acres included an airstrip for $129,900. And a large three-bedroom with a 31-foot Florida room, a separate office, and an oversize two-car garage on a beautiful lot listed for $87,500. Although there are luxury homes here in the high $200,000 range, they are in short supply and usually include lots of land or large lakefront settings. You'd have to really work overtime to spend this much on a home (or estate) in Lake Placid. Approaching this town's high end, there was one four-bedroom four-bath executive home on a one acre lot for $211,900. Property taxes in Lake Placid are $23.55 per $1,000 nonexempt valuation.

Culture and Entertainment. South Florida Community College is to Highlands County what Rollins College is to Winter Park and the University of Florida is to Gainesville. It is the cultural and educational backbone of the county and one of the driving forces in the continuing redevelopment of its communities. The college's 1,500-seat auditorium on the college's main campus between Avon Park and Sebring is home to an annual cultural series, which includes Broadway shows, concerts, and dance performances. The lobby of the auditorium serves as a community art gallery with changing exhibitions of works by students, local artists, and touring art shows. The college's drama department stages plays, and the music department presents cabaret shows and an annual Christmas Madrigal Dinner. Affiliates of the college's Adult and Continuing Education Department—including the Highlands County Concert Band, the Highlands Chorale, the Sweet Adelines, and the "The Highlandaires," a '30s and '40s style band—perform at the college.

In Sebring the lakefront Allen C. Altvater Cultural Center houses the Highlands Little Theater, the Highlands County Library, a community civic center, and the headquarters of the Highlands Art League. The Art League has a gallery for changing art shows.

In both Avon Park and Lake Placid early 1900s railroad stations have been converted into historical museums.

Sports and Recreation. Fishing, boating, waterskiing, and swimming in Highlands County's seventy-seven lakes are just some of the attractions of this area. There are thirteen golf courses in Highlands County with year-round play. Highlands Hammock State Park, a few miles west of Sebring, was Florida's first state park. It is a 4,600-acre nature preserve with 3½ miles of trails for hiking. There are facilities for camping and picnicking. Each year the 12 Hour Grand Prix of Endurance Race brings more than 100,000 automobile racing fans to Sebring.

Law Enforcement and Safety. In 1996 there were 110 criminal offenses reported per 1,000 year-round residents in Avon Park and 135 per 1,000 in Sebring. The 1996 report from the Florida Department of Law Enforcement did not provide any criminal offense data for Lake Placid.

Senior Centers. Senior Scene, a monthly tabloid newspaper for seniors published in Lake Placid, gives considerable information about all of the services available to seniors in Highlands County. The newspaper is supported by advertising and is free to readers. Highlands County is in the area coordinated by the West Central Florida Area Agency on Aging, Inc. Elder Helplines are maintained in Avon Park, Sebring, and Lake Placid.

Addresses and Connections

Chambers of Commerce: Avon Park Chamber of Commerce, 28 East Main Street, Avon Park, FL 33825; (941) 453–3350; Fax, (941) 453–0973; E-mail: apcc@ct.net

Greater Sebring Chamber of Commerce, 309 South Circle, Sebring, FL 33870; (941) 385–8448; Fax, (941) 385–8810; http://www. sebring.com; E-mail: sebcc@ct.net

Greater Lake Placid Chamber of Commerce, 10 East Interlake Boulevard, Lake Placid, FL 33852; (941) 465–4331; Fax, (941) 465–2588; http://www.lake-placid-fl.com; E-mail: lpcc@ct.net

Newspapers: *The Highlands County News-Sun* (Wednesday, Friday, and Sunday), 2227 U.S. Highway 27 South, Sebring, FL 33870; (941) 385-6155; Fax, (941) 385–1954

Highlands Today (daily), 231 U.S. Highway 27 North, Sebring, FL 33870; (941) 382–1164

Lake Placid Journal (weekly), P.O. Box 696, Lake Placid, FL 33862; (941) 465–2423

Senior Scene (monthly), 3109 Old State Road 8, Lake Placid, FL 33852; (941) 465–7586; E-mail: seniorscene@hotmail.com

ADDITIONAL RESOURCES

Books

Douglas, Marjory Stoneman. *River of Grass*. R. Bemis Publishing Ltd., Marietta, GA, 1974.

Floyd, Susan S. (Editor). *1997 Florida Statistical Abstract*. University of Florida, Gainesville, FL, 1997.

Gannon, Michael. *Florida, A Short History*. University Press of Florida, Gainesville, FL, 1993.

Jahoda, Gloria. *The Other Florida*. Florida Classics Library, Port Salerno, FL, 1984.

Longino, Charles F., Jr. *Retirement Migration in America*., Vacation Publications, Inc., Houston, TX, 1995.

Matschat, Cecile H. *Suwannee River: Strange Green Land*. University of Georgia Press, Athens, GA, 1980.

Pratt, Theodore. *The Barefoot Mailman*. Florida Classics Library, Port Salerno, FL, 1993.

Rawlings, Marjorie Kinnan. *Cross Creek*. Macmillan Publishing Company, New York, 1961.

Savageau, David. *Retirement Places Rated*. Macmillan Publishing Company, New York, 1995.

Brochures and Guides

Destination: Florida Golf, 1998. Published by Hillsboro Publishing Group for the Florida Sports Foundation, 2964 Wellington Circle North, Tallahassee, FL, 32308; (904) 488-8347.

1997 Florida Camping Directory. Florida Association of RV Parks & Campgrounds, 1340 Vickers Drive, Tallahassee, FL 32303-3401; (904) 562–7151; Fax: (904) 562–7179. Web site: http://www.floridacamping.com

1996 Florida Fishing Guide. Published by Outdoor Media Group, Inc., for the Florida Sports Foundation, 2964 Wellington Circle North, Tallahassee, FL 32308; (904) 488–8347.

1996–97 Florida Sports Vacation Guide. Published by Ulrich

Communications Corporation for the Florida Sports Foundation, 2964 Wellington Circle North, Tallahassee, FL 32308; (904) 488–8347.

1997 Florida Vacation Guide. Published by Worth International Communications Corporation for the Florida Tourism Industry Marketing Corporation. P.O. Box 1100, Tallahassee, FL 32302-1100.

1997–98 Insuring Your Home Consumers' Guide. The Florida Department of Insurance, Consumer Outreach and Education, 200 East Gaines Street, Tallahassee, FL 32399-0323.

Official Guide Map to Florida Attractions. Florida Attractions Association, Inc., P.O. Box 10295, Tallahassee, FL 32302-2295; (904) 224–0519. E-mail: attractions@nettally.com

Periodicals

Ellis, Rafaela. "Gulf Coast State of Mind," *Car & Travel,* September/October 1997, 6–6b.

Florida Living: The Magazine of Life and Travel in Florida. North Florida Publishing Company, 102 Northeast 10th Avenue, Suite 6, Gainesville, FL 32601; (352) 372–8865; Fax: (352) 372–3453. E-mail: flliving@earthlink.net; Website: http://www.floridaliving.org

Mobile Home Lifestyles of Pinellas. Volume 2, Issue 1 (undated). Marketplace Publication, 2882-A Gulf to Bay Boulevard, Clearwater, FL 33759; (813) 797-3300.

Reports

Comparative Climatic Data for the United Sates through 1995. National Oceanic and Atmospheric Administration; National Environmental Satellite, Data and Information Service; National Climatic Data Center, Asheville, NC 28801-5001.

County and Municipal Offense Data, 1996 Annual Report. Florida Department of Law Enforcement, Statistical Analysis Center, P.O. Box 1489; Tallahassee, FL 32302; (904) 487-1179.

1997 Florida Community Colleges Directory. Division of Community Colleges, 1314 Turlington Building, Department of Education, 325 West Gaines Street, Tallahassee, FL 32399-0400; (850) 488-1721.

The 1996 Florida Price Level Index. Office of Education Budget and
Management; Florida Department of Education, The Capitol
Building, Tallahassee, FL 32399-0400. (This report can be found
on the Internet at www.firn.edu/doe/bin00047/fplifnl.htm
#96FPLI.)

Agencies

Florida Department of Revenue, 5050 West Tennessee Street, Building K,
Tallahassee, FL 33399-0100; (904) 488–6800.

Index to Counties, Cities, and Towns

ABOUT THE AUTHOR

James F. Gollattscheck is a fourth-generation Floridian. He earned undergraduate and graduate degrees from the University of Florida and a Ph.D. from Florida State University. He was president of Valencia Community College in Orlando and later served as an executive officer of the American Association of Community and Junior Colleges in Washington, D.C. He is the author of several books on higher education and recently co-authored *America's Community Colleges: The First Century*. Following his retirement in 1993, Dr. Gollattscheck lived for several years in Europe where he wrote *Europe the European Way; A Traveler's Guide to Living Affordably in the World's Great Cities*, now a Globe Pequot Press book. With obvious affection for his native state, he drove thousands of miles throughout Florida visiting the more than 250 cities, towns, and other sites described in this book. He currently resides in Sarasota, Florida.